OLIVER TWIST & ME

Also by Nicholas Blincoe

Acid Casuals

Jello Salad

Manchester Slingback

The Dope Priest

White Mice

Burning Paris

NON-FICTION

All Hail the New Puritans (co-editor with Matt Thorne)

Bethlehem: Biography of a Town

More Noble than War: The Story of Football in Israel and Palestine

OLIVER TWIST & ME

*The True Story of my Family and
Charles Dickens's Best-Loved Novel*

NICHOLAS BLINCOE

THE BRIDGE STREET PRESS

First published in Great Britain in 2025 by The Bridge Street Press

1 3 5 7 9 10 8 6 4 2

Copyright © Nicholas Blincoe 2025

The moral right of the author has been asserted.

All rights reserved.
No part of this publication may be reproduced, stored in a
retrieval system, or transmitted, in any form, or by any means, without
the prior permission in writing of the publisher, nor be otherwise circulated
in any form of binding or cover other than that in which it is published
and without a similar condition including this condition being
imposed on the subsequent purchaser.

A CIP catalogue record for this book
is available from the British Library.

ISBN 978-0-349-13638-7

Typeset in Jenson by M Rules
Printed and bound in Great Britain by
Clays Ltd, Elcograf S.p.A.

Papers used by The Bridge Street Press are from well-managed forests
and other responsible sources.

The Bridge Street Press
An imprint of
Little, Brown Book Group
Carmelite House
50 Victoria Embankment
London EC4Y 0DZ

The authorised representative
in the EEA is
Hachette Ireland
8 Castlecourt Centre
Dublin 15, D15 XTP3, Ireland
(email: info@hbgi.ie)

An Hachette UK Company
www.hachette.co.uk

www.littlebrown.co.uk

To Janet and Fredo

CONTENTS

	Introduction: 1974	1
1.	The Two Workhouses: 1790s/1830s	17
2.	Two Families: Barrow and Dickens, 1790–1801	37
3.	Factory Boy: 1799–1803	53
4.	Portsmouth: 1805–14	73
5.	The High Peak: 1804–14	94
6.	Dickens Loses Three Friends: 1816–22	111
7.	Rag Trade: Manchester, 1819–22	138
8.	Dickens Alone: 1824	154
9.	Fleet Street: 1824–28	179
10.	Publishing Robert's Story: 1828–33	196
11.	Dickens's Lift-off: 1834–44	210
12.	Whited Sepulchres: 1857–68	238
13.	Up the Orphans! 1870	269
	Sources	281
	Acknowledgements	315
	Index	317

INTRODUCTION: 1974

Family visits to my grandmother's home revolved around television, a meat-and-potato pie served with two different vegetables (one of them also potato) and my father asleep in an armchair. That Easter, we started with a tour of the upstairs to admire her decorating. She had painted her bedroom a Hanna-Barbera purple with the help of her best friend, Mrs Whittle, who held the stepladder. A bright new palm cross was pinned to the wall above her pillow, so pale that it seemed to hover above the fresh paintwork. She was a Manchester woman, and Palm Sunday is the most Manchester of Holy Days: it reminds us that even Christ had to be brought down a peg after his big entrance into Jerusalem. My gran saw it as a duty to cut tall poppies down to size. Ask, 'What's for dinner?' and she'd say: 'Two jumps at the cupboard door and a bite of the knob.' I might timidly wonder, 'I thought we were having chips?' and she'd reply: 'You know what thought did: followed a muck cart because it thought it was a wedding.'

I know I make my gran sound like Mrs Gummidge, the mordant widow of *David Copperfield*. But she spoke the way all the women of her generation spoke. She was a small, plump woman with a kindly face, a nylon housecoat, and coils of white permed hair. She was born Violet Foulkes in Ancoats in Manchester in 1910. It was a Dickensian world – a city over-populated, smoke-filled and skyless. She spoke about 'muck carts' as though nightsoil men still rumbled through the dark alleys to empty the lavatory pails. Her family followed a beady-eyed old-time evangelical Christianity that wasn't so old at all, but a response to city life when the cities themselves were new and alien, and everyone came from somewhere else. There was no real privacy. She couldn't step outside her community, her city, her *class*, any more than she could shed her skin. Debates and slanging matches were conducted in public. Lovers waited at lampposts, kids played on the kerb stones, and women chatted over the back wall. Barbed retorts helped to hide real feelings, and a tight lip was always the best defence. *Ask me no questions and I'll tell you no lies.* Even when Ancoats was long behind her, my grandmother relied on codes of decency to bring a sense of space and distance to her world. Even the closest of her friends were addressed as 'Mrs'; the front step was polished to a shine; the church calendar faithfully kept. The television provided an echo of her childhood. She liked hubbub: she hated the humdrum.

That Easter of 1974, the television was tuned to the musical *Oliver!* which she had circled in the *TV Times* as one to watch. I was hooked from the first number, 'Food, Glorious Food', as Oliver made his long walk to the gruel pot and addressed Bumble, the Beadle: 'Please sir, I want some more.' I had no idea what a beadle might be: possibly the dog in the *Peanuts* cartoon. But I knew the sign above the poorhouse door that read *God is Love* was phooey – and when the fat man got his hands on Oliver it would end badly.

As the ominous chant of '*Oli-ver, Oli-ver*' rose, my father opened an eye and looked at the television. 'Oliver Twist is a Blincoe,' he said. 'He's my great-great-grandfather.'

*

My *great*-great-great-grandfather Robert Blincoe was a workhouse child. His was one of only seven working-class memoirs published in the 1820s. As the book brought him a degree of fame, he became a campaigner for industrial reform and appeared as a witness before a parliamentary committee. The memoir was also a key source for the early life of Oliver Twist. If you know the novel *Oliver Twist*, then you know Robert's story. He was born in the London parish of St Pancras in 1792, an orphan and almost certainly a foundling: the parish books have no record of his baptism or who his parents were. His early years were spent in a baby farm, an orphanage run by a wet-nurse paid for by the parish board. In 1796, around the age of four, he was transferred to the workhouse and became an 'oakum picker', pulling apart old ships' ropes to recycle the fibres for caulking. This was a job reserved for paupers and criminals: naval ropes were waterproofed with a coating of tar and picking the strands apart would shred your fingers and tear off your nails. The expense of looking after workhouse children fell on the parish, and the parishioners, so the board would get rid of them as soon as possible by offering them as 'parish apprentices' to local tradesmen. Robert was just six years old when the local chimney-sweeps came to look him over. St Pancras Parish, roughly equivalent to the present-day Borough of Camden, was the fastest-growing part of the city and the new houses needed a steady supply of boys to climb up the chimneys and clean them.

The opening chapters of Robert's life story, *A Memoir of Robert Blincoe; An Orphan Boy*, and Charles Dickens's *Oliver Twist; or, The Parish Boy's Progress* unfold in lockstep: the same events are told in the same order. Even the account of how the boys came by their names is similar. Dickens's beadle, who I now know is the parish policeman, is asked how Oliver came by his name if he had no mother or father. The beadle replies: 'I inwented it... Mrs Mann. We name our fondlings in alphabetical order. The last was a S, – Swubble, I named him. This was a T, – Twist, I named *him*. The next one as comes will be Unwin, and the next Vilkins. I have got names ready made to the end of the alphabet, and all the way through it again, when we come to Z.' Mrs Mann can't help but express her admiration. 'Why, you're quite a literary character, sir!'

Robert was the first Blincoe. He had never even heard of the name until he was given his papers at the age of twenty-one. 'Blincoe', a name conjured up by another literary representative of the parish, has stuck. It's been a mixed blessing. No one can spell it, nor even quite remember it, yet no one ever completely forgets it, either. I've been told it's a good name for a writer – but just as often I'm asked if it's real, which I guess it isn't.

Robert's *Memoir* tells how he was raised in a London workhouse before being sent as a seven-year-old apprentice to the northern cotton mills. Dickens drew on Robert's opening chapters because they provided an insight into the parish workhouse, an institution that functioned like a prison, and so was off-limits to civilians. By reading Robert's story, Dickens could imagine the lives of parish orphans, and especially the childhood of a young workhouse girl around his age that his parents recruited as their domestic servant. Dickens commemorated his relationship with this girl in two of his novels: as the Marchioness in *The Old Curiosity Shop* (1841) and the Orfling in *David Copperfield* (1849). She disappeared from his life when he was twelve years old. Robert's book struck a chord, perhaps because Robert's workhouse was in the same London streets that Dickens shared with her.

Robert Blincoe's *Memoir* was written in 1822 but not published until 1828, when it appeared as a weekly serial in the *Lion* newspaper based in Fleet Street. That year, Dickens's uncle John Henry Barrow began publishing his own newspaper, *The Mirror of Parliament*, close by, on Whitehall. Over the next five years, Robert's story went through another four editions, including an 1832 edition published by a trade union organiser named John Doherty as part of the campaign for the Ten Hour Act. By this time, Dickens had joined his uncle's paper as a reporter, where he covered speeches by Lord Ashley (later Shaftesbury), the champion of the act in Parliament and an associate of Doherty. In the summer of 1833, Robert's portrait appeared on banners at a major demonstration in support of Ashley's bill. After *The Pickwick Papers* made Dickens famous, Ashley arranged fact-finding tours of the industrial north for him in late 1838. Dickens wasn't the only author looking for material on working-class lives. In early 1839, Ashley also organised a tour for the rival best-selling novelist Frances 'Fanny' Trollope, the mother of Anthony Trollope. She got to know Doherty and went on to borrow chunks of Robert's *Memoir* for her own serialised novel, *The Life and Adventures of Michael Armstrong, The Factory Boy*. The serialisation of both *Oliver Twist* and *Nicholas Nickleby* overlapped with Trollope's work and Dickens was angry that she was stepping on his toes.

The germ of the idea for *Oliver Twist* can be dated back to 1833. The twenty-one-year-old Dickens had the idea almost before he had written anything else. He felt a strong affinity for the parish orphan or foundling child. That year saw him stage a family production of Richard Brinsley Peake's play *Amateurs and Actors* (1818), which features a parish orphan named Geoffrey Muffincap (a plum role taken by another of his uncles,

Edward Barrow). His first sketches of London appeared that December, and he adopted his pen name, Boz, a corruption of Moses, the most famous foundling in religious myth. Through 1834 and 1835, he took to asking friends as well as his fiancée Catherine Hogarth to see parallels between himself and the poet Richard Savage, who had claimed to be the abandoned child of an aristocratic mother. In 1836, in the run-up to the serialisation of *Oliver Twist*, Dickens wrote a short autobiographical piece drawn from his Camden childhood, recounting a meeting with a sweep's apprentice. The boy tells Dickens that he does not know his father, and Dickens takes this as evidence he is another lost child of an aristocrat.

Dickens continued to draw upon stories of abandoned orphans and parish apprentices throughout his career. A possible reason for this lifelong obsession was disclosed two years after his death in 1870, when his close friend John Forster sensationally revealed that Dickens had been abandoned by his parents and dumped in a London bottling plant when he was eleven years old. Forster claimed many of the events of *David Copperfield* were drawn from life, hidden in plain sight in an essentially autobiographical novel. In Forster's account, Dickens began working in the bottling plant when his parents were imprisoned for debt. His job was to paste labels on pots of blacking – the stuff used to waterproof and polish boots and kitchen grates.

The story of Dickens's miserable childhood forms the opening chapters of Forster's *Life of Charles Dickens* (1872). There are many problems with Forster's account, first among them his claim that Dickens was forced to work because of his parents' money troubles. We now know that Dickens's apprenticeship in the blacking factory was intended to teach him the bottling business and was planned before his parents got into difficulties.

Forster's biography has been taken as gospel, because Forster claimed to have access to an original lost memoir containing passages identical to those in *David Copperfield*. When, in 1941, Edmund Wilson wrote his haughtily camp essay on Dickens, *The Two Scrooges*, he could plausibly claim there had never been an authoritative biography of Dickens, dismissing Forster's as an 'elaborate memoir' and 'never ... a real biography'. Yet, despite throwing shade on Forster's book, Wilson accepts its thesis that the months he spent in the blacking factory were both the trauma and the pivot of Dickens's entire life: 'the work of Dickens' whole career was an attempt to digest these early shocks and hardships, to explain them to himself, to justify himself in relation to them, to give an intelligible and tolerable picture of a world in which such things could occur.' This psychological explanation for Dickens's genius is Forster's legacy, succinctly restated by John Carey: 'the blacking factory permanently wounded Dickens' mind, and helped make him a great novelist.'

Every subsequent biography of Dickens has run with the idea that if we understand the damaged child, then we understand the great author. All rest upon Forster's claim to have access to what Dickens scholars refer to as the 'autobiographical fragment'. But this claim is suspect. The text Forster quotes from is itself fragmented, non-sequential and taken from different documents. Forster presents direct quotes from *David Copperfield*, with a comment that the original autobiographical piece said the same thing. Other excerpts turn out to be Forster's transcriptions of recalled conversations, which Forster claims 'I can describe in *his* own words' (my emphasis). There are even rewrites of *David Copperfield* with Forster's own interpolations. The passages do not always read much like Dickens, with inconsequential lists and odd repetitions ('my poor white hat, little jacket, poor corduroy trowsers' appears twice). Why does Forster quote piecemeal from a supposedly original text that he claims to have seen but no longer has in his possession? Forster preserved letters from Dickens yet seems to have mislaid reams of personal memoir handwritten by Dickens himself, with his famous goose quill. If we ask how the original text came to lie in fragments, we might conclude that it was never whole. Rather, it's Forster's own assemblage of quotes, texts he claims to remember seeing, rewrites of the supposedly autobiographical episodes in the novels, as well as posthumous accounts of his private conversations with Dickens. Even if Forster had been shown a few pages of memoir in the 1840s, the text he presents thirty years later is a simulacrum. But once Dickens was dead, who would contradict him?

It becomes clear that Forster has cobbled together glosses and inventions when he recounts the influence of a figure named James Lamert. This young man was Dickens's cousin-by-marriage and a close ally through his childhood, despite being nine years senior. At the age of twenty, Lamert landed a job as the manager of the infamous blacking factory. In official records, from court documents to civil registers, James is only ever known as 'George', a fact which evidently confused Forster. Faced with the mystery of the Two Lamerts, he identified George as a shareholder in the factory, and James as the manager. In order to support this invention, he then ventriloquises a reference to George in Dickens's voice, so the non-existent man is identified as 'the cousin and brother-in-law of James'. Dickens loved his cousin and would have known there was only one man. Behind the convoluted attempts to explain the existence of George we can see Forster's brain whirring as though caught in a nonsensical dream, creating a solution so improbable that he must place it in Dickens's mouth if it is to ring true.

The existence of a once complete, now lost, memoir is an object of faith among Dickens's biographers, and Forster is our apostle. We never ask if there was an original because it feels so true. Why else this obsession with foundlings, orphans and abandoned children? Where else could it come from? Peter Ackroyd's account of Dickens's life, like Forster's original, is also an elaborate memoir: he mischievously gives it the subtitle, 'A Memoir of Middle Age'; that is, his own mid-life and not Dickens's. Ackroyd seems to speak for all writers when he asserts: 'If he was the chronicler of his age, he also stood apart from it ... always in some sense the solitary observer.' Dickens had a large circle of friends and family and took a desperate pleasure in their company. Yet Ackroyd chooses to draw upon the image of the great writer as someone essentially alone, doomed to isolation because of his genius. Forster's account of the blacking factory story has become sacred because it provides us with a wellspring for the troubled and lonely man. The idea that the psychological development of an adult begins in childhood trauma is now familiar, but it was once novel. In Forster's account, Dickens's childhood trauma not only individuated him, it also made him great.

But was Dickens really as miserable in the factory as David Copperfield? After all, Dickens was not an orphan, he did not have a vindictive stepfather, he was not a stranger to London but had aunts and uncles all around, and he worked alongside a favourite family member. The story of Dickens and the blacking factory is essentially about emotional and psychological suffering, a kind of trauma distinct from that of figures like Robert Blincoe or the Dickens family's orphan maid, a girl whose name has been lost. The historical accounts of child workers focus on appalling physical abuse. Robert Blincoe's memoir is a harrowing account of years and years of unimaginable violence. Protesters carried his picture at demonstrations because he was crippled, his buckled and twisted legs a common result of a childhood spent spinning cotton using the Arkwright water frame.

Dickens knew the abuse and negligence suffered by parish apprentices. The Dickens family's maid was dismissed during or shortly after the parents' imprisonment. She was a lone girl, uneducated and essentially unskilled. John and Elizabeth Dickens had taken her from Chatham workhouse and brought her to London, leaving her stranded far from her hometown and any relatives. Like Nancy, the prostitute of *Oliver Twist*, she would find herself old before her time, victimised by pimps, abusers and boyfriends. Dickens must have felt as though she had been murdered ... the fate he ultimately visits on Nancy.

Forster quotes Dickens as saying: 'It is wonderful to me how I could so easily have been cast away at such an age. It is wonderful to me, that, even after my descent into the poor little drudge since we came to London, no one had compassion enough on me – a child of singular abilities, quick, eager, delicate, and soon hurt, bodily or mentally.' Like other child workers, Dickens felt pain and hunger, but the worst of the experience was the damage to his sense of self. We are asked to see the mental scars as the more lasting, because they cannot be forgotten. Memory doesn't heal. This is Dickens the writer, who transcends the brutal reality of his time, turning his hopes and disappointments into great works of fiction. And so, while his abandonment as a child scarred him, it was also a necessary wound for the writer. Forster gives us a lengthy quote that he claims is from the autobiographical fragment, but which appears, almost word for word, in *David Copperfield*. It begins with a description of the author's feelings towards his work and workmates in the bottling plant:

> No words can express the secret agony of my soul as I sunk into this companionship; compared these every day associates with those of my happier childhood; and felt my early hopes of growing up to be a learned and distinguished man, crushed in my breast. The deep remembrance of the sense I had of being utterly neglected and hopeless; of the shame I felt in my position; of the misery it was to my young heart to believe that, day by day, what I had learned, and thought, and delighted in, and raised my fancy and emulation up by, was passing away from me, never to be brought back any more; cannot be written.

Forster concludes the passage with a new, final sentence that does not appear in *David Copperfield*: 'My whole nature was so penetrated with the grief and humiliation of such considerations, that even now, famous and caressed and happy, I often forget in my dreams that I have a dear wife and children; even that I am a man; and wander desolately back to that time of my life.'

'Famous, caressed and happy' was not, though, the fate of most child workers. Unknown, ignored and desolate would be more accurate. Which is why the lives of these parish boys and girls and other vulnerable children have a political as well as a personal dimension. Their injuries speak of unfettered industrialisation, a lack of social care, and the cruelty and indifference of a rigidly class-based society. Copies of the *Memoir of Robert Blincoe*, like the handful of similar accounts that followed over the two decades it took Parliament to pass the Ten Hours Act, were circulated to fight for the rights of a class of people. But by presenting *David Copperfield* as pure autobiography, Forster gives us a Dickens who is always in revolt against this class: he flat-out rejects the companionship of the other child workers. Did Forster simply lift a passage from *Copperfield* and twist it? The claim to be 'famous and caressed and happy' reads like a piece of projection, rather than anything one might say of oneself. Especially as Forster knew, better than anyone, how shabbily Dickens had treated his wife in the years following the publication of this novel. Yet the underlying idea is one that we imagine would speak to Dickens. The factories are pressing out mass-produced tubs and bottles, yarns and cloths, while physically turning a class of people into identikit factory fodder. Dickens transcends the masses because he turns his suffering into a kind of sensitive self-awareness, which in turn leads to work that is not mass produced and repeatable, but has its own distinctive, genuine quality. Dickens frees himself through writing, no longer answering to a boss – and certainly not to his parents – but only to his inner light. Physical suffering belongs to a world of mass production and class conflict; mental suffering to a classless society of individuals, endlessly refashioning themselves as self-realising projects. Early in his career, Dickens began to call himself 'the Inimitable', showing a talent for what we would nowadays call *branding*, but also revealing his belief in himself as a self-made creative man. He's a one-off, because what he does is beyond anyone else, as unique as a signature. One may doubt the provenance of Forster's 'autobiographical fragment', but the distinction it makes between physical labour and artistic creation is Dickensian – not his invention, true, but a romantic philosophy that Dickens embraced and made his own.

Stories of child workers captured the public imagination and helped drive popular appeals for factory reform. Dickens repurposed these accounts to tell the story of a new kind of worker. His was a story not of class action but individual realisation, not solidarity but entrepreneurialism, not mass production and physical hardship, but aesthetic production and mental anguish. It is a flattering if ambivalent portrait of the life of a writer or artist. Contemporary self-employed creatives, the arts and media freelancers and the digital nomads, are not as free as they like to think. Their work still exists in the real world, beset by parents and dependents, and continues to rely upon mass-production, high speed communication – not to mention the financial infrastructure of mortgages, overdrafts, pension plans and share prices. Artists don't suffer a superior form of anxiety that lifts them out of the rat race and closer to genius. And yet... the idea that one is set apart, striving to be inimitable, seems real – at least to those doing the work of creation.

(I'm talking about myself. Inevitably. All biographies of Dickens turn out to be elaborate memoirs of the writers toiling in his shadow.)

I had three newspaper rounds as a kid, and prior to starting university I worked for my father in the exhaust pipe factory that he inherited from his grandfather, learning to electro-weld, cut pipes and drive a van – all quite disastrously and often dangerously. But since I graduated, I've only ever earned money as – *cough* – a 'man of letters'. To create and sell your ideas, to put yourself out there as a voice or style or dramatic presence, to have no resources and no capital other than the next idea, the next story, the next *thing*: it's not without its anxieties. To be a writer or artist, a musician or actor, perhaps even an *influencer*, feels like the absolute personification of freedom. We've moved out of the hardships of the physical realm and the wage slave.

We've canned the bosses, so why doesn't it feel more *fun*? I can't help feeling the harsh relationship between boss and worker has been internalised, and now it's all about scrutinising oneself, beating oneself up to become ever more productive, inventive or original.

To talk about my life as a writer alongside Oliver Twist is not simply to reflect on the relation between the fictional Oliver and his original, Robert, my real-life ancestor. Nor even to ask about the connection between the most *inimitable* of writers and myself, hopelessly flailing away hundreds of floors below in the tower of stories. It's also about the way that Dickens's first real novel caught the popular revulsion at the exploitation of children. He cared about the working child. The story of his family's maid genuinely tore at his soul and disturbed his mind. And yet, in working through this pain, he ended up creating something else, a new economy of *creators*. Dickens was born into a world where poets, artists and writers still had to toady to the rich and powerful to gain space, permission and an audience for their work – and he broke free. He was a pathfinder, reaching a vast popular audience on his own terms. His example haunts every other writer. After Dickens, we not only live in a world where we are exploited for what we can physically *do* in a working day, but one in which we are also exploited for what we *hope* for, we *dream* of, what we *imagine* or *desire*. We live vicariously as the aspirational version of ourselves, endlessly throwing out ideas, looking for affirmation while risking envy or opprobrium. Endlessly making a show of ourselves: the very thing our grandmothers warned us not to do.

I hear my grandmother asking, 'You know what thought did?'

In the 1830s, Dickens was part of a London literary scene that encompassed the theatre, music, books and magazines, illustrators, printers, publishers and impresarios. During the serialisation of *Oliver Twist*, Dickens got married and had two of his ten children, while the last Hanoverian king died, and the eighteen-year-old Queen Victoria ascended the throne. *Oliver Twist* marks the beginning of a new era not only for Dickens but for the entire country. A centralised metropolitan police force replaces the old and amateurish parish beadles. Travel by horse-drawn coach gives way to steam trains. The Atlantic is crossed for the first time by ocean liners. It's the beginning of a new global popular culture. *Oliver Twist* spans this change, but also captures it. The story of parish apprentices is taken and repurposed to tell a different story, not about physical hardship and systemic abuse, as was the case with Robert Blincoe's memoir, but about self-reliance, overcoming one's parents, and backing oneself to succeed. It's the story of Dickens himself, a new kind of self-made, self-exploiting project. But it's a story that Dickens can only tell by taking someone else's story and, if we are charitable, absorbing it as his own. Less charitably, we might say he *appropriated* it.

Oliver Twist is the most loved, and the most enduring, of all of Dickens's works, with endless revivals of the musical, retellings of the book, and even spin-off projects in what we should probably call the Dickens Multimedia Universe. As I write this, there is a new *Oliver!* musical in development for the West End, and two competing Artful Dodger TV series running simultaneously, a prequel on the BBC and a sequel on Disney+. *Oliver Twist* is Dickens's signature work, the novel that encompasses his entire career, threads itself through everything, and explains it all: the man, his times, his influence. Dickens sketched a plan for the book at twenty-one, before he'd published another word, and he returned to it at the end of his life. The national reading tour he undertook in the late 1860s culminated with a dramatic *tour de force*, the murder of Nancy. Of all the great set pieces in his novels, this was the one he chose to close his performances. Why, if not to take responsibility for the life of the orphan child-maid that his parents had thrown onto the streets? The readings proved lethal: the physical strain brought on the stroke that ultimately killed him at fifty-eight.

The age I am, as I write these lines.

1

The Two Workhouses: 1790s/1830s

At twenty-two years old, Charles Dickens was an aspiring writer with a single big idea. He sketched it out in a letter to his friend Henry Kolle. It would be a novel based on his parish, St Pancras, the semi-rural district – he uses the word 'suburban' – that was his family's home for a decade from the early 1820s. His plan was to sell chapters to magazines as he wrote them, where they would sit alongside the other sketches of London life that were beginning to make his name. The 'parish' series appeared shortly afterwards in the *Monthly Magazine*, though Dickens was never actually paid for them. While his focus is local politics and neighbourhood gossip, the interconnected tales are shot through with the disconcerting rumbles of change. St Pancras is the fastest-growing district in London. Newcomers arrive from the countryside, tenants slip in and out of rented homes, children multiply, and the number of poor keeps growing. Although Dickens underplays the disquiet, his readers would know the truth: the parish is on the cusp of being swallowed by the sprawling megalopolis to the south. The comedy lies in the way the parishioners potter on oblivious to the storm around them.

The parish series evolves into *Oliver Twist*, where the focus soon shifts to the teeming alleyways and thieves' kitchens of Fagin and the Artful Dodger. The plan to capture a parish in the process of change has been reworked and condensed until, finally, it only occupies the opening chapters of *Oliver Twist* – with brief periodic returns to the workhouse and Mrs Bumble's chambers. Dickens has seen that his parish no longer really exists. Who would ever speak about St Pancras as an area, today? It's always Camden, thanks to 'Camden Town', London's national goods depot, drawing the east and the west of the capital together, and linking the metropolis with the industrial heartland of the north.

The end of the parish system was driven by the Poor Law of August 1834. When Dickens wrote to Kolle, he had been living in and around Camden Town for a little over a decade. He knew his wonky colourful parish no longer had the finances or the professionals to care for a growing urban population, especially the paupers, the elderly and the children. The new Poor Law effectively nationalised the parish workhouses by creating administrative units, known as Poor Law Unions, larger than the old parishes and answerable to a central administration. Almost immediately, the unions were used to register births, deaths and marriages – usurping other services that the parish council had once supplied. The parishes, which had been the basic unit of local government since medieval times, were suddenly over. In essence, the Poor Law was a first attempt at a welfare state, but faceless, authoritarian and punitive. Dickens was not especially idealistic: he saw as clearly as anyone that the parish system was already broken. Yet he also felt that something had been lost. Wasn't there something laudable in the idea of the old-fashioned parish? A self-governing Christian community, dedicated to good works, prayer and the fellowship of man? This utopian ideal is the unlikely happy ending to Oliver Twist (*spoiler alert*): the virtuous characters leave London to establish a self-governing Christian commune in a rural idyll. This ideal family is the counterpart to the only other family in Oliver Twist: Fagin and his boys, dedicated to laughter and sin, and ultimately destroyed by murder, betrayal, deportation and the gallows.

In the original parish stories, the workhouse itself lies in the shadows. When the beadle – 'one of the most, perhaps THE most, important member of the local administration' – arrests an old drunk woman and takes her to the workhouse, we don't follow her inside. We learn the workhouse is run by a thin angry overseer, with his own secret recipe for workhouse soup, and governed by the Vestry, or parish board. When the beadle dies following his exertions with the old lady, the soup's secret ingredients become the focal point in the elections for a new beadle, with a political fight between the Tories, represented by a local landlord, and the more combative parishioners, represented by a retired naval captain. But what happens inside the workhouse is as mysterious as the soup. The building is a kind of prison – one that Dickens has never seen inside. As his plans for the parish stories evolve into Oliver Twist, he finds he needs an insider's account. This is what Robert Blincoe's Memoir supplies.

A generation earlier, in the 1790s, St Pancras Workhouse was based in temporary premises in a fork in the road on the way to Hampstead. It was a near-derelict building that had once been a mansion, and more recently an inn. The parish board acquired it in the 1770s on a short-term lease but kept it for thirty years.

Today the easiest way to visit the site is by Underground: it's where the present-day Camden Town Tube station stands. My girlfriend Janet and I visited on a Saturday after walking our dog on Hampstead Heath and it began to go wrong the moment the doors opened at Camden Town. We had made a mistake. We realised it: even the dog realised it. I had to cradle him because there were no gaps between the bodies packed on to the platform, and no space for his paws between the outsized trainers and platform-soled Dr Martens. A pair of young women cooed and tickled Fredo's ears as we were crushed and jostled. Janet and I have lived in London most of our lives, but we like to see ourselves as Northerners. Specifically, we like to see ourselves as Mancs: mad-for-it, bucket-hatted City supporters, wearing 'On the Seventh Day God Created Manchester' T-shirts. Perhaps it takes a trip to Camden to prove it. Real Londoners know it's no longer possible to visit Camden at the weekend.

The archaeology of ancient cities is so fascinating because each new iteration of the city is built on the dust and refuse of older generations. The city writes its own timeline over the centuries, which can be read by excavating a trench and counting the layers. Which is why I thought it was such a good idea to enter Camden from below. I forgot that Camden isn't very old, and what little history it has disrupts the old timelines. It's not even possible to read the striated sediments as we travel up the station's escalators. There are posters advertising West End shows, adult health vitamins and gym memberships, but the deeper structure is sealed behind air pipes, electricity cables and plaster. I keep hold of Fredo because the escalator ends in sharp teeth, and he gets frightened. He only skips out of my hands as we reach the ticket hall and we start searching for our phones to swipe out of the barriers.

The parish opened the temporary workhouse after the original, built in 1731, became uninhabitable due to flooding from the River Fleet. I want to find a spot where I can imagine how this ramshackle building would have looked in Robert's day. I decide there is a place in front of the traffic lights, wedged against the market-day barriers. Janet, Fredo and I push through the queue of people trying to enter the Tube and take up a position where the art deco station building appears like the prow of a ship. Camden High Street flows to its left, and the road to Kentish Town to the right. There's been a cashpoint at the tip of the building for as long as I can remember: when I was young I would scrape out money in £5 increments for ill-judged nights out. The junction has been crazy for as long as I can remember, with six roads converging into a narrow traffic-choked point. It was a lot simpler in the days of the workhouse. Camden High Street was then the main turnpike between London and Hampstead, and the road to Kentish Town was a lane branching off to the right.

Where we are standing, in the 'V', was once the village pound, designed to hold lost and stray livestock. To our right, where the World's End pub now stands, there was a famous inn called the Mother Red Cap, named after a reputed witch. Robert's workhouse rose up behind the animal pound. It was a large square building, three storeys high and surrounded by a six-foot wall. It had been designed as a home for perhaps thirty people, a well-to-do family and their servants. By the 1790s, the same building was home to 450 paupers, of whom around half were children, including thirty or forty orphans. The inmates were forced to share beds infested with fleas and lice. Although the workhouse had moved to avoid flooding, the temporary building was still close enough to the river that its basement regularly filled with foul-smelling water, seeping up through the floorboards into the workhouse rooms. The walls creaked and cracked: when the paupers were finally moved to a new workhouse in 1809, it was discovered that so many internal walls had been removed that the roof was in danger of falling. An audit of the available beds revealed that a mix of 149 doubles and singles could be salvaged for the new premises, 'if cleansed of vermin', but another seventy-five were only fit for burning.

The temporary workhouse was a makeshift solution that bridged the gap between two purpose-built parish workhouses, both built on the same site on what is now St Pancras Way. The workhouse as Charles Dickens knew it survives as the oldest parts of the present-day St Pancras Hospital. St Pancras was once a rural village. The site of the present church dates back to the Roman era. For more than a thousand years, it overlooked the River Fleet from the small hill, facing meadows where dairy cattle grazed. As London grew, the meadows became a flood plain. They lay halfway between the paved hills of Hampstead to the north and the congested heart of London to the south. In the eighteenth century the meadows became stagnant shit-filled swamps as the Fleet swept sewage down from Hampstead above, and then was unable to drain away because the entrance to the Thames downstream was so choked, forcing the river to back up and overflow. The Roman church and the surrounding village were abandoned, along with the parish buildings and its first workhouse. Between Robert's day in the late 1790s and Dickens's arrival in London in the early 1820s, a series of large-scale solutions to the area were found. The river was tamed by burying it in a pipe underground, while a new navigable waterway – the Regent's Canal – was cut through Camden, and an inland dock was created in the canal basin of Camden Lock. When a network of railways was also cut through the district from the 1830s onwards, Camden effectively became one of the busiest ports in the country.

London's growth in these years marks a radical break with older cities. There was no sense of a slow, natural expansion, nor a well-ordered timeline with a visible chronology. London was expanding in all directions, and even the city grid, the one immutable part of the city, was changing as rivers disappeared, enabling new roads and waterways to appear where none had existed before. The London that I know has its roots in this period, a city shaped by capital projects, international money, and immigrants from both the countryside and abroad. It created a topsy-turvy, unreadable city – the kind of space that Dickens evoked with such consistent brilliance that we simply call it *Dickensian*. However, Dickens was acutely aware that his city was new, and to his mind unnatural. Perhaps he sensed it so keenly because he had spent a big chunk of his childhood outside London in Hampshire and Kent. Perhaps also because he knew and loved the novels of Tobias Smollett, Henry Fielding and Oliver Goldsmith, which so clearly belonged to another, quieter world. But he also felt the world had changed because his parents' generation had lost or squandered something – that a world had ended as they came on to the scene. Given the cramped and filthy state of the workhouse in Robert Blincoe's day, it would seem curious that Dickens believed there had been a golden age for parish apprentices and paupers before the Poor Law of 1834. But as appalling as the conditions in Robert's temporary workhouse were, the situation was a great deal worse after the Act. Dickens knew this, which is why he was so opposed to it; still, he also knew the crisis had been a long time in the making. If he dates the beginning of this long-term decline back to the 1780s and 1790s, when his parents were born, one can make a case for that. The end of the old parish system represents a world caught in flux, as the very last shreds of the old order disappear, and modernity is born out of the chaos. The new Dickensian London was rising, filled with dirt and violence, but also with children, colour and possibilities.

In 1791, an abandoned child was found 'dropt at a Gentleman's Door in John Street, Tottenham Court Road'. The street, now named Whitfield Street, lies at the edge of St Pancras, close to the border with St George, Bloomsbury. One of the beadle's jobs was to remove anyone who might be a burden on the parish purse, whether a pauper, a destitute pregnant woman or an abandoned child. The bundle may have been smuggled over the boundary of the neighbouring parish. Was the child Robert Blincoe? There is no record of anyone baptised Robert Blincoe in St Pancras. Robert insisted his mother must have been resident in the parish when he was born, otherwise he would never have been accepted as a parish orphan. Perhaps the John Street gentleman knew more than he claimed and bribed the beadle to take the child, no questions asked. Ten pounds was the going figure at the time. The baby was just a few months old, wrapped in a pair of caps, an old handkerchief, three shirts and a linen jacket – a bundle of rags large enough to keep it warm. The famous Foundling Hospital at Coram's Fields was also in the parish of St Pancras, but would only take a child if a fifty-pound donation was pinned on its blanket – a clean and convenient way for families to get rid of unwanted or illegitimate children such as those born to their servant girls. The Foundling Hospital baptised the children they accepted, which Robert envied because it gave them a name in law and the sight of God. Without a baptism, he felt he had no recognised name. It was a constant source of anxiety. He worried that he had no status in this life, and that he might not be recognised in the next.

Robert was thought to be around four years old in 1796 when

he was brought to the workhouse by a woman. There were no tears or drama when she left. In Robert's memory, she was just one of a chain of women whose hands he had passed through. Like Mrs Mann in *Oliver Twist*, she is likely to have been the owner of one of the private orphanages known as 'baby farms'. The parish paid for wet-nurses to look after parentless children until they were old enough to be transferred to the workhouse. Children like Robert were more likely to survive as infant mortality rates declined. London was fast becoming a city of children, a development propelled in part by new brick homes which harboured less mould and fewer disease-carrying bugs than houses made of mud, dung and straw – many of which had been cleared out by the Great Fire a century earlier. St Pancras was the centre of the brickmaking industry in London. The heavy clay soil was stripped from its waterlogged meadows, mixed with coal cinders, and baked in open-air stacks known as clamps. The industry destroyed the land and filled the air with acrid smoke. There's an irony in the fact that, just as the brick homes were helping the city's babies survive, the brickworks were lending the still largely rural parish of St Pancras a distinctly toxic flavour. Yet the parish kept growing, up from 5,000 inhabitants in the 1780s to 30,000 by the close of the century, an astonishing six-fold rise.

The workhouse was paid for through the local rates and administered by a board of local dignitaries, who in turn appointed overseers. By the 1790s St Pancras had fourteen overseers, who were responsible for managing the beadle, his constables and the church wardens. The workhouse only provided shelter for those who could not look after themselves. This meant that half the inmates were children, and the rest a mix of the elderly and the infirm, with ten 'lunatics'. Anyone healthy enough to actively look for work took what was known as 'outdoor relief', which might come in the form of food, clothes or cash (outdoor relief ended after 1834). Life inside the workhouse was undeniably harsh but not as harsh as it would become. David Lean's 1948 film of *Oliver Twist* depicts a vast hall of children picking oakum: rubbing tarred rope against barbed hooks. But this is a picture of life in the workhouse following the 1834 Act. In Robert's day, whether there was any actual work depended on the local overseers, who had to go out and find contracts for the inmates to fill. Often there was nothing to do. Robert states that he was cleanly dressed, and even that his shared bed was comfortable. Most importantly, and unlike Oliver, he had decent food. There was porridge made with milk for breakfast, a lunch which included meat or mutton on four days of the week, and a supper of bread and cheese in the evening. He could be grateful for the beer allowance, three-quarters of a pint for children, and special treats for holidays such as plum pudding for Christmas, alongside a gift of tuppence. Robert was even inoculated against smallpox at the new hospital in Battle Bridge, opened just a couple of years earlier. The widespread adoption of vaccines was another reason for the population growth. The smallpox hospital survived on the Battle Bridge site until the mid-nineteenth century when it was demolished to make way for the St Pancras railway terminus.

Robert's days were regimented, and boring. He was marched between the canteen, the factory floor and the schoolhouse. The lessons focused on the Bible, duty and gratitude, but Robert gained the basics of an education. When he left the workhouse at the age of seven, he knew his letters and was more than capable of simple arithmetic. He also had leisure time to play with the other children or even to sit alone. The high walls prevented him from interacting with locals but from the third-floor windows he had a view towards London, down the road which became Camden High Street. He was fascinated by the life he saw outside, and he wanted to be a part of it.

Robert's *Memoir* and *Oliver Twist* repeat the same scenes, from the baby farm to arriving alone at the workhouse, and in both a woman appears with news about the death of their mother. The women also come with tokens; in Oliver's case, he is given a gold locket with two locks of hair and a wedding ring; in Robert's case, the woman gives him a penny and tells him that his mother is dead, and that his name is 'Saint'. Throughout his apprenticeship, Robert was known as 'Parson'. It's unclear whether he believed it was a nickname or his family name. It was only when he saw his apprenticeship papers at the age of twenty-one that he began to use 'Robert Blincoe', the only name he had that had ever been written down.

The *Memoir* is a collaboration with a journalist named John Brown, and though packed with direct quotes, the language is often odd and artificial. Brown is compelled to admit he cannot guarantee these are the very words Robert used. Instead, he claims they 'faithfully convey the spirit and tendency of his language'. Robert agreed. Interviewed over several days, he subsequently read and approved Brown's text. He went on record three times to say the account was accurate. Almost the first thing Robert says of himself in the *Memoir* is that he is a Parish Orphan. Without a name, parents or wider family, this was his only identity. The subtitle describes him as 'An orphan boy; sent from the workhouse of St Pancras'. When Dickens republished the *Oliver Twist* serial as a novel in 1838, he added the subtitle, 'The Parish Boy's Progress'. A workhouse boy who is a ward of the parish is no one. Robert is quoted as saying:

> When the friends, relatives, parents of other [workhouse] children came to visit them, the caresses that were sometimes exchanged, the joy that beamed on the faces of those so favoured, went as daggers to my heart ... and, young as I was, the voice of nature, instinct, if you will, forced me to consider myself as a moral outcast, as a scathed and blighted tree in the midst of a verdant lawn.

The workhouse of the 1790s wasn't intended to be unbearable. But it seemed that way to Robert. He felt like an outcast, and it weighed on his spirit. That outsider feeling underpins the biggest difference between Oliver Twist and Robert Blincoe: their responses to the visit by the chimney-sweeps looking for child apprentices.

The sweeps come calling two years into both children's stay in the workhouse. In Dickens's version, Oliver does everything he can to avoid becoming a sweep. He recognises that the life of a sweep's boy means certain death by suffocation, burning or illness, and Oliver wants his life. In *Oliver Twist* the action in the workhouse takes place just three months after the changes brought about by the new Poor Law which abolished outdoor relief: healthy adult paupers could only receive welfare if they gave up their freedom. Whereas the older regime had been custodial, providing a home (of sorts) for infants, the elderly and lunatics, the new law punished people for accepting welfare. The decision to remain free or accept welfare was framed as a rational choice. As the workhouse overseer in *Oliver Twist* says: 'the alternative (for they would compel nobody, not they,) of being starved in a gradual process in the house, or by a quick one out of it'. It is left to the artless and pompous Mr Bumble to admit that death in the workhouse is not necessarily slow, though it is certain.

He assures the undertaker, Sowerberry, Oliver's subsequent master, that the new system will make his fortune. Sowerberry retorts that the contract to bury the workhouse dead is small, and Bumble replies: 'So are the coffins.' Of course they are small; the inmates are dying of hunger. Bumble shows off a medal he received on the death of a local homeless man. The medal is engraved with the image of the Good Samaritan. Bumble is proud to receive the medal, though if the reader knows the story of the Good Samaritan, they will recognise that he has been commended for passing by on the other side. Sowerberry recalls the details of the inquest: '"They made it a special verdict, I think," said the undertaker, "by adding some words to the effect, that if the relieving officer had –" "Tush – foolery!" interposed the beadle angrily.'

It's as if, by ignoring a dying man, the beadle has respected his freedom, and left him to his own choice.

In the case of children, the workhouse board was the child's legal guardian, and had to make decisions on their behalf. When the chimney-sweep Gamfield offers to employ Oliver in return for a £5 consideration, he is questioned by Limbkins, the head of the board. Haven't children died of suffocation inside the chimneys? Gamfield admits this is so, but the fault is using damp straw when a child is stuck. The smoke from damp straw has a soporific effect; at least, the child loses consciousness. 'That's vot he likes. Boys is wery obstinit, and wery lazy.' Gamfield favours building a good hot blaze, which has the benefit of making a boy struggle and perhaps free himself. Gamfield is known to have killed three or four boys by beating them to death, so when Limbkins rejects his proposal and condemns chimney sweeping as 'a nasty trade', it seems that, finally, someone is acting out of concern for Oliver. But no, Limbkins is simply looking to strike a better deal. Rather than £5, he offers Gamfield a reduced rate of £3 10s. If Oliver's life is the responsibility of the board, then by setting the market price of an asset, everyone is a winner. The board was creating a market, and as agents and middlemen stepped in to match workhouse children with factory owners, something very like slavery emerged in the trafficking and selling of children to the industrial north.

As the price is set, Gamfield grumbles and accepts the terms. The plan goes wrong, however. Before a parish orphan like Robert or Oliver can become an apprentice, bound to a master by law until they are adults, their indenture papers must be signed by a magistrate. Oliver is duly taken before a magistrate but begins crying and shaking so much that even a half-blind old man can see his distress. In Oliver Twist, Dickens has created a child astute enough to know how to make an economic judgement, and judge that life in the workhouse offers a marginal improvement on the life that Gamfield is offering outside.

In complete contrast, Robert is desperate to be chosen by the sweeps. He joins a parade with enthusiasm, even standing on his tiptoes to appear older. He has seen another world from the top floor of the workhouse and wants to get out. Maybe he saw the brickmakers tending their clamps, the architects and surveyors laying out the grid of streets that make up Camden Town, as well as the fast carriages on the turnpike to the genteel suburbs of Hampstead and Highgate. In the *Memoir*, Robert describes the beggar children selling matches door-to-door, and the sweeps' boys running after their masters in all weathers. When he insists that he would have swapped his life for theirs in an instant, the journalist Brown cannot let these words go, and insists these are 'perverted feelings', the product of 'a diseased imagination'. What does Brown mean? Robert admits he was falling ill at the

The Two Workhouses: 1790s/1830s

time of his decision. He says that his appetite began to decline, that he was surly with the staff and avoided games in the yard. He was determined to break free from the workhouse. His state of mind reflects his loneliness. Almost all of the children in the workhouse had parents living in the parish. Even the other orphans had relatives close by. Being so alone was unnatural; or, at least, Robert – and Oliver – are made to feel that it is unnatural.

We should remember that Robert was only six years old when he tried to become a sweep's boy. He could see the other children were scared, yet it didn't stop him from trying to get picked. Robert smiled as these dirty, fearsome men prodded and examined him. He held his head high and stood on his toes while the other boys shuffled and cried, but though he was complimented on his spirit, they turned him down because he was too young and small, even for a sweep's boy. He took an irrational risk for freedom, where Oliver takes a rational decision to preserve what little safety he has. Dickens may place rational-seeming arguments in the mouth of the clown Bumble, and lampoon a government bill that punishes the poor, yet he accepts the underlying philosophy that a rational actor will be risk-averse. Oliver's timidity contrasts with Robert's bravery. Robert will take an irrational risk, and perhaps I am irrational, too, but isn't this what freedom means?

Our Saturday walk continues down Camden High Street. The Mother Black Cap, sister pub to the Mother Red Cap, stands on the western side of the street. One of London's oldest gay pubs, in its heyday between the 1960s and the 1980s it was known as the Palladium of Drag, with a tiny stage where the drag queens would perform. The pub closed years ago but hasn't been redeveloped yet. It's sealed up with shutters welded over the windows.

Janet went to a party there a few years ago, thrown without the permission of the owners of the premises. The basement filled with sewage as the evening wore on. Foul water is a perennial feature of Camden.

When Robert Blincoe lived in the workhouse, there was a brickmakers' field almost opposite the Mother Black Cap; more recently it was the site of an old Waterstones bookshop where I did a few readings in the 1990s, with Charlie Higson and David Peace. The best bookshop back then was Compendium, also now closed, in the block before the canal bridge. Long before I met Janet, we would both buy counter-culture novels and books of radical French philosophy from there and chat with the man who ran it, Mike Hart. Camden had a reputation as the radical edge of London through the 1980s and 90s. Janet had a clothes stall on the market. I played in punk bands and later a hip-hop group in its pubs. We both went to club nights at the Camden Palace. Although we didn't know each other, we were never far from each other.

The Camden Palace – now called Koko – stands at the end of the small grid of roads developed by Charles Pratt, 1st Earl of Camden. South of Koko is Somers Town, where the brickfields were owned by the Rhodes family, Hackney farmers who learned to sweat their assets in St Pancras before turning their attention to Africa and diamond mines under Cecil Rhodes. There were attempts to develop Somers Town as a fashionable address with the building of the Regency crescent known as the Polygon, but the smell of the brick clamps and the wasteland of open clay pits ensured that the spot never became fashionable. The Polygon and the rest of Somers Town became home to several thousand French priests fleeing the French Revolution; they rubbed shoulders with English radicals like Mary Wollstonecraft and

William Godwin, who also made their home in the Polygon. French priests and English Radicals alike were attracted to Somers Town for the cheap rents, but also because once the parish church had been abandoned, St Pancras afforded more religious freedom than anywhere else in London. The French community succeeded in opening a Catholic chapel in 1798, and there's still a church on the site – St Aloysius, the oldest post-Reformation Catholic church in England. In the workhouse, there was a rumour that Robert Blincoe was the bastard child of a clergyman, which is why he was named Saint and Parson. Perhaps he was a child of one of these refugee priests?

We turn left at the Camden Palace and walk down to the old churchyard. The church stands on a little hill, with the river curving around, overlooking dairy meadows on the far side of the bend. This is one of the spots where it's possible to work out the route of the now-subterranean River Fleet because the road now known as St Pancras Way ran beside the river. (In Robert's day, it was Kingsway.) We let Fredo run wild around the graveyard. The last time I was here, I came for the Hardy Tree, an ash standing at the centre of a circle of old gravestones. The story is that Thomas Hardy designed this strange monument as a young surveyor, when he supervised the clearance of half of the cemetery to make way for the rail tracks to St Pancras station – the tracks which led to the demolition of the smallpox hospital. The gravestones are packed tight and upright, like the slides in a carousel projector. The tree stood at the centre like a hub but is now gone. It was brought down by storms in the winter of 2022. I thought of the lines in Yeats's poem, 'Things fall apart: the centre cannot hold'. Janet and I even had our own rough beast, Fredo, snouting out the scent of other dogs in the gaps between the gravestones.

The parish church is a true Roman temple. It is highly likely to be the oldest Christian church in England. After the eighteenth-century floods forced its closure, the villagers established an acting parish church in Kentish Town. This provisional solution lasted until the 1820s when a grand new church was built on the southern side of New Road, now Euston Road. Later in the century, the original church was renovated by enthusiastic Victorians, ensuring that almost nothing of its original character remains. The churchyard appears in *A Tale of Two Cities*, Dickens's novel set in the 1790s, coinciding with Robert Blincoe's time in London. A pair of grave robbers hang around a funeral because they know there is little chance of anyone noticing them dig up the body in the godforsaken district with its abandoned church and graveyard set beside a flooded, shit-filled swamp.

The span of twenty years leading up to Dickens's birth saw the greatest upheavals in European history, perhaps until the Second World War. Perhaps ever. If you tried to explain the turmoil, you might focus on revolution, or technology, on economics, war, the history of ideas, the flourishing of Romantic and Idealist philosophy, the beginning of the labour movement, on grand strategy, the transatlantic slave trade, the rape of Africa, the Raj and colonial imperialism. For the most part, Dickens doesn't say what has happened – but his two historical novels, both set in the years of his parents' (and Robert's) birth and infancy, focus on violence, revolution and mob rule. *Barnaby Rudge* is set against London's Gordon Riots, while *A Tale of Two Cities* takes place during the French Revolution. Dickens describes a world in which authority breaks down, and power moves into the hands of the people or, at worst, the mob. To see revolution as chaos, and change as a falling away from a more natural order, implies a particular perspective: a romantic conservatism. Although Dickens is a very young man when he writes *Oliver Twist*, just twenty-one when he begins work on the Parish series, he already has the romantic conservative streak that will see him become the English laureate of family gatherings and feast days.

But it's a little more complicated than that. If Dickens hopes to recapture lost values, he is not trying to recapture a lost past. Perhaps he is not sure what exactly is lost, or even if anything good or perfect ever actually existed. His ideal families are invented families, 'logical families' to use the phrase popularised by Armistead Maupin. This is the paradox, especially of the young Dickens: he is a staunch anti-Tory, even at times a Radical, despite his conservative sympathies. For good and ill, Dickens was born into an age governed by reason rather than faith, and by the agenda of the Radicals with their ideas of freedom and self-determination. He wants to build a better world than the brutal workhouses, or the haughty utilitarian calculations of what is good for the mass of people. But by turning the big set piece of Robert Blincoe's memoirs on its head, by making Oliver afraid of the sweeps, he shows that he is fearful of the irrational leap that freedom requires.

Janet's birth parents put her up for adoption before she was born. Although she was secure in her adoptive parents, she felt the wider family could be cruel. At Christmas, she separated herself from the family circle, playing cards and board games without caring about the result, and feeling that no one cared about her. She was too young to understand, but she felt they had made a judgement: she had already gone to the bad. The term 'moral outcast' doesn't seem over the top; to her mind, they had decided that she wasn't clever enough, or sociable enough, and Christmas Day games brought this home. If I listen to Janet, Robert Blincoe draws closer to me. It's not as though sharing pieces of genetic material affords me any insight into his life. But when I hear about a six-year-old Janet being judged and ostracised without understanding why, it makes Robert more real. He reacted with a kind of courageous irrationality, the one thing that neither John Brown nor even Charles Dickens understood – but Janet does.

2

Two Families: Barrow and Dickens, 1790–1801

Dickens believed a venerable old world ended around the moment that his parents entered it: in the last decades of the eighteenth century. What made his mother and father such harbingers of disaster?

Showing an almost mystical faith in patrilineal descent, Dickens's biographers have focused on John Dickens's family. Peter Ackroyd is typical in claiming, 'the figures who influenced him most are found on the father's side of the family'. In contrast, the Barrows, his mother Elizabeth's family, have been minimised or even erased, a bias that goes back all the way to Forster's first biography of Dickens, which omitted figures like John Henry Barrow, the uncle who gave Dickens his start as a writer. Dickens grew up surrounded by his mother's brothers and sisters – she was the second oldest of ten – and her family had an enormous influence on his career. I don't want to say that Dickens was a nepo baby, but then again – perhaps I do. There are strong reasons to put the Barrows at the centre of Dickens's story, because of their deep connections to the worlds of show business, publishing and journalism. But it's also worth exploring why the story of the Barrows has tended to be suppressed. The reason is that great tabloid-style story: *My Secret Shame*. Dickens had good – and bad – reasons to be ashamed of his mother's family.

First, though, John Dickens. The few things that we know about him have been curated over two centuries to provide comparisons and counterpoints with his son. If Charles was irrepressible, sociable, grandiose, then these are characteristics he inherited from his father. John was like a cork which, 'when submerged, bobs up to the surface again, none the worse for the dip'. As often as not, he was deep under water: John Dickens might be the most famous bankrupt in British history. He was ready to lie and beg to borrow money, and invariably failed to pay when the debt was called in. He is said to be the source of the famous 'Micawber Principle' from *David Copperfield*: 'Annual income twenty pounds, annual expenditure nineteen pounds and six, result happiness. Annual income twenty pounds, annual expenditure twenty pounds nought and six, result misery.' Ackroyd sees their contrasting financial acuity as the great division between Charles Dickens and his father, but it is difficult to argue that either man had any money smarts. Dickens signed contracts for cash, constantly demanded more money after putting down his signature, looked for bonuses on top of his escalating fee, and would break a contract in a heartbeat if he sniffed a better deal. Nor was his freewheeling approach to contracts accompanied by a shrewd business brain. When Dickens died, he left less than £100,000, which sounds a lot – indeed a multimillion estate in today's money. But £20,000 of that had been earned just two years previously from a single tour of America – and he would have banked almost twice as much if he had not impetuously converted his dollars into gold. If Charles Dickens never had to apply the Micawber Principle to his own life, it's because he never had to keep to a strict annual expenditure. John had to worry about a fixed income; Charles had a near-unbounded capacity for earning more money – which he always spent.

The real difference between the two men is that the father was a clerk, while the son was one of the most famous men of his age. Charles Dickens wasn't more honest or careful than John, but he didn't need to be: he lived on another planet – there was no one like him. Yet if Charles stood alone, at the pinnacle of talent and celebrity, he was rarely actually alone. He grew up in a large family and, in later life, spent freely to ensure he was always surrounded by friends, lovers and close relatives. He travelled constantly, surrounded by male companions or family members, and kept three homes: one for his estranged wife in London; a very public set-up in Kent run by his sister-in-law, who was also his housekeeper; and a semi-secret peripatetic household that he had taken over, comprising a woman named Frances Eleanor Ternan and her two daughters. Long after Dickens's death, his second daughter, Kate, revealed that her father had taken the youngest Ternan girl as his mistress, a woman named Ellen or 'Nelly' Ternan. He was a paradox, a man who saw himself as lonely and alone, yet hated actually being alone. He surrounded himself with people, but they were all essentially his juniors, and they were beholden to him, and often living off him, which allowed him complete control over his network. In contrast, John Dickens cuts a far more solitary figure. 'It is often claimed that Dickens draws his fictional orphans from his own blighted experience as a boy,' writes Ackroyd, 'but can we not also see in his father's partial orphanhood a ready source of fantasies and stories?'

John Dickens was not an orphan but his father died a few

weeks before he was born. William Dickens was the senior servant in the house of John Crewe, an influential Whig politician who became Baron Crewe in later life. Crewe had a London home in Grosvenor Square, another in Hampstead where his wife liked to entertain, and a palatial family home in Crewe Hall near Nantwich in Cheshire, reputed to be the largest and finest house in England. William Dickens was a dedicated servant, who proved his devotion by remaining a bachelor until well into his sixties. Among the Crewe family's neighbours in Grosvenor Square was an elderly Dutch widow named Maria Catherina Haeck de Jong, styled Lady Blandford after her first, short marriage to William Godolphin, the Marquess of Blandford. When Lady Blandford died in 1779 at the age of eighty-four, her maid, Elizabeth Ball, moved into the Crewe household. Two years later, William and Elizabeth gained the family's blessing for a marriage. It was far from common for servants to remain in service after they had married. Perhaps the Crewes believed the union would be childless; William was in his mid-sixties, while Elizabeth was thirty-six. In the event, their first child was born two years later in 1783, a son, also named William. Then came John, born shortly after his father's death in 1785.

The world only discovered that Dickens's grandparents had been servants thanks to John Forster's *Life*. Like the story of the blacking factory, Forster's revelation seemed to say something about Dickens. But what? John Dickens had never known his father, and there is no reason to think Charles ever knew anything at all about this long-dead butler. The reasons for emphasising the lives of two servants lie in the English class system, never far from the surface in any consideration of English literature. The Dickens family brings the author into closer proximity with the British aristocracy and, thus, suggest that his father's spendthrift ways were an unfortunate reflection of his age. It was left unexplained why the child of servants should have absorbed the habits of their masters. It took Claire Tomalin to make the connection explicit in her 2011 biography. John Dickens, she suggests, was possibly the bastard son of John Crewe. Or a friend. Or maybe a house guest. It's all highly speculative. Tomalin asks us to consider that the forty-year-old Elizabeth had a child by a Crewe family member or close friend, and not only raised the illegitimate child within their household but remained the senior maid to Frances Crewe for another thirty years. The theory is intended to elevate John over his immediate family, reimagining him as a Regency buck or dandy. If we cast John Dickens as a kind of occluded nobleman, then we throw a romantic glow over his reckless spirit and interpret Dickens's exorbitant talent as a kind of aristocracy of the mind. Tracing Charles Dickens to the illegitimate line of one of the great landed families makes perfect sense in a country that still takes seriously the idea that Sir Francis Bacon or the Earl of Oxford wrote the plays of Shakespeare.

Except that it makes no sense whatsoever.

Elizabeth Ball led a peripatetic life as a maid to Frances Crewe. She was a distant mother, as her work forced her to live much of the time apart from her sons. The oldest son, William, was born in Cheshire though it was two years before he was baptised, in Marylebone, London, on the same day as his baby brother John. The boys were probably in town to attend their father's funeral. With a dead father and an absent mother, it is possible to think of the Dickens boys as near-orphans. Growing up on a great estate, they may have been nursed locally, and perhaps lodged with the class of servants who were allowed to have wives and children; those who lived outside the house, such as gamekeepers, foresters and gardeners. At the age of seven, the boys could move into the house and begin work as apprentice servants. It is likely that John Dickens served an entire apprenticeship as a footman or page because he arrived in London at the age of twenty-one, the age when an apprenticeship ends. John Dickens rejected the life of a servant, and though it would be another hundred or so years before the world of masters and servants finally died, his choice shows that it was already, in a sense, part of the past.

John arrived in London in 1805, just as the long war against revolutionary France was evolving into a conflict with the Napoleonic empire. The civil service was expanding and John soon found work as a clerk in the Navy Pay Office, part of the Navy Treasury based in Somerset House. It was a time when government jobs were filled through friendships and favour, which has freed the imagination of Dickens's biographers to see the hand of an aristocratic benefactor. However, John had only an entry-level job. At the age of twenty-one, he was starting at the same rank as a child. His fellow clerk Thomas Barrow was just twelve years old, though he had the advantage of being the son of the department head. Charles Barrow held sway over his government fiefdom, free to employ his own children, and if John Dickens didn't get his job directly through Barrow, he would at least have needed his approval. John was a young man, a northern lad, new to the big city. He arrived without friends or relatives but was almost immediately drawn into the orbit of Barrow's family. It wasn't long before he was courting – or encouraged to court – Barrow's sixteen-year-old daughter, Elizabeth.

Charles Barrow was only in his forties but had already led a colourful life. He was born in 1759 by the docks in Bristol. His father, William, was a barber-surgeon, in his mid-twenties when Charles was born. The surgeon's trade would soon become professionalised, but it was still a barbaric business in a port during the Seven Years War, with returning invalids, industrial accidents, and the general antics of drunken sailors on shore leave. Charles Barrow's twenty-three-year-old mother, Ann Casteels, was of Spanish Jewish heritage. Her family were picture-framers and gilders whose escape from the Spain of the Inquisition had taken them first to the Netherlands, and then through London before arriving in Bristol. Other members of the family settled in Dublin. It is possible that her Christian marriage to William Barrow in St Leonard's Church followed an elopement; a first child, named Ann, may have been born a year earlier. If so, Charles was the second child, born a year after his parents wed, and baptised in the same Bristol church. At twelve, Charles became an apprentice merchant seaman, sailing on the world's great trading routes at one of the decisive junctures in history, from the rise of the Raj in India to the seeds of the American revolution in the protests against East Indian tea in Boston harbour. He must have been apprenticed as a ship's musician because by his mid-twenties he is working as a musician and sheet music publisher and salesman in London.

In the mid-1780s, Charles Barrow found work with a music company based in Cheapside, opposite the Church of St Mary Le Bow. It was a partnership of West Country men like himself, and he quickly became close to the senior partner, Thomas Culliford. The company made harpsichords, published sheet music, especially practice pieces for the piano or harp, and manufactured a forerunner of the guitar, the 'guittar'. Barrow was proficient across a range of instruments and must have been a good salesman, but his career really took off after he married Culliford's daughter. Mary Culliford had just turned sixteen; Charles was in his late twenties. The family made their home in Lambeth where they eventually had ten children, all baptised at the Church of St Mary the Less at the end of Lambeth Walk. Perhaps Lambeth was the first part of London Barrow reached after leaving Bristol, but it offered plenty of work for a professional musician and salesman thanks to the famous Vauxhall Pleasure Gardens, site of a seasonal festival that ran between May and September each year. Instrument makers like Culliford & Co. employed professional musicians to showcase their products, and Barrow must have found a stream of customers among other musicians, as well as from pleasure-seekers on their summer excursion.

Lambeth was London's night-time capital, home not only to the Pleasure Gardens but also to many inns and theatres. The invention of gaslight helped to create the first night-time economy, in an area conveniently placed across the river from the West End – putting it outside the responsibility of the Lord Chamberlain, who governed what could and could not be seen on the London stage.

If we want to make Charles Dickens's genius a matter of genealogy we should forget the Dickens family and look instead to the Barrows and Cullifords, and their connections to this new world of show business and popular culture. The extended family included many of the notable musical instrument makers of the day, a large and intermarried network of English and German families. Their friends included many of the city's best musicians. Barrow had hit the perfect time to marry into a musical instrument-making dynasty as the industry was moving rapidly thanks to a sensational invention: the piano. By the early 1790s, Culliford & Co. was the largest manufacturer of pianos in London, which effectively made Thomas Culliford the biggest manufacturer in the world. Soon the company was moving away from itinerant salesmen and investing in glossy showrooms. Here they would hire the most fashionable musicians to promote the new pianos. The aim was to dazzle and charm the young women and their mothers who were their principal customers.

The sheet music publishing side of the company lay the foundations for what would, a generation later in the 1820s, become the new family business. Barrow's sons John Henry, Edward and Robert all worked in the publishing industry. It's not a fanciful observation to say that Dickens's entire career can be traced back to a rather shady Lambeth-based sheet music peddler, and that his feel for popular taste owes as much to comic routines and hit songs delivered by patter merchants in pleasure gardens, as to his favourite older novelists, like Smollett and Fielding. More broadly, Dickens emerged from a network of small manufacturers working in music and entertainment. Charles Dickens is neither an aristocrat nor, really, a worker. He represents a new class: a scion of urban salesmen, small manufacturers and shopkeepers, squeezed between the mass of new city-dwellers and the class with all the power and the wealth that sits above them.

It's easy to explore the site of Vauxhall Pleasure Gardens. It's the park behind London's most famous gay pub, the Royal Vauxhall Tavern. Today is Sunday, and there are a few strung-out looking men sitting in the sun, as though they have not yet made it home, but the Tavern was closed last night – and for most of the week – because so many drag queens were boycotting a planned Eurovision party in protest at Israel's conduct in its war on Gaza, now in its seventh month. It's the hottest day of the year so far, drawing the sunbathers out in force. The park is unusual in that it is filled with decorative knolls, between winding paths and flat lawns. I assume the tiny hills are artificial and reflect the landscaping of the original pleasure gardens. The gardens were much larger in the eighteenth century, when they sat behind walls and a pay booth. It was essentially a festival site which ran all summer long and included dancing pavilions, musical theatres, bars, restaurants, and shady groves for illicit night-time escapades. I don't know how much of London's original street grid survives but the contours of the original pleasure gardens seem to live on behind the Royal Vauxhall Tavern, and continue to shield sexual trysts. Fredo may be contemplating an archaeology of London's sex life. He is going wild, though this may have something to do with chicken bones in the rubbish bins.

Janet suggests the old pleasure gardens may have had merch stalls. Why not? I can see Charles Barrow selling song sheets and instruments inside the park, to visitors who hoped to continue the party once they got home. Summertime festivals are still a big thing in London, across all the city's parks. It's tempting to think that a city never changes but it's more accurate to think of commercial summer festivals as an idea born in late eighteenth-century Vauxhall. This was the beginning of mass popular entertainment for a young urban population.

Janet buys Magnum ice-creams from a shop on Black Prince Road, once Lambeth Butts, the eastern edge of the old pleasure gardens, and we head along Lambeth Walk. In the 1780s, this was a market street called Three Coney Walk. It has the strange distinction of providing the names for two dances: there's the Lambeth Walk, of course, while the earlier Three Coney Walk was an eighteenth-century square dance. A 'coney' is a rabbit bred for eating, but also a slang term for a street thief or con man. The name conjures up a long history of Vauxhall as a lairy night-time experience, but the street was a working market, supplied by the surrounding commercial vegetable gardens. Before the Thames embankment was built, Three Coney Walk was the main route into central London. There were three windmills, to pump out ground water and keep the soil dry. The area became heavily built-up in the nineteenth century and was bombed in the London blitz. It is now filled with an array of mid-twentieth-century social housing. I'm pleased to find that almost the first shop on Lambeth Walk offers piano lessons.

I'm worried I am going to smear ice-cream all over my face. It's a hot day so our Magnums are melting quicker than we can lick them. Janet is fighting a combination of heat, pollen and pollution and her streaming eyes are leaving mascara stripes down her cheeks. She looks a little goth, but still chic. We pass a doctor's surgery named Lambeth Walk Group Practice and I joke that the medical team comes out early each morning to practise cockney dance moves. It turns out that Janet has never heard of the Lambeth Walk. I have to show her a YouTube clip of Robert Lindsay in *Me and My Girl*. We've both loved Lindsay since childhood, but his performance is so hokey, it's an object lesson in how to be a song-and-dance man, if you want to ensure that being a song-and-dance man will never be cool again.

When Charles Barrow began work at Culliford & Co., he had to make his way from Lambeth to Cheapside, a distance of three miles. As a salesman, perhaps he did not go into the office every day but kept to his beat in Lambeth. After his marriage, when the company started to specialise in pianos and his father-in-law made him a partner, he would have been wealthy enough to take a carriage to the showroom on Cheapside. In 1792, Cullifords signed a contract to build pianos for Longman & Broderip, an innovative company which never made their own instruments, but instead bought patents in the most advanced technology, effectively creating the modern piano by combining the best innovations in a single instrument. Culliford opened several workshops around Cheapside to cope with the booming order book. Unfortunately, Longman & Broderip spent so much money designing the new piano that they went bankrupt in 1795. The gifted and celebrated musician Muzio Clementi was recruited to run Longman & Broderip in administration, and he took over the company in 1798. This long-lived company went through a series of partners, eventually evolving into Chappells, perhaps the most significant names in pianos and publishing in British musical history.

Clementi offered Culliford & Co. £600 in lieu of what they were owed. In 1796, Thomas Culliford and Charles Barrow started a new partnership, and opened a new piano showroom at 172 The Strand. In 1798, that business also collapsed. Culliford and Barrow were declared bankrupt and imprisoned. While Robert Blincoe was living in the workhouse in Camden Town, Charles Dickens's grandfather and great-grandfather were imprisoned downstream in the Fleet Prison, both buildings susceptible to flooding by the same foul water of the River Fleet. Their stay in prison was just a few weeks, but almost immediately Thomas Culliford's wife died. Her name was Mary Goldsworth, a member of another musical instrument-making dynasty. Culliford had lived through a rollercoaster decade, as the piano business exploded across the globe like a tech industry of the present day. He had seen immense wealth, been imprisoned for bankruptcy, and was now widowed. It must have affected him because he left London to live a quieter life as an itinerant piano tuner. He moved to Hampshire, between Winchester and Portsmouth, where he would have tuned many of the pianos that his company had made. He would certainly have serviced pianos heard by Jane Austen in country house recitals, and perhaps even kept her family's home piano in good order.

Charles Barrow also turned to piano tuning, as well as continuing to publish song sheets and give music lessons. I want to trace his story between the 1780s and the turn of the nineteenth century by following his route to work in the Strand; that is what my walk with Janet is all about. The most pleasant route on a hot, smog-laden day would take us through the Archbishop's Park but the bishop's gardens were not then open to the public. We turn on to Westminster Bridge Road, with Janet's eyes streaming, and sirens wailing from the ambulances at St Thomas' Hospital.

Until the middle of the eighteenth century, London Bridge was the only bridge across the Thames east of Putney. The 550-year-old bridge was an institution, filled with shops. Walking across the bridge could easily take an hour. For this reason, most people would cross the river on boats, operated by watermen – figures that seemed to both intrigue and repel Dickens, if his novel *Our Mutual Friend* is a guide, where the watermen make money by taking anything of value from the corpses that they fish from the Thames. Barrow might have hired a waterman and taken this old-fashioned route, sailing from Lambeth Marsh to one of the piers below the Strand. The blacking factory stood above one of these piers, on Hungerford Stairs, and Forster's biography notes that the brother-in-law of one of Dickens's co-workers was a waterman, while the father of another was a fireman, a coincidence that appealed to Dickens. The Guild of Watermen had to be bribed to agree to the construction of Westminster Bridge, because it would have such a negative impact on their business. The new bridge opened in 1750, followed by Blackfriars Bridge in 1769. Either bridge would have got Barrow to his shop at the top of the Strand.

Janet, Fredo and I take Westminster Bridge.

A Sunday afternoon stroll on Westminster Bridge puts you

at the heart of the London tourist experience. We photobomb a dozen holiday selfies without even trying. I carry Fredo at the crossing on Victoria Embankment, because the crowd is at least a hundred people strong. We struggle up Whitehall and across the southern edge of Trafalgar Square, hot, bothered and discombobulated.

The name of the Strand comes from an old word for beach. It was once the northern edge of the Thames. At Chancery Lane, the Strand becomes Fleet Street, which puts it close to the heart of the two businesses – and the professional classes – we tend to associate with Dickens, namely lawyers and journalists. Yet the Strand is really the old heart of theatreland, the profession Dickens truly loved. The Strand is where the West End begins and in Dickens's work it represents London life as a spectacle. It features in almost all his books, and always as a place where things are seen. If one character spots another in a contrived coincidence, you can bet it is on the Strand. It is where David Copperfield glimpses his manservant wearing his clothes, and is an area that Dick Swiveller must avoid, because he may be seen by his many creditors. It is home to the Adelphi Theatre, which staged pirated versions of Dickens's works throughout the 1830s, and the Adelphi itself, a wharf-side area of coal barges and riverside pubs. The shadowy arches of the Adelphi represent an underworld to the fashionable street above, an experience which, like the Golden Cross Inn, had all but disappeared by the time Dickens wrote about it, but that he remembered from his childhood in the blacking factory. The Strand was home to a row of grand seventeenth-century mansions that had established the West End as the fashionable part of town. Oliver Twist's benefactor Mr Brownlow takes two separate houses just off the Strand, but it is the street life that appears in Dickens's novels, rather than the events behind the mansion doors. Dickens was never comfortable around the aristocracy. His self-consciousness made him fearful of being exposed or sneered at, and this is reflected in his stories which cover all human life yet stop at the upper crust. His grandfather and great-grandfather opened their piano shop on the Strand because this is where their customers lived – and it proved their downfall.

Number 172 no longer exists. I didn't expect it to, but it hadn't occurred to me that I knew exactly what stood in its place: 180 Studios, which is a gallery space, a Soho House-owned members' club, and a restaurant, Toklas, named after Gertrude Stein's lover, and owned by the Slotovers, the couple who created the Frieze Art Fair. The building is a modern brutalist block that has had a renaissance in the last few years by hosting (I am sure someone would say 'curating') these separate but interconnected businesses. 180 Studios represents the kind of risky bet on a cultural moment that characterised the early days of the piano business. Are there enough of the kind of people that want to buy a lifestyle to support all these businesses? The partnership between Thomas Culliford and Charles Barrow went bankrupt within two years, but Barrow soon returned to the area. 180 Studios is next door to Somerset House; indeed, 172 was the corner building, opposite Somerset House. It was 1801 when, in a surprise career change, Charles Barrow abandoned piano tuning and music lessons for a job in the Navy Pay Office. It was a low-level job, but even more surprisingly, he rose through the department at a miraculous pace. Within a few years, he was overseeing the entire payroll for all the ports in the south-west of England.

Even after he began work in the Navy Pay Office, Barrow continued to publish sheet music, which he distributed through a family-run 'circulating library', loaning it out on a subscription model to the musicians of London. It's worth noting that engraving a musical score involves the same skills as the printing of bank notes, bonds and promissory notes. Anyone capable of producing the rondos and sonatas that filled the inventory of Culliford and Barrow could equally turn their hand to forgery – but this is getting ahead of the story.

3

FACTORY BOY: 1799–1803

The crowds promenading beneath the lights of Vauxhall Pleasure Gardens each season represent the positive side of the youthful city's long population boom. Robert's story represents the other side, the excess population reviled for their sins, and exploited for their labour.

At the turn of the eighteenth century, half the male population of London was under twenty-five, and the ensuing century was shaped not only by their energy, but also by the fear of what they represented: a potential rebel army at the disposal of any preacher or demagogue who could harness their power, as Dickens describes in *Barnaby Rudge*, in his account of the Gordon Riots of June 1780. The population boom might have been celebrated as a sign of public health and declining infant mortality, but instead the growing number of young people was taken as a symptom of social decay, sexual incontinence and the breakdown of authority. Inevitably, a potential political threat was framed as a moral fault. The 1790s ended with Thomas Malthus writing his famous essay on the dangers of population growth with its promise of an exponential crisis of famine and poverty. Malthus's text went through a series of editions and revisions over the next thirty years, gaining influence and admirers, until it became the key theoretical text behind the 1834 Poor Law.

Robert Blincoe never knew his parents, and this counted against him. If both his mother and father had disappeared, it was proof they were no good, and Robert most likely shared their feckless dishonesty. As Noah Claypole tells Oliver, his mother was 'a regular right down bad 'un'. She had died unmarried, leaving a workhouse bastard behind as a burden on the parish. Society judged Oliver and Robert as though it was their fault they had been abandoned. It's easy enough to see the fault in the reasoning. How's the child to blame? But identifying poor logic is one thing, stepping beyond it quite another. Dickens has fun with Noah Claypole, whose superiority rests on the fact he 'can trace his genealogy all the way back to his parents'. If Oliver's mother is bad, then Noah's grandmother is no better. Being one degree removed is not much to boast about, and so it proves as Noah runs away to London to embark on a life of crime – infuriating Fagin by insisting on only doing the lowest-risk jobs, mugging younger children.

Dickens's work may be filled with orphans, but the dead or absent parents are always around somewhere, like a toxic cloud colouring and influencing their surviving children's lives. In *Oliver Twist*, the whole sad story of the dead teenage mother is revealed at the end so that Oliver can take on her sins and exonerate her: she was weak enough to have an illegitimate child, but also strong enough to bear him alone and express her love with her last breath. Oliver can honour her for that much. The classic Dickens story is one where the characters choose to shoulder the shame of their family – to heroically take on their sins and make it their own story. From *Oliver Twist* to *Our Mutual Friend*, from first to last, it's the brave choice that elevates his characters.

Which doesn't do much for a real orphan like Robert Blincoe, who had no benevolent patron to act as an adoptive father.

Robert can't become a decent person until he takes on his family's shame, but as he will never know anything about his family, he will always remain an outcast. It's a classic double bind. The pay-off that Dickens gets from the story of abandoned children, the blend of pain and victory that comes from transcending a bad lot, is only available to pretend orphans, like Dickens himself, not to real ones like Robert. But if Robert had no family, he at least had friends. He was part of a new and rapidly growing demographic: the working class.

St Pancras was slow to join London's population boom. The area was one of the largest parishes in London by area, but it remained overwhelmingly rural until the last decade of the eighteenth century. There were 150 inmates in the workhouse throughout the 1780s, but the number grew rapidly over the next decade. By 1796, when Robert arrived, there were 450 inmates, half of them children. This jumped again to 623 by 1802, by which point the parish was £2,100 in debt. Something had to be done. The answer seemed to lie in the system of child apprenticeships, which were repurposed to allow parishes to send children like Robert to the northern textile mills.

Apprenticeships were a rite of passage for most young men until well into the eighteenth century. Charles Barrow served his in the Merchant Navy, and John Dickens had likely been an apprentice footman at Crewe Hall. The system dated back to the end of the Middle Ages and reflected the rising new world of powerful cities and trading fortunes, overseen by the guilds, the new professional associations. Children, most often boys, were bound to a master craftsman through a contract and punished if they refused to work, or tried to abscond. These 'indentures' varied in length from seven to fourteen years and cost between a few pounds and several hundred, depending on the quality of the training and the wealth and status that an apprentice hoped to enjoy when they became a master in their turn. The system was designed to maintain standards and restrict competition, ensuring no one could muscle in on someone else's business without a lengthy apprenticeship. But it also helped to ensure public order by placing the urban youth in a city-wide institutional system, overseen by masters and backed by the power of the beadles and their watchmen. It was a mentoring scheme that in many ways resembled a private penal system, with all the power of the law that implied.

By the mid-eighteenth century, the process of industrialisation meant there was little need for lengthy training across a whole swathe of professions. Newer and innovative professions often had no guilds at all. Piano-makers joined any guild that would take them, from furriers to spectacle-makers. Yet rather than phase out the number of apprenticeships and focus only on those specialised trades that required high-quality training, the opposite happened. The old apprenticeship system was amended to increase the number of both boys and also now girls, and the number of years they would serve. The upper limit of fourteen years became a standard even in trades that required no skills or training. What had begun as a way of protecting trades and training new workers had ended in a system that segregated the young poor by gender and turned the most vulnerable people into unpaid labourers.

The original trades' apprenticeships were purchased by a parent, compensating the master for housing and training their child. As the apprentice system was redesigned to get pauper children off the parish books, the local councils began to pay the fee. In the case of orphans like Robert or Oliver, the parish was also the legal guardian, and they could dispose of children as they wished, though a magistrate had to sign the indenture papers. Where children had parents, the parish promised that the children would enjoy a better way of life. If that didn't work, parishes resorted to threats to withhold welfare from the rest of the family. Girls would become servants, on the understanding that they would be trained in housework. Boys were advertised to local tradesmen, but the parishes also began to look for ways to get rid of boys in bulk. It was hoped this would be a root-and-branch solution to poverty: by simply sending menfolk away, the problem of soaring birth rates and poverty would cease to exist. Boys from the giant Bishopsgate workhouse were conscripted into the navy. The City of London was engaged in a series of colonial projects which allowed them to send unwanted pauper boys to plantations in Virginia and Derry, which was renamed Londonderry in honour of the City and its guilds.

Between the 1790s and the 1820s, workhouses across London looked to the industrial cities of the north to unload their children. Parishes advertised in provincial newspapers that children were ready and available for work, and a network of agents sprang up, acting for northern textile mills, and taking a slice of the apprentice fee. In Camden, there were a pair of agents named Gorton and Haslam. When Robert Blincoe was sent north in 1798, the approach came from a local man acting on behalf of his cousins, three brothers by the name of Lambert who operated a mill deep in the Nottinghamshire countryside. A deal was struck and the children were offered at thirty shillings a head, a quarter of what a child cost a year to keep in the workhouse. The process began with an inspection of the children, to ensure no disabled inmates had been smuggled into the consignment, whether physically or mentally impaired. The children were promised a healthy country life in Nottingham, a lie to sway the parents who were unlikely to ever see their children again. Robert was happy to go, seduced by the idea of freedom as much as by the false promises of horse-riding, silver watches and roast beef. He says, 'We refused to associate with children who, from sickness, or being underage, had not been accepted; they were commanded to keep their distance; told to know their betters.' One of the most popular songs of the day was 'The Roast Beef of Old England', with lyrics written by Henry Fielding. A variation for the piano was published by Culliford & Co., and distributed by Charles Barrow through his circulating library. I like to imagine Robert singing the song as he looked forward to life in Nottingham, rubbing his good fortune in the faces of the children who were not picked. The children felt they were little swells, especially as they were given two new suits, one for working and one for the weekend, alongside a shilling, a handkerchief and a piece of gingerbread.

I travel to Nottingham with my brother, another Robert Blincoe. There's been a Robert Blincoe in every generation of our family since the first. My Rob is a civil service statistician. In a nice Dickensian parallel, he is visiting Nottingham for the May council elections, as Dickens also toured elections in his time as a journalist. Tomorrow morning he will go round Nottingham's polling stations as his department tries to gauge the impact of the new photo ID requirement on voter turnout. He's taken a half-day off to explore with me, and we're visiting a village called Gonalston, eight and a half miles outside the city.

We meet in the lobby of our hotel. I'm older, but only by sixteen months. Rob is a much bigger man at six foot four. He's not only tall, but also broad: even his head is big. We hug, and I have the sense I'm reaching up, as I always do. He looks like a Blincoe. Our father, Edward, is also tall and physically big, and from the photographs we have of our grandfather, also Edward, our great-grandfather, Robert, and our great-great-grandfather, another Robert, they are all imposing men with big, bearded heads and stern noses, often quite heavy round their centres. But my brother must be the biggest Blincoe yet. The exception, aside from me, is the original orphan Robert. But while I resemble my mother's side of the family, Robert was short due to malnourishment and deformities caused by operating heavy machinery. I am five eleven, which isn't exactly short, but aggravating if you come from a family of tall men. I was only taller than my brother until I was fourteen, at which point I had to turn to sarcasm and cruelty to keep the upper hand. Our teenage fights or, to be honest, my bullying might have soured our relationship but when we moved to London in our twenties, we shared a flat and became friends. Those two years were among the happiest of my life and healed most of the problems of our childhood. But we are very different in ways that seem to be emphasised by our difference in size. For instance, in personality (he thinks mine is bigger) and heart (I worry mine might be smaller). We mainly speak to each other about pop culture – books, records and films – but we also have a semi-comic routine of discussing brothers who have spectacularly fallen out, like the Gallaghers (we're both on Liam's side), the Milibands (split on age lines) or Prince Harry and Prince William (probably another vote for the younger brother). Maybe it's odd that the great binding quality of the working class, *fraternity*, is based on the relationship between brothers, because it's a relationship that often ends in disaster. But what else is there, except brotherhood and sisterhood? We love each other, we fight for each other, and though we've had our problems, we've hopefully got enough sense to work them through.

The local train takes us north-east out of the city, through Burton Joyce to Lowdham, names that we know from the *Memoir*. Lowdham has a picturesque station, with a cream and burgundy signal box fitted out with brass-and-wood levers. Robert Blincoe's party travelled up from London in a covered wagon, like the ones in cowboy films, a journey that took four days. They arrived late in central Nottingham and slept the night in the Lamberts' warehouse, close to the city's Lace Market, moving on to Gonalston the next afternoon after the Lamberts had, somewhat improbably, arranged a guided tour around the city's historic attractions. The *Memoir* describes the Lambert brothers' mill as being ten miles outside Nottingham, which reflects the distance when the road from Nottingham snaked across the River Trent's flood plain, navigating the countless becks that feed the river. John Brown, the journalist who took down Robert Blincoe's story, never visited the area, so he only had Robert's word for anything. The fact that it proves accurate, in the smallest details is reassuring. It matters, not just for what the *Memoir* says about the lives of young people two hundred years ago, but because it is one of the very earliest accounts of the life of the industrial working class.

On the train to Nottingham, I had read the novel *James* by Percival Everett, a retelling of *Huckleberry Finn* from the perspective of Jim, and was struck by Everett's criticism of the famous slave memoir of Venture Smith, published the same year Robert was trafficked to Nottingham. Venture Smith paid someone to write his memoir and, as Everett says, there is a big difference between 'related by' and 'written by'. Actually, between Venture Smith and Robert Blincoe, there's a whole series of issues of authorship, influence and copying. Not only did Robert not write his own memoir, but the *Memoir* itself is modelled on a slave memoir, a genre which Venture Smith's book did much to create. Working-class memoirs were so new when it was written in 1822 that John Brown repeatedly evokes the stories of black men and women as a model to articulate Robert's experiences. We don't know how accurately the memoir conveys Robert's voice and personality, which adds a question mark to our trip. We're retracing his journey to pay homage, but also, inevitably, to test Brown's account, and to try to hear Robert for ourselves. If it is a story that follows an established format, it is also the story of a real man, and we're the proof. The Blincoes. Especially the Robert Blincoes.

We walk north from the station, turning east on to the road between Nottingham and Southwell. This is now the A612, a fast straight highway where long tracts have a 60 mph speed limit. Brown writes Southwell as 'Surhill' and his misspelling has never been corrected, despite the number of editions the book has been through. It seems no one thought to follow Robert's travels on a map and check the place names. The slip is an indication that Brown was using shorthand to take down Blincoe's testimony as he heard it. In Nottinghamshire, Southwell is pronounced 'Suthill' with a voiceless 'th' that Robert Blincoe has softened to the point it has become 'Surhill', at least to Brown's ears. We walk for a few hundred metres before a fork breaks off the new highway and we take the original Nottingham–Southwell road as it follows the course of a stream called Dover Beck. Almost immediately, we see the Lamberts' mill. It is a broad brick building of three storeys, standing on an arched bridge, two spans wide. The beck is narrow and deep, and fast enough to drive a water wheel. A series of flour mills have stood on the site since the eleventh century, but the present building was built as a textile mill in 1784 by Richard Lambert, the father of the owners in Robert's time. The mill has gone through a number of names. It was then called Lowdham Mill, as Dover Beck marks the border between the villages of Gonalston and Lowdham. It is now called Cliff Mill, a name embossed on a metal plate set into the brickwork. I had read that the mill had been converted into a single family home, but it is currently a building site, in the process of being turned into apartments. There's a black Tesla parked on the bridge but no sign anyone is working. Rob rings the doorbell and we stand around awkwardly, waiting for someone to appear. No one does.

It was an August summer evening when the truck reached the mill. Robert's first glimpse of the building was a decorative dome on the roof, and he asked if it was a church. The trucker laughed and said he didn't doubt the young cockneys would be regular attendants. The wagon rolled on another half mile to the apprentice house. We follow the route down the centre of a sunny road between green fields towards Gonalston. A hundred yards past the mill, the road turns and crosses over the beck at a stone bridge. Ahead of us, a blue Ferrari appears and slips away in the direction of Southwell. The locals are clearly wealthy, but there was always a manor house in Gonalston and so perhaps Ferraris, or the caleche, their eighteenth-century equivalent, were never out of place. The truck rumbled on until it reached the apprentice house, which Robert was dismayed to find looked just like a workhouse. He was told this would be their home for the next fourteen years.

The tone of the *Memoir* changes in this chapter: there is an outbreak of reported speech to evoke the rush of memories as

Robert recalls what people said, and how they said it. Robert and the other children were hearing northern accents for the first time, as locals gathered to peer at the 'cocknies', pitying them as poor wretches. Gonalston has never had a large population, peaking at 134 in 1851. The 2021 census put the figure at 83. The Lamberts' apprentices would have had an enormous impact on the village, doubling the population. The historian John Waller has found records for thirty-one children in the batch that arrived with Robert. They joined another fifty already employed at the mill and living in the apprentice house. That first evening, they were fed boiled potatoes, which the existing inmates collected in the tails of their shirts or the aprons of their smocks. Robert had left an institution that had covered the tables with cloths, and served food with plates and cutlery. The dirt of the buildings, the smell of the children, the poverty of the food – all hit Robert hard.

The old farmhouses are now well-cared-for villas, with their barns converted into studios and guest bedrooms. My brother asks if I can identify which buildings are contemporary with Robert's story. I don't know; can he? A number of low, long barns are very old. We pass a terrace of cottages that might also be very old, though the original roof has been replaced with Victorian tiles. There are a few grand houses, which may be rebuilds of the original manor house and rectory. Researching the village later, I find this seems to be the case. As we walk around, there is one building that keeps drawing us back: a two-storey brick barn. It is the only building that is both old enough and large enough to provide room for eighty children, and it has the blank, prison-like aspect that fits Robert's description of a workhouse. It's now at the edge of the garden of one of Gonalston's grander houses, close to a side road. We can walk around two-thirds of it, and get a glimpse of the rest by peering over a high wall. The children ate at long tables in a dining hall downstairs, and slept in the room above in shared bunk beds. The governor was a retired drill sergeant, who carried a horse whip which he would beat on the table when he spoke. He divided the children so they slept with strangers rather than children they knew. They were woken at five, and would wash at a pump in the yard, before being given watery porridge that Robert describes as looking 'blue'. I don't know how we could prove we've found the apprentice house, except maybe by Robert-to-Robert vibes. Rob obligingly tries to pick up tremors of his namesake. The Lambert brothers didn't build their own apprentice house, and there would be a limited number of existing buildings to rent in such a small village. If this isn't the building, we agree, the one they stayed in would have been all but identical.

Rob sees a spire poking up beyond the hedgerow at the far end of a waterlogged field. I hadn't expected to find a church in such a small village but I discover that it's clearly marked on the map. The *Memoir* states the children went 'pretty regularly' to Lowdham church, which goes by the name of St Mary's and is well over a mile from where we are in Gonalston. It would make more sense for the children to attend the church in the parish where they were living, but perhaps they were excluded for this very reason: because they almost outnumbered the locals. In any case, we decide to take a look at Gonalston's church. The problem is, while we can see the spire, we cannot work out how to reach it. We take the road out of the village, back to the A612 where we have to walk on a banked verge because there is no footpath, as cars scream by at high speed. In fifty yards, we are parallel with the church, but there is no obvious entrance. Then I see a rough footbridge, actually a few planks across a ditch, with a single handrail. This leads through some shrubs to the back of a graveyard. The small church is named St Laurence's and is clearly very old, though it has the inevitable Victorian additions. The porch is locked, so we sit on a bench in the sun and I do some research on my phone. It's a thirteenth-century church built by a Norman family named de Heriz who became the lords of the manor after the Conquest. Maybe dedicating the church to St Laurence was their reminder to the locals that it took the foreign-born St Laurence to bring the Saxons to God. Inside the church are funerary statues dedicated to the family's exploits in the Crusades. Which we have to imagine, as we cannot get inside. The church was remodelled in the middle of the nineteenth century by a local architect. We look for another path out of the churchyard and find a verdant grass track between manicured hedges, leading through the grounds of the old rectory. A blue Ferrari stands on the gravel. Probably the same Ferrari we saw leave the village, though maybe not. Anyone who can afford one Ferrari tends to have several, in the way that people always have more than one Kelly bag, or Rolex watch.

The Lamberts must have faced resistance when they rented the apprentice house; these issues mattered when a parish became responsible for anyone who could claim residency. With Dover Beck marking the boundary between Lowdham and Gonalston, the mill's location on the bridge puts it in a grey zone. However, the original medieval flour mill belonged to Lowdham: it was the property of the Black Canons of Thurgarton Priory, an order of monks who controlled Lowdham church. The issue was finally settled in 1802 when the Lambert brothers closed the apprentice house and constructed a new purpose-built house on the Lowdham side of the mill.

We return to the mill. Rob wants to get a picture of us together.

'Big grins and thumbs up?' I ask.

'What's the appropriate face for: this is where my ancestor was whipped and beaten?'

When he started his civil service job, Rob was asked to speak about something personal, and he gave a presentation about Robert Blincoe. The *Memoir* is still fresh in his memory. If there is someone at the mill, he plans to get them to take our picture, and then ask if we can take a look around. He used to be a journalist and is trained to ask questions – something I hate doing. But when we get back, the Tesla is gone. Rob is annoyed we didn't hang around a while longer. I figure, if there is no one about, why don't we just poke around? The gate is unlatched, so I walk through, and Rob follows. We're in a large and attractive garden with an old ash tree at its centre, nestled in a curve in Dover Beck. We can hear the rush of water in the mill race below us. The end of the mill has been removed and replaced with modern glazed windows and balcony doors. There's still a lot of work to do, and the back of the mill is completely covered in scaffolding.

Of course we climb the scaffolding to look in the upper windows.

The Lambert brothers rarely visited their mill, relying on a manager named Mr Baker who ran the mill through violence, believing that beatings were essential to meet the production targets the brothers had set. The overseers – called 'overlookers' in the industry – also used violence, punching, kicking and pulling the children around by the hair. Robert says his body was so bruised that he looked like a leopard. At seven, he was the youngest child at the mill, but the average age was still only eleven. Water mills are susceptible to bad weather, not only to drought but also heavy rain as the wheel cannot turn if the water level is too high in the lower race. The children were expected to make up for slack periods, and so working for sixteen hours at a stretch was not uncommon. The Lamberts' father had built the mill for spinning cotton, but the sons had diversified into hosiery, the speciality in Nottingham. The finer machinery needed to be cleaned every other week, and again the children were forced to work longer hours to make up for lost time. Robert's first job was as a scavenger: he had to dart about under the spinning frame clearing up cotton fibres while the machinery whirred and cranked above him. Later, he was promoted to winder, responsible for ensuring the frame had a constant supply of the long cotton fibres known as *rovings* that were spun into thread. He was beaten for not keeping up with the spinning machines, but the problem was that he was too short and had to stand on a box to reach the bobbins. In London, he had been regarded as a tall child, and perhaps he would also have been a big man – the first in the line of these Blincoe giants – if he hadn't been so undernourished, if his legs hadn't been so twisted.

We swing up the scaffolding, two men in our fifties. It's fun trespassing with Rob, a memory riff back to our own childhoods. We used to play in derelict buildings, and scrabble under fences to get into building sites. The year I was seven, we moved twice, which makes it easy to recall the years when I was the same age as Robert Blincoe. I reach the very top of the scaffold and peer through the windows. The interior of the mill has been boarded out and divided into flats. There's nothing much left to help me imagine the shop floor, the thrumming machinery, drawing, and spinning and weaving. But the view down to the beck is unchanged. The *Memoir* states that Robert contemplated taking his life as he looked down from the upper-floor windows but lacked the courage to jump. I peer at the water churning into the mill race. If he had jumped, the fast-running water would have pulled him underneath the mill, sweeping him into the blades of the water wheel.

When we return to the lower floors, I'm surprised to discover the water wheel is still in place, jagged and ferrous, its blades thinner and sharper than I expected. There's a scene in *James* when James and his fellow runaway Norman steer their boat into the wheel of a Mississippi paddle steamer and are almost cut to pieces. Looking at the wheel, I remember the story of one of Robert's friends from Camden, a girl named Mary Richards. Towards the end of a day, when she was tired, she was taking the weights off a drawing frame. This is a machine that prepares the rovings for spinning, and the weights maintain tension as the roving is drawn through a series of rollers. As Mary worked, her apron got caught in the drive shaft, pulling her under the machine. The turning of the shaft sent her spinning over and over, beating her like a doll against the floor and the whirring machine. Robert said, 'I saw her blood thrown about like water from a twirled mop.' I'm looking through the dirty windows of the ground floor, perhaps into the very room where that happened. Mary broke almost every bone in her body and her skull was crushed, but somehow she survived as a disfigured cripple. She came back to work in the mill.

We take our grinning selfie with the mill behind us. Which celebrity brothers are we today? I'm thinking the Chuckle Brothers but without their natural solemnity. I send the pictures to our mum, and we start walking towards Lowdham, following the route Robert Blincoe took on the day he escaped.

Robert had planned his escape, but only haphazardly – remember he was still only seven or eight years old. He slipped out of the mill when the overlookers were busy, hoping to get as far as possible before the light gave out. He took the main road because it was the only route he knew to Nottingham and for the first half mile he kept looking over his shoulder. Lowdham is still sparsely built up and has a large sweeping common on the north side of the road, so Robert must have felt particularly vulnerable in this stretch. It is four-thirty in the afternoon, and schoolchildren are walking up from the station, wearing the bizarre uniform of the English middle-class child, like three-quarter-sized solicitors in a world where nylon has finally become the future. It's a warm evening and we walk briskly, wondering how fast a child in dirty rag clothes would travel, and whether he would stand out. Two miles past Lowdham, the original road parts way with the A612 again to follow another of the becks that feed the Trent. Crossing over a bridge, it passes through the tiny hamlet of Bulcote. A number of the houses look old enough to have seen Robert scarpering past. Somewhere between here and Burton Joyce, a tailor stepped out of a cottage and blocked his way, calling him by his name: still, 'Parson'.

Could the tailor really have recognised Robert, one of eighty children in the mill?

This scene is one of the liveliest in the book. You can hear Robert telling a story he has told before, performing for a new audience. The tailor speaks like a preacher with a distinctly northern voice. 'Oh, young Parson, where art thou running so fast this way? . . . I saw Satan behind thee, jobbing his prong into thy arse! I saw thee running headlong into hell when I stept forth to save thee.' I can see Robert acting a role, taking the part of a man he describes as having a 'long shaggy neck . . . black greasy locks . . . a lanthorn jaw'. One who wears a 'malicious grin upon his long, lank visage'. In short, a man who looks like the devil.

We discover that the tailor is a Methodist, a fact which Robert says has turned him against Methodists for life. The Methodist movement encourages laymen to preach the gospels and the tailor clearly fancies himself as a sermoniser. The *Memoir* says that he worked for Lowdham Mill. It seems likely that he was a pieceworker whose job was sewing up the stocking seams. When he catches Robert, he has been working at his 'shop-board', an old term for a tailor's table, which would be set up in a window to catch the light. The tailor has a reputation for returning absconding children for the bounty of a few shillings. He's the local child-catcher and maybe he has made it his business to know the children's names. Perhaps Robert was memorable because he was the youngest in the mill, or because he was known as 'Parson' and the preacher delighted in catching him out, seeing Satan 'jobbing at his arse' ('job' is the older term for 'jab', which again suggests that Brown is transcribing an imitation). Ultimately, I think the tailor knew Robert's name simply because the world was still small enough to recollect the names of everyone you met. Robert was returned to the apprentice house, where he received a kick from the old drill sergeant, and jeers from the older apprentices.

Robert's stories are filled with names and characters, because people knew each other and had developed strong attachments – they had made friends, brothers, sisters ... and enemies. Even the way that the tailor could recall Robert's name is evidence of a class of people being formed, not simply an abstract socio-economic group, but rather a community of workers. Robert recounts a story of two St Pancras girls, sisters named Fanny and Mary Collier. They managed to write to their mother, who walked from London to see her girls' working conditions for herself. She stayed two weeks, then walked back to London to take what she had seen to the St Pancras board.

St Pancras sent inspectors to follow up on Mrs Collier's complaints. Perhaps their report was a factor in the Lamberts' decision to build a new apprentice house beside the mill. They also sacked the drill sergeant and hired a new man, an ex-apprentice named Robert Woodward. They were also aware of the provisions of Robert Peel's impending Act for the Health and Morals of Apprentices, a bill aimed at children in the textile industry. Robert Peel was the father of the more famous Peel, also Robert, the future prime minister and creator of the Metropolitan Police. Peel senior was a northern mill owner himself, but successfully piloted an act that limited working hours for children to twelve hours a day, set aside hours for education, specified that apprentice houses should be ventilated and cleaned, and made provisions for regular inspections. In addition, two copies of the act had to be prominently displayed so the apprentices would be informed of their rights. The Lamberts set out to comply with the bill, but rapidly changed tack. In 1803, they abandoned the mill. The fact was, water mills were being superseded by steam power. A water mill requires live-in apprentices because the fast-running streams required tend to be found in the most remote countryside, exactly the kind of places where it is difficult to find and retain sufficient workers. As the water mills became obsolete, the cotton industry moved into the centre of cities. Instead of looking to house pauper children, the mill owners began to employ children that lived at home with their parents – and consequently weren't bound by Peel's new apprentice act. But as long as water mills survived, children would be trafficked between isolated sites. When the Lamberts closed their mill, a few children were reclaimed by their families, but the bulk were sent into the remote High Peak of Derbyshire, Robert among them.

The Lamberts remained one of the most prominent families in Nottingham for the next hundred years, building the city's Theatre Royal. They boasted that they would employ no children younger than thirteen. Brother Rob suggests we track down their descendants and ask for reparations. We can superglue ourselves to their door.

4

PORTSMOUTH: 1805-14

John Dickens joined the Navy Pay Office in 1805. He soon began dating his boss's sixteen-year-old daughter. Claire Tomalin speculates that, 'as daughters often do', Elizabeth Barrow was drawn to the echoes of her father she saw in her new boyfriend, but perhaps we ought to ask what attracted Charles Barrow to the man he would make his son-in-law. What made him encourage the newbie in the office, and wrap him in the warm embrace of his family?

Both Charles and John were sociable men. Charles Barrow could sing and play instruments, always at the centre of things, with a large family and a wide circle of theatrical and musical friends. John Dickens also earned a reputation as a good companion, with a turn of phrase that made everyone laugh. He was good-looking, but he was also physically imposing, evident in the pictures of Mr Micawber that accompanied the serialisation of *David Copperfield*. The illustrator 'Phiz', aka Hablot Knight Browne, was hand-picked by Charles Dickens because he could be relied upon to follow Dickens's instructions. Phiz knew John Dickens personally and when he depicts Mr Micawber as the broadest and tallest figure in a room, we can be confident that he has captured the energy and presence of Micawber's model. John Dickens's physical presence played a role in his transfer and promotion in 1809 to the pay office in Portsmouth. His job was to go down to the docks with the strong boxes and the pay packets. He put his safety on the line, handing out wages in dockside warehouses and on ships. He paid the sailors and port workers, as well as the contractors, through their gangmasters. Disputes could flare in a second, and their target would be Dickens, rolling through the port in a wagon filled with large sums of money. Any working dock was filled with heavy plant, but Portsmouth was also the world's largest armoury. John was a man in his mid-twenties, and yet he was trusted because he had the air of someone who could take care of himself, whether that took charm or force.

He was still seeing Elizabeth Barrow, a woman always described with words like small, pretty, petite – the opposite of John. One Saturday morning in the early summer of 1809, he travelled back to London and cemented his connection to her, and to the Barrow family. The marriage took place on 13 June, a Tuesday, which gave the couple a few days either side of the wedding for celebrations, as well as time to settle into their new Portsmouth home, before John returned to work the following Monday. They were married in St Mary Le Strand, the church opposite Somerset House.

I hook Fredo's lead over the boot scrape outside St Mary Le Strand. It's five-thirty on a Sunday evening, and Evensong has begun. Janet chooses a pew at the back of the church, and I follow her. I don't believe in God, but like Joey Zasa in *The Godfather*, I like to cut a *bella figura* and I make the sign of the cross as I cross the aisle. Perhaps I find the sign comforting. The priest tells us that he once worked in Calcutta and goes on to describe the local icons that depict Christ in traditional Indian styles. His argument seems to be that Christ's universality is revealed in the way that artists can paint him in different formats for different markets. The church is baroque, but simple. The real centrepiece is the ceiling, which has carved ornamental reliefs. The patterns are so deep, you feel that if you could only swim up to explore them, then you might get lost. This is where Charles Barrow gave his daughter away to a young clerk, sitting in the front row with his ten children and his wife, Mary Culliford Barrow, who was still in her thirties. The choice of church reflects Charles Barrow's controlling hand. This was not a marriage for a young couple and their friends, nor was it their local Lambeth church, where Mary worshipped and their children had been baptised. The event was geared around Barrow's professional world, bringing the other clerks and managers to celebrate the marriage of their boss's son, and no doubt inviting the top brass to come and drink a toast with Barrow. The celebrations are likely to have continued across the river with music and dancing, and the next day, or the one after, the couple would board a wagon with their wedding gifts and no doubt a new piano and set out to Portsmouth to start married life together.

There was every reason for Charles Barrow to make a show and win friends in the office. Just seven months after the marriage, on 11 January 1810, he was detained at work. He had presented the accounts as usual, with a petty cash demand for £900. The petty cash was usually signed off without comment, but this time someone checked, and suspected a serious discrepancy. The Pay Office called in the sheriff, whose investigation discovered that Barrow had been systematically tampering with the petty cash ledger and forging documentation to cover his tracks for at least seven years. The investigators came up with the figure of £5,689 3s. 3d. An online calculator tells me this has the purchasing power of half a million pounds today.

Barrow admitted the crime but made a plea for clemency. He argued that he had been driven to act because he had ten children and that a demand for immediate payment of the full amount 'might drive me into gaol, strip my family of what little furniture, clothes or other resources they may possess for their immediate subsistence. They are now unprovided for and severer steps, by preventing my exertions for their future maintenance, would indeed confound us all in one overwhelming calamity.' The plea must have found favour with his seniors, because he was not immediately arrested. Perhaps they believed his claim that his brother, John Barrow, a merchant in Bristol, could make good the missing money. The brother did later become wealthy, but in 1810 he would have had little hope of covering for his brother's crimes. He had his own problems as a director of the Bristol Dock Company, which looked as though it would go bankrupt while building a floating harbour in the city. Barrow simply wanted to buy time. Within days, he was on the run, reported to be heading for France, beyond the scope of British justice as the Napoleonic War raged on. The family of ten that he claimed to care so much about were left to pick up the pieces.

I head to Portsmouth with Fredo. It's the first day of the summer season of the Charles Dickens Birthplace Museum, which opened in 1904, making it one of the oldest Dickens museums in the country. From the beginning, it had the support of Dickens's people. His executor, his housekeeper/sister-in-law, presented the new museum with the couch that had once held Dickens's dead body.

Portsmouth was the naval armoury in John Dickens's time and is still a militarised city, filled with current and ex-servicemen, and heavily policed military zones that are off-limits to civilians and dogs. On the train down, a man stands to begin a plea for cash to get into a homeless shelter: he's not an addict, he says, but ex-forces and he's working on his mental health. I guess the mental health issues are related to anger management, because his hands are swollen and his knuckles cut up and grazed. When he sees Fredo he coos and strokes his head. Fredo is my first dog, and for a long time I was surprised when people asked me if they could pet him. I didn't know there was an etiquette. Now I take it for granted. This man doesn't ask, and Fredo responds to the informality with a growl. The man tells me that the dog is all right. 'He clearly fucking isn't if he growled,' I snap.

We've all got our anger issues.

There's a split second before he apologises and backs away to continue his plea for money. There's a tenner folded up with my driving licence, and I give it to him.

The truth is, I am on edge because I am on the wrong train: I bought a ticket for a specific time and ended up catching the earlier train. I am also worried because I know Fredo won't be allowed in the museum, and I don't know how I will work around that. Luckily there is no ticket inspector on the train, so I reach Portsmouth with one worry cancelled out. The museum is on Old Commercial Road, and the station is on Commercial Road. Google Maps show that this is basically the same road, give or take a few roundabouts and a pedestrianised strip. I pass a shop called Vape N' Beans and try to guess the link: products designed to create emissions at either end of a human body? The local paper has a story about a group of children dancing into the shop and cheerfully stealing a box of vapes worth £500, leading to the arrest of two girls, aged thirteen and sixteen. A local politician, George Madgwick, founder and leader of the Portsmouth Independents Party, posted online that the shopkeeper 'should have smashed two bells of crap into the little scroats. Defend your business and deal with the consequences after. If people are willing to steal from you they have to be willing to take a beating.'

The Portsmouth name Madgwick has been described as 'one of the most localised names in the country'. The family have been horse traders since at least the mid-eighteenth century, and later became hauliers. If John Dickens hired a removal wagon in Portsmouth to transport his bride and furniture to their new home, then he may have gone to the Madgwick family. The name is conspicuously close to that of the escaped convict in *Great Expectations* (1861): Magwitch, who becomes Pip's secret benefactor. Why did Dickens choose such a distinctive name? He was too young when he left the city to remember any actual Madgwicks, but he may have seen the name on haulier wagons or come across the family on a visit he made to Portsmouth at the end of the 1850s, as he began work on *Great Expectations*. The character Magwitch has been associated with his errant grandfather and it is easy to see why: two criminals, haunting the lives of the people they left behind. The story of *Great Expectations* is, in many ways, the exoneration of a criminal. Though guilty, Magwitch is also a kind of innocent. Magwitch's weakness is to operate according to a thief's honour code which his associates exploit, hypocritically turning the code to their advantage. They know he won't betray them, and they falsely claim that Magwitch was their ringleader. Once Pip exonerates Magwitch, he finds that he can also forgive him.

If Magwitch is a version of Charles Barrow, then perhaps the family believed he was also less guilty than he appeared. After all, there is something odd about his story: odd enough to suggest there were powerful figures in the know, and perhaps were beneficiaries of his thefts. When Barrow got his start in the Navy Pay Office he was a forty-year-old man, jobbing around the fringes of London's music industry with a background in sales and sheet music publishing. We might wonder why he rose so quickly, how he escaped so easily, and why the two men most likely to be his accomplices – his son Thomas, and his son-in-law John Dickens – never seem to have come under suspicion; indeed, both continued to work in the same department for a decade after the theft was discovered. Perhaps these questions suggest nothing but that the Navy Treasury wished to sweep an embarrassing episode under the carpet. But in one important aspect, the family *was* guilty, because Thomas, John, and everyone else in the Barrow family knew that he had never fled abroad. He hid out in Brighton for a few years, before moving to the Isle of Man where he reunited with his wife and all of his younger children. The entire family were always in close contact. To put it bluntly, they were conspiring with a felon, which is also the plot of *Great Expectations*: Pip is forced into being an accomplice because Magwitch is not in Australia; he has broken the terms of his licence and is hiding out in England.

The map says it's less than a mile from Portsmouth station to the Dickens Birthplace Museum along a straight road. The casual day-tripper might be tempted to saunter through the delights of the city centre. It would be a mistake. The first obstacle is an ornamental fountain celebrating the 1977 Silver Jubilee: an ugly concrete tub surrounded by eight heraldic monsters. The animals are copies of a series designed for the 1952 Coronation by sculptor James Woodford, repurposed at half size for this fountain by an anonymous town planner, a man that I suspect also had anger issues. Woodford designed ten beasts, but here there are only seven (the Lion of England appears twice). It's an apt symbol for post-war Portsmouth: the ugliness is so loaded, it hits you even before you recognise it. It's pre-emptively ugly.

I continue my inhospitable trawl along a dual carriageway, negotiating roundabouts that have no obvious crossing points, requiring long detours. It seems most people in Portsmouth save time by using mobility scooters, which they drive with a reckless disregard for anyone on foot. If Fredo was less fussy about where he poos, I might have been seriously injured, but fortunately he keeps dragging me off the path into bushes and flowerbeds. Portsmouth is so disorientating for a delicate dog that he can't find the perfect spot. The route to the museum is mapped out on my phone, and I follow it as the juice drains from the battery. Old Commercial Road begins with a stretch of cobblestones into which are set a short length of tram tracks. The tracks end abruptly, mid-road, just like the tyre marks of the DeLorean in *Back to the Future*. Evidently, the tram jumped time to escape Portsmouth.

Charles Dickens's birthplace is a three-storey Georgian house plus basement, with a wide, neatly paved front yard. The museum entrance is in the old kitchen basement. I hook Fredo's lead around the railing spikes and descend the cellar step to a paved room with a metal range in its fireplace. The desk is manned by two people. I tell them I have a dog: should I carry him or leave him tied up in the garden? It turns out neither option is acceptable. I tell them I am writing a book about Dickens. I also mention that Fredo is very small, as they can see for themselves. I point to the high narrow window on to the yard.

'I can't see a dog,' one says.

I move a small cardboard sign so that Fredo's face appears. It does the trick: their hearts are melted. We negotiate. A dog cannot be left at the top of the steps, where someone might trip, but it will be okay if I move him to the other side of the yard. I am also allowed to charge my phone at a socket under their desk. It was a bad start, but now we are friends.

Throughout my visit, I can hear Fredo crying. He is a quiet dog, so I suspect it's constipation. I spend less time in the museum than I might have done, but that's all right. There really isn't much to see. It is a small museum: eight rooms, two on each floor with two off-limits. So, six. The basement comprises a front kitchen and back scullery, which is now the museum loos but would have been the utility room where clothes would be washed, with access to the garden clothes-lines – and beyond, access to the city sewers. The maid-of-all-work, a child, would have slept in the kitchen. There's a narrow staircase between these two rooms up to the raised first floor. The front parlour is where the Dickenses would entertain guests. Elizabeth played the piano well and it is the one essential luxury that her relatives in the Culliford and Goldsworth families could present at her wedding. The museum has left the back parlour largely unfurnished. There is a small display of photographs and the famous death couch. Dickens is supposed to have expired lying on this couch, though Claire Tomalin suggests he may have been laid out after his death, having been smuggled from his secret second home with the Ternans.

Up one more floor on the narrow staircase are two bedrooms. The front bedroom is papered in an ornate scrolling pattern, a replica of a contemporary wallpaper. There is a wooden cot at the foot of the bed. Charles's older sister, Frances Dickens, was born in this house in August 1810. She was always called Fanny after Elizabeth's older sister who lived with the family – though Aunt Fanny's real name was Mary. It was common for women to help the transition to a new life by moving in with their married sisters, and after their father absconded the pair had even more reason to cling together. Shortly after their father disappeared, their mother, Mary Culliford Barrow, also fled London with the youngest children. Portsmouth would have been a natural destination, not only to be close to Elizabeth and Fanny but also because her own father, Charles Culliford, lived close by on the road between Winchester and Portsmouth. As I look through the museum, I wonder how many of the ten Barrow children passed through the couple's house. The attic rooms are under the eaves, small rooms with limited head height. One room is locked, and the other is almost bare, with just a few stools and a bookcase displaying later editions of Dickens's novels. These rooms may have been set aside for a servant, or a nursery. I imagine the crying I hear is the sound of children. It's not. It's a backed-up dog tied to the front railings.

Dickens was born in this house in February 1812, eighteen months after Fanny. The two years in Portsmouth may have been the beginning of a life of debt for John and Elizabeth. After all, they were responsible for Elizabeth's mother and her younger brothers and sisters. But Portsmouth was also lively. It was a navy town, filled with young officers, and there were parties and balls. Aunt Fanny was soon engaged to a naval lieutenant, Thomas Allen, the officer in charge of a ten-gun cutter, HMS *Dart*. They married in May 1812, a few months after Dickens's birth. Once Aunt Fanny moved out, and when their lease ended, the family opted for a lodging house on Hawke Street, closer to the docks and the Navy Pay Office. It was also cheaper than the £35 annual rent on their first home.

The walk from the museum to the docks is even worse than the walk from the station. I follow an inner-city ring road punctuated by roundabouts, pushed to the edge of the pavements by mobility scooters. But now I am also circling the edge of a naval base, with high walls topped by barbed wire. Modern Portsmouth is an extraordinarily bleak city, but my problems aren't all existential. I also have practical problems. Before I left the museum, I bought two books on Dickens and a souvenir mug with the words, 'Please Sir I Want Some More'. The added weight proves too much for my shoulder bag. The clasp snaps just as Fredo finds a spot that suits his purposes. I am pinned to a spot between a closed military zone and a four-lane highway, trying to hold a broken bag together and oversee a shitting dog, while waving mobility scooters around the turds. Once I clear up the mess, I set off, now with two bags: a broken shoulder bag filled with books and souvenirs and a biodegradable bag of poo.

There is nothing much on Hawke Street except a pub dating to 1781 and a block of flats dating to the 1950s. Though the lodgings were cheap and convenient for John's work, the Dickens family didn't stay on Hawke Street long. Aunt Fanny's new husband was lost with his ship off the coast of Brazil in 1813, making her a widow at just twenty-five. She returned to live with John and Elizabeth, who found a new home on Wish Street in Portsea, close to the current Portsmouth university campus. This will be my next stop, the site of the third and final Dickens house in Portsmouth. I take the scenic route by the water. There's a spectacularly brooding sky over the historic ship at anchor in the harbour. Nelson's flagship, HMS

Victory, is close by, in dry dock inside the museum, alongside the Tudor ship, the *Mary Rose*, one of the earliest examples of a purpose-built warship. I might have known more about these ships, except this museum also forbids dogs and this time Fredo failed to melt any hearts.

The Dickenses had a third child while they were living in Wish Street, born in 1814 and named Alfred Allen to commemorate Aunt Fanny's lost husband. Arthur died at the age of six months and was buried in a village named Widley, six miles outside Portsmouth. The tenth-century church and churchyard no longer exist. It would be odd for a family to bury a child a good two-hour walk away in the countryside, rather than in their local church, St Mary's, where both Fanny and Charles had been baptised. It suggests the sisters had family living in Hampshire; Elizabeth and Fanny must have stashed their mother and younger siblings in the countryside. Widley is almost halfway to Bishop Waltham, the town where their grandfather was later buried (in 1821), so we can guess he was close enough to provide support.

There is a reason that I keep worrying away, trying to pinpoint the various members of the Barrow family after Charles Barrow's disappearance. Ultimately, it comes back to the blacking factory, and how it was presented by Dickens in his novels, and later by Forster in his biography. When the family went into the debtors' prison in 1824, twelve-year-old Charles Dickens lodged in Camden with a widow he disliked named Elizabeth Roylance. This same woman had sheltered the fugitive Charles Barrow from 1810, during the years he was hiding in Brighton, fifty miles along the coast from Portsmouth.

It seems unlikely that Barrow ever intended to leave England. The fact that the authorities believed he was hiding in Napoleonic

France must have been misinformation spread by his family, in the hope the hunt would cool. The news that he had been hiding out in Brighton with Elizabeth Roylance only emerged in 1872, when her granddaughter contacted Forster to complain about a reference in the biography. In the book, Forster notes that an early plan for *Dombey and Son* had given the name Roylance to Mrs Pipchin, the witch-like old lady of Brighton who is responsible for the young Dombey children. The Roylance granddaughter got her husband to write to Forster to say her grandmother was nothing like the portrait of Pipchin, but was a kindly woman who had welcomed the Dickens family into her London home in 1824, not as lodgers but as welcome guests. The letter added that a home in Brighton had earlier 'proved the sanctuary to a respected relation, Mr. Barrow, a paymaster of the Admiralty, while under a dense cloud'. It was not then widely known that Charles Barrow had been a fugitive; indeed, it didn't appear in any book until the 1930s, when it was revealed by Gladys Storey, a friend of Dickens's daughter Kate. The fact that Roylance's family were privy to the family secret, and yet regarded Barrow as an honourable man whose name had been traduced, suggests that the connection between Barrow and Roylance was intimate and deep. Their friendship lasted long enough for Roylance to step in once again when the Dickens family needed her, after the debtors' prison.

Even in his absence, Charles Barrow exercised a decades-spanning influence on his family. My instinct is that Roylance was Barrow's mistress, though Dickens's savage portrait of Pipchin makes her an unlikely sexual figure: 'a marvellously ill-favoured, ill-conditioned old lady, of a stooping figure, with a mottled face, like bad marble, a hook nose and a hard grey eye, that looked as if it had been hammered on an anvil without sustaining any injury'. Yet equally, the description could be an expression of discomfort or hatred, because Roylance was an unwelcome intruder into his family.

The American publisher James T. Fields, a friend of Dickens in his last years, also mentioned Mrs Pipchin. Dickens had boasted that his description of her was a reliable childhood memory:

> Speaking of memory one day, [Dickens] said the memory of children was prodigious; it was a mistake to fancy children ever forgot anything. When he was delineating the character of Mrs. Pipchin, he had in his mind an old lodging-house keeper in an English watering-place where he was living with his father and mother when he was but two years old. After the book was written he sent it to his sister, who wrote back at once: 'Good heavens! what does this mean? you have painted our lodging-house keeper, and you were but two years old at that time!'

On the face of it, this passage suggests Roylance was not in fact the model for Pipchin. The connection between the Dickens family and Mrs Roylance spanned decades, and so Fanny would never be surprised that her brother could describe her. When Charles was two, the Dickens family was living in the lodgings on Hawke Street, which suggests that Mrs Pipchin is actually drawn from their Hawke Street landlady. Yet the term 'watering-place' describes a holiday resort like Brighton rather than a naval port. It seems more likely that Fanny is amazed at the two-year-old Dickens's recollection of Roylance's Brighton home, rather than his recall of Roylance herself. Fields possibly misunderstood the context, and thought Dickens was talking about a woman when he meant a house. Dickens is certainly talking about Roylance's house in an earlier letter to Forster: 'I hope you will like Mrs Pipchin's establishment. It is from the life and I was there – I don't suppose I was eight years.' What is significant is the number of different ages that Dickens assigns to his memories of Mrs Roylance. Especially as he says, 'the memory of children [is] prodigious'. It suggests that Dickens stayed with Roylance frequently, right across his childhood, in a variety of different homes, from the age of two, then when he was eight, and again at twelve years old when he worked in the blacking factory. Roylance emerges as a kind of step-grandmother – a constant presence, but someone he could never warm to because of the context of her appearance in the family. She looks after him each time his parents are away. Rather than associate her with a single traumatic event, his parents' imprisonment and his miserable year in the blacking factory, we should see her as a sign of a longer and more nuanced anxiety that reverberates throughout Dickens's life and to which he returns in memory as well as his novels. An essay by Robert L. Patten from 2012, written in the light of the doubts over Forster's account of James Lamert and the blacking factory, makes this point: what has been painted as a single traumatic event is more likely to be a series of events that Dickens's stories keep returning to and trying to work through. The appearance of Roylance signals unhappiness: when she's on the scene, his parents are missing. And behind Roylance is an even shadier figure, the controlling fugitive grandfather.

At some point, perhaps as early as 1814, Barrow escaped to the Isle of Man, where he was eventually joined by his wife and his younger children. If Fanny and Charles were regularly left alone with Roylance, as Florence and Paul Dombey are left with

Mrs Pipchin, then this may have been because his mother and aunt regularly visited the Isle of Man. It was an arduous journey. The stretch to Liverpool by stagecoach was bad enough, but it was followed by a nine- or ten-hour sailing time to the port of Douglas. The women may have stayed for weeks, deepening Charles's resentment. John Dickens had a deep fondness for the island, visiting it long after Charles Barrow's death with his daughter Fanny, when his mother-in-law Mary had returned to live in London as a widow.

The existence of the Portsmouth Madgwicks inevitably leads to a re-evaluation of Magwitch and his connection to Barrow. But there is another career criminal who may represent a disguised version of Dickens's grandfather. We now think of Fagin as an ambivalent figure, in the way that Magwitch is ambivalent, because sixty years of sympathetic portrayals on television, stage and film have somehow softened the original descriptions. This was not true in Dickens's lifetime. Eliza Davis, a Jewish woman who corresponded with Dickens over the last decade of his life, saw Fagin as a figure of one-dimensional evil, writing: 'Fagin I fear admits of only one interpretation.' He is not simply criminal: Fagin is born to evil. Yet even in the original book, he exercises such an influence over his 'family' that we are supposed to understand he is genuinely loved. How are we supposed to read this love: that his children have been groomed? Or that he offers something they need so desperately that even in its very worst form, it is better than nothing?

However evil Fagin might be, he is still family, which is why Oliver visits him in Newgate at the end of the novel while he is awaiting execution. There is a parallel to a scene in *Great Expectations* when Pip visits Magwitch in Newgate before he dies in prison. It suggests that the idea of an ageing errant relative mouldering in prison is a recurring nightmare for Dickens. We can add to this pair a figure from *Barnaby Rudge*, Lord George Gordon, leader of the Gordon Riots as the head of the violently militant Great Protestant Association. Gordon escapes to the continent but also returns, having converted to Judaism. He ends up in Newgate, and the final chapter of *Barnaby Rudge* depicts him in his cell.

Fagin lacks the ambivalent idealism of Gordon, or the ambivalent virtue of Magwitch, yet he is nevertheless an ambivalent figure: Dickens has created a kind of literary code-switcher. He is both feminine and masculine, both cooing mother and proud father, as well as the manipulative and murderous figure we associate with the evil stepmothers of fairy tales. This ambivalence is undeniably antisemitic: indeed, it depends upon the antisemitic trope that sees Jewish men as both too soft and too seductive, and regards Jews as weak people who are yet capable of secretly controlling the world. Fagin is a racist cartoon. Yet when we see the positive reimaginings of Fagin in *Oliver!* it feels as though this sympathetic Fagin is somehow embedded in the original book, even if it took two Jewish geniuses – composer Lionel Bart and actor Ron Moody – to reinterpret the material. The reinvention of Fagin by Moody and Bart has kept him alive through endless revivals of the musical, as well as the competing BBC and Disney+ series that focus on the Dodger–Fagin double-act.

Because we know Charles Barrow has Jewish heritage, we could read Fagin as another version of the errant grandfather. In a racist society, there is a double shame in being tainted as a criminal and a Jew, making Fagin a rawer expression of anger and shame than the convict Magwitch. Dickens conceived Fagin so much earlier in his career than Magwitch, when the influence of the errant grandfather could still be felt. If Fagin is Charles

Barrow, then the Barrow family are his gang, groomed and controlled, covering for a man they love, whose love is making their lives a misery and pulling them into criminality and poverty. Perhaps the double-act of Fagin and the Dodger is Barrow and John Dickens, the endlessly entertaining father who is secretly also a lonely and vulnerable figure.

Readers and historians have suggested other real-life prototypes for Fagin. There is Ikey Solomon, a career criminal and fence who twice escaped deportation in a career that was still sensational news when Dickens was writing *Oliver Twist*. The problem here is that Solomon is neither as grubby nor as old as Fagin: he was born in the same year as John Dickens and was also known for his charm and good looks. His life story could not help but make him a romantic figure. Another possibility is Henry Worms, the Jewish owner of a marine store, the name for the very lowest kind of second-hand junk shop. Worms was a great-uncle by marriage to the cousin James Lamert and went to trial at least twice on charges of receiving stolen property. Another promising suggestion came in 2011, when the archive editor of *The Times* found a story of a black criminal, Henry Murphy, who was said to have run a gang of boys. Dickens might easily have seen reports of Murphy in *The Times* in 1834. He may also have read the 1836 book *London and The Londoners* by Scottish journalist Robert Mudie, which provides an account of a man with an 'Israelite' cast who runs a thieves' kitchen.

So there are numerous possible models for Fagin, and all are from London's minority communities: black or Jewish. In his reply to Eliza Davis, Dickens writes, 'Fagin in *Oliver Twist* is a Jew, because it unfortunately was true of the time to which that story refers, that that class of criminal almost invariably was a Jew.' But there is something disingenuous in this response: no one is making him write about a class of criminal who grooms and sustains an artificial family. That's his decision. Placing a Jew at the centre of this family merely amplifies racist stereotypes. Fagin is not an example of reportage. Dickens senses this, but in his letter to Davis chooses to dig a deeper hole, writing: 'he is called "The Jew", not because of his religion, but because of his race.'

What kind of distinction does Dickens think he is making? Percival Everett's novel *James* comes to help me again. A rattlesnake bite results in a fever dream where James meets the philosopher Voltaire, who tells him that all people are equal, but only in theory. Someone from an inferior race may become the equal of a European, but it is not a given, only a possibility – if they work hard at it. If they raise themselves up. I can see Dickens agreeing with Voltaire, while being just as oblivious to the fact that these ideas of equality do not define Reason, or Civilisation, or Logic, but only justify a distance from non-Europeans. What Dickens means, when he says Fagin is a Jew by virtue of his race rather than his faith, is that he is non-European and uncivilised, while paying Mrs Davis the compliment of regarding her as fully European. Or, to be more blunt: she passes, Fagin does not.

Dickens returns again and again to the idea that we carry the sins of our parents or grandparents. So many of these stories of young people trying to make their way in the world can be read as accounts of what it means to feel ashamed. This isn't just the story of *Oliver Twist*, written in the 1830s, but also of *Great Expectations* and his last completed novel, *Our Mutual Friend*. We can try and exonerate those who cared for us, and understand they acted out of poverty, or ignorance, or passion, yet we will still feel ashamed. I have no doubt that Dickens is writing out of his own sense of shame that his grandfather was a criminal, but I wonder if he is also exorcising his secret shame that his family have Sephardic roots. Fagin is depicted as one step beyond a Spanish Jewish refugee: he is an Arab Jew, wearing a gown rather than European trousers, making his coffee in a pan in the Turkish or Arabic style, and characterised by the constant repetition of 'my dear', which echoes the Arabic use of *habibi*.

I walk to Wish Street via Gunwharf Quay, once the largest armoury in the world, supplying the cannon and explosives for the Royal Navy, now a shopping centre. I buy a new bag in the Nike store and transfer my books and mug as I sit on a bench and listen to a busker sing Taylor Swift. The walk to Wish Street is pointless. The area was bombed heavily and later redeveloped. Wish Street stood somewhere between Landport Terrace and Green Road, in the university district. Turning back towards the station, there's a rather good statue of Dickens wrapped in a cloak, a book casually dangled from his hand. He has a strong bearded face staring into the distance. Dickens was a smaller and more fragile man than the statue suggests. He resembled his delicate and diminutive part-Jewish mother rather than his father. Dickens was praised for his androgynous beauty as a young man, but subject to snide remarks in later life as he lost his looks and began to look older than his years. Yet he always managed to project the figure seen in the Portsmouth statue, the great writer, not only in print but also on stage during his final, epic reading tours.

Pip's shame over Magwitch. The shame of Harmon and Hexam over their fathers in *Our Mutual Friend*. One might wonder, why keep picking at a child's shame: what good does it do him? Throughout Dickens's career, there's this urge to tempt fate, and keep posting hints about his family secrets and the anguish they caused him. But the shame and the writer are part of the same package. It's a strange kind of paradox: he has a story by virtue of the pain and the shame that he feels, but also because he is capable of turning that shame around. He's no longer a victim, but a storyteller. The greatest storyteller of his time.

5

THE HIGH PEAK: 1804-14

Robert Blincoe's indenture papers were transferred from the Lambert brothers to a gentleman farmer named Ellis Needham of Hargate Wall in Derbyshire. In November 1803, the children of Lowdham Mill were loaded once more onto covered wagons for a two-day journey west. Travelling with them was their latest overseer, Robert Woodward, the replacement for the retired drill sergeant with his bull whip. Woodward's brother William was employed as a manager at Ellis Needham's spinning mill on the River Wye close to his Hargate estate. The road to Derbyshire took eleven-year-old Robert and the other children through Arnold, the birthplace of the paramilitary Luddites, a secret organisation of pieceworkers and small weavers who had been forced out of business by the mills, and now sought retribution by smashing machinery and threatening owners. The children spent the night in Cromford, a town on the River Derwent that was planned around the cotton industry. The boys were found space in local stables, while the girls were lodged in the town. Cromford was the site of Richard Arkwright's mill, which harnessed the power of the river to spin cotton on his invention, the water frame. A fifteen-mile stretch of the Derwent from Matlock Bath, where Arkwright opened his second, larger mill, to Derby is a UNESCO heritage site, celebrated as the cradle of the industrial revolution. Needham paraded Robert and the other apprentices through Cromford's main street to advertise his fresh start after twenty years in the cotton trade with his new, young workforce. The street is a wide thoroughfare, flanked by sandstone warehouses, terraced houses, shops, a pub, a church and a school – an area now recognised as the first planned industrial community. Yet by this time, towns like Cromford were in decline. These children were Needham's last desperate gamble to make money. The turn towards steam meant the industry that had begun in these Peak District villages was now dying there.

As described by the journalist John Brown in the *Memoir*, the abiding image of this landscape is death. Needham's mill was set in a valley: 'Its situation, at the bottom of a sequestered glen, and surrounded by rugged rocks, remote from any human habitation, marked a place fitted for the foul crimes which hurried so many ... to an untimely grave.'

The idea that a valley is the road into the underworld is part of Christian imagery, connecting the 'valley of the shadow of death' of Psalm 23 to the Valley of Gehenna below Jerusalem, long associated with death. In Fanny Trollope's novel *The Life and Adventures of Michael Armstrong*, Ellis Needham has become Elgood Sharpton, a kind of real-life devil, and the location of his mill is called 'Deep Valley', an image that turns the High Peak upside down, into a vision of hell:

> Sharpton's factory at Deep Valley is one of the most perfect institutions, I take it, that the ingenuity of man ever produced.

It is perfect, sir, just perfect. In the first place it is built in a wild and desolate spot, where the chances are about ten thousand to one against any of the travelling torments who take upon themselves to meddle and make about what does not concern them – it is a hundred thousand to one against them ever catching sight of it. . . . 'Tis such a hole that I don't believe the sunshine was ever known to get to the bottom of it.

The speaker of these lines is Sir Matthew Dowling. At the opening of Trollope's novel, Sir Matthew is trying to ingratiate himself with Lady Clarissa, a charitably minded aristocrat. This leads him to foster the child Michael Armstrong, a decision he immediately regrets. He feels the child sees through him to his rotten soul. Unable to control his impulses to beat and maltreat Michael, he decides it would be cleaner to get the boy out of the way, and fixes on the idea of binding him to Sharpton, an industrial-scale child-catcher. The *Memoir* doesn't go much into Needham's background, which leaves Trollope free to construct her own portrait of Sharpton. Her industrialist is a severe and calculating figure, one of the post-Malthusian utilitarians whose ideas were in the ascendancy at the time Dickens and Trollope were beginning their careers in the 1830s. The real-life Needham may have been as cruel as Sharpton, but he was far more hapless. He and a cousin named Frith had turned to the cotton industry in 1783. They quickly regretted the decision, and within three years advertised the business as a going concern in newspapers in Derbyshire, Nottingham and Lancashire. Failing to find a buyer, they changed tack and began recruiting apprentices from London. Their mill was so isolated they could not find a ready workforce close at hand, and certainly not one flexible enough to work in a water mill, with all the uncertainty of water power. A captive supply of children kept the mill working. It was simply a happy accident that there was no one to witness his treatment of these children. In contrast, Sharpton has deliberately selected a spot where no one can see his crimes.

Sir Matthew says:

> There's many you know, that say this one thing, this nasty filthy excess of pauper population is the very mischief that is eating up the country and destroying our prosperity. But who's the greatest political economist ... the man who talks of the evil, or he who sets about finding a remedy? ... mark what [Sharpton] has done. First, he finds out this capital spot for the job, and builds a factory there; next he either goes himself, or sends agents, good, capable, understanding men, to all the parishes that he finds are overburdened with poor. Then, sir, he enters philosophically into the subject with the parish authorities, but of course with proper discretion, and proves to them that in no way could they do their duty by the parish children, particularly the orphans, or those whose parents don't trouble them, so well as by apprenticing them to a GOOD TRADE.

Trollope's novel was criticised when it was first serialised because the water mills it described had been driven out of business, and she was targeting practices that no longer existed. Yet her portrait of a sinister economist is spot-on in the period after the 1834 Poor Law. Elgood Sharpton is the original for all the subsequent crazed industrialists in Victorian literature.

This was an age that had absorbed Adam Smith's message that a healthy economy had to allow entrepreneurs to judge their own needs and agree their own targets. Victorian industrialists were assured this was the surest way to greater efficiency and increased productivity in the economy as a whole, as though 'led by an invisible hand'. Sharpton's critique is the corollary of Smith's message: he argues that if parts of the economy are allowed to skate by without ever setting goals, meeting targets or being driven by manufacturers, then they will poison the political body, rotting it from within. The factory owners claim that the only way to a healthy economy is to give a free hand to the industrialists, and forget sick, soggy ideas about paupers and children. The result, as Trollope sees, gives industrialists complete power over the workers, especially the urban poor. If elements of Trollope's depiction of Sharpton are anachronistic, the essential picture of a man determined to expunge all charity from the economic system hits home. *Michael Armstrong* created a new genre, the industrial novel, and Sharpton became the template for characters like Thomas Gradgrind in Dickens's *Hard Times* (1854). As the editor of *Household Words* magazine, Dickens commissioned and edited Elizabeth Gaskell's *North and South* (1854–5), one of the key factory novels, and even chose its title, in a deliberate echo of Disraeli's earlier factory novel, *Sybil, or The Two Nations* (1845). The genre survived well into the twentieth century, where tales of fiery abused working women would fill my grandmother's bag on her weekly trips to the library.

Sharpton hid his mill to ensure no one knew how many of his apprentices died. Needham had his own ingenious method for disguising the high number of deaths, distributing the bodies between different graveyards. His estate was in the village of Wormhill, and he built his mill in nearby Litton, an unsuitable choice which led to the added expense of building a weir to ensure a steady supply of water. He and his cousin used agents to recruit apprentices from London, which required an apprentice house. They built the first one beside the mill, but this caused problems with their neighbours. The cousins were both members of the old local gentry, and the arrival of so many children threatened their standing in the parish of Tideswell. The parish knew full well how easily child workers could become dependents of the community. Since they could not afford to see their stock fall with their neighbours and congregants, Needham and Frith opted to build a second apprentice house on the opposite side of the river, which placed it in the neighbouring parish of Taddington. Inevitably, they received even more complaints from the locals: as late as 1810, a local landowner railed to an inspector (one of the 'travelling torments' mentioned by Sir Matthew) that Needham had dumped so many paupers on Taddington the cost was equal to the community rents. A child's death was registered for each of the years Needham ran Litton Mill, with five buried in Tideswell, one in Wormhill and twenty-one in Taddington, suggesting sick children were swiftly moved across the river. A death per year in a mill that employed fewer than a hundred children is high: somewhere between double and four times the figure of nearby mills. The *Memoir* puts the mortality rate even higher, which may be Robert's mistake or an exaggeration. Yet as the *Memoir* is generally so often reliable, and Robert could count, it suggests Needham had found other ways to hide excess deaths.

The cousins ended their partnership in 1799. Frith continued farming and spinning in a modest way. In contrast, Needham borrowed heavily against his land, and brought his adult sons into the business as partners. This is the new regime that Robert Blincoe joined, moving into the Taddington apprentice house after his journey from Nottingham. Litton Mill is still standing, though it was significantly rebuilt in the nineteenth century by later owners. It is a large stone building of millstone grit, now subdivided into apartments and holiday lets. I book an overnight stay for myself and my brother on Airbnb. It's a large apartment over the fast-running stream, with a private riverside path. An aerial shot shows the mill, almost completely hidden in the trees on a river bend. It's far from the hellhole described by Brown or Trollope.

My brother is already worried about our night in the mill. He fears he will be too sensitive to the vibes of torture and death. Reading the reviews online, though, the gruesome history hasn't noticeably bothered the tourists. On the contrary. The mill is deep in the countryside and the apprentices would break out of their houses to scavenge the fields and hedgerows. They stole from the surrounding fields, hiding turnips in the latrine and washing the shit off later in the Wye. In Jonathan Glazer's film on Auschwitz, *The Zone of Interest*, prisoners are seen bustling around under night-vision cameras hiding scrap food, a scene similar to those described by the original Robert Blincoe in 1822. The way that the Nazi work camps segued easily into death camps suggests the power to murder the inmates was built-in, and the description as 'work camps' helped inure society to the horrors to come. This is what Trollope saw in Robert's *Memoir*: that death was the entelechy of these mills. The scenes which most affected her were Robert's account of stealing food from Needham's pigs. The Needhams kept both cows and pigs near the mill, neither of which were to feed the apprentices – the produce was sent to the nearby town of Buxton. The pigs were treated better than the children; at least, they could not be beaten into silence when they clamoured to be fed. They made so much noise that they were always fed first. 'The pigs are served, it will be us next,' the children said. The pigs were fed on patties of meal and dough, and Robert would steal the patties and hide them as they hid the turnips to eat later. This scene constitutes a set piece in *Michael Armstrong*, illustrated by Trollope's younger French lover, the artist Auguste Hervieu. The bright young child Michael of the earlier drawings is reduced to a feral creature, scrabbling with other children, all far fiercer than the pigs. Robert relates how the pigs became wise to the thieves and learned to hide their food, setting up a chorus of screams and squeals to alert the overlookers whenever a child approached.

Was Trollope wrong to see Litton Mill as a death camp rather than a workplace? The Needhams made little attempt to treat sick children: children were isolated if they came down with a fever, but only after they were too weak to be beaten into working. The only medicine seems to have been treacle in hot water. Robert claims that at one time, forty children were off work and the mill had to stop production. There are records of smallpox in the area in 1803. Infestations such as lice were treated by using pitch caps to rip the hair out of the children's heads. Perhaps death was not certain or intended, but the factory fulfilled the common view that the children did not matter. Sir Matthew fixes on Sharpton because Sharpton has no qualms about burying pauper children in isolated and sunless holes. For his scheme to work, Sir Matthew must first make Michael his apprentice, and then sign the indenture papers over to Sharpton – just as Robert Blincoe's indentures were transferred from the Lambert brothers to Ellis Needham. This exchange becomes the fulcrum of the plot, turning *Michael Armstrong* into something far closer to a slave memoir: Trollope's previous novel had been set among the avaricious slave-owning class of Mississippi and her villains in *Michael Armstrong* continue the theme of inhumanity walking hand-in-hand with greed.

The musical *Oliver!* sees the beadle attempt to hold a slave auction in the snow, with the song 'Boy for Sale'. Lionel Bart misrepresents the situation. In *Oliver Twist*, as in real life, the parish paid potential masters to take the children, rather than sell them. The only aim was to get rid of children, rather than create slaves. However, when the children's papers were traded in a secondary market, the situation became something like slavery. The parallel between child apprentices and the transatlantic slave trade was not invented by Trollope: John Brown makes the analogy throughout the *Memoir*, as does its first publisher, Richard Carlile in his 1828 introduction. Indeed, both argue that Robert's situation is in many ways worse than a slave's. John Brown writes, 'If I were to assert that it would be difficult, if not impossible, from the record of sufferings inflicted upon Negro slaves, to quote instances of greater atrocity ... I should not exaggerate.'

After insisting that Robert is effectively a slave, Brown segues to a more general discussion of the misery of the cotton industry. The avarice of 'a few great and unfeeling capitalists', he argues, has reduced 'so many hundred thousand weavers to a state of destitution so extreme as to render the condition of the most destitute ... worse than that of a field slave in the West Indian plantations, who had the good fortune to belong to a humane proprietor'.

The idea that factory work, in general, is a variation of slavery was new in the early nineteenth century. John Brown's aside must be one of the earliest references to what would be called 'wage slavery'. Reading Brown's formulation, it is striking how poor the analogy is. He takes as a given that the world is run through binary relations between the powerful and the powerless, and in consequence sees nothing off-kilter about an African working for an English master on a Caribbean island. When comparing field slavery to other industries, the key factor is only the work conditions. Brown has passed over what is most unnatural and shocking in transatlantic slavery, that people have been torn from their homes, transported thousands of miles, separated from their families, to be worked, raped and bred for profit.

The idea that power hierarchies, based on economic relations, are the constitutive feature of human societies was new in the early nineteenth century, but was fast becoming widespread. If masters are defined by their freedom – the freedom championed by Adam Smith to pursue their desires and make their contracts – then the people who work for them are characterised by their lack of freedom, and the violence needed to keep them in bondage. The comparison to slavery made this observation about life in industrial cities, with their class-based violence, more vivid. Looking to slavery seemed useful because it had an explanatory power. Yet slavery is not simply factory work with no wages, and to claim they are comparable ends up downgrading the real horror of slavery. It's an analysis that passes for realism only as long as we ignore that slaves are captured by force, not by trade. They have no stake in the relationship, not even the unequal and exploitative relationship that exists between a factory-owner and his workforce. Being a wage slave can be mitigated by improved industrial relations, and perhaps even overturned by a more equitable share in the economy, but nothing changes the status of a real slave, not even 'the good fortune to belong to a humane proprietor'. The analogy with slavery was important for early industrial reformers because it provided a model: not simply because of the tradition of slave narratives, but more importantly because the abolitionists had built an organised politics of protest. Modern labour politics begins with a debt to the politics opposing transatlantic slavery, but a debt it misinterprets and, thus, resists properly acknowledging or paying.

On the other hand, Robert Blincoe's situation is as close to real slavery as is possible for someone who is white and English. He is a helpless child reduced to nothing, just meat for the industrial grinder. Robert is the link that allows us to compare slaves and factory workers – as long as we read about Robert, we can buy the analogy.

Brown's remarks on slavery are more than just asides, they give shape and an argument to the *Memoir*. Robert's time in the High Peak is the heart of the book. Though just two chapters long, it comprises almost half of the whole. These sections are by far the toughest to read not simply because they represent an account of a cruel and indifferent system, but also because they show how the masters and their overlookers enjoyed torturing the children – it was sport. The chief sadists are Robert Woodward, who had travelled with the children from Nottingham and whose brother was the factory manager; and John Needham, one of Ellis's sons. Woodward acted in concert with two other young men who had grown up in the system as apprentices, but Woodward was always the instigator. He would insist, as a game, that Robert clean out all the cotton dust beneath a machine within one cycle of the frame. He would beat or punish him if he failed to do it in time. The punishments would often involve weights which he would tie to Robert's shoulders or screw to his ears with clamps. Weighted down like this, Robert would be forced to work full days of sixteen hours. When, as an adult in the 1830s, a quarter of a century later, Robert gave evidence to a parliamentary committee, he showed the committee the scars, which he usually hid by wearing his hair long over his ears.

Another game involved Robert standing on one of the metal canisters used to store rovings, the drawn-out fibres that were spun on the spinning frames. He was made to balance on this can, at times with his arms tied and at others holding a broom out straight, within range of the machine's drive, so that he would be knocked over each time the shaft returned. Robert risked falling into the machine or onto the floor. Beatings were constant, using belts, switches and whips. Ellis Needham would punch and beat the children as he passed by, used horse whips on the children, pinched their ears until his fingernails met, and would lift children off the ground by their hair. His son John Needham was just as vicious, and once insisted Robert strip naked while Woodward was sent to cut switches from a nearby thicket to use on his back. Robert had recently been beaten by Woodward and as there was no part of his body that wasn't cut or bruised, Needham changed his mind and ordered him to dress again. The *Memoir* only alludes briefly to John's worst crimes: he was a rapist. 'To boys, he was a tyrant and an oppressor. To the girls the same, with the additional odium of treating them with an indecency as disgusting as his cruelty was terrific.' To this is added, in parentheses, '[Those unhappy creatures were at once the victims of his ferocity and his lust.]'

The reference throws into relief the story of a girl named Phebe Rag. The *Memoir* relates that she was a handsome woman of twenty, which seems like a random observation, but is perhaps a way of coding a reference to rape; in the sense that she is singled out, thereby blaming the victim. What Needham wants her for is simply glossed over as her 'ill treatment'. Rag had made persistent attempts to escape to her hometown of Cromford, and as a result Needham issued an order to place her in irons. Similar to those used on convicts, the irons were welded on to anyone regarded as a flight risk; the job was done by a local blacksmith who rented premises at the mill. Rag then tried to commit suicide by throwing herself into the mill pond. She was dragged out and revived, but Ellis Needham ordered her removal. The *Memoir* says she was returned to Cromford.

Another apprentice, nicknamed Blackey, was bullied so severely he became catatonic: 'his head was as soft as boiled turnip'. He was beaten in summer, usually around the head, and in winter thrown naked into the mill pond and dragged backwards and forwards with a rope, before being sat under the pump and sluiced with cold water. The treatment left him unable to work, so he simply became a figure for sport, which he attempted to avoid by spending his time trying to hide in corners and holes. The treatment left him incontinent, 'inflicted of incontinency of stools and urine', and the Needhams ordered him to be starved. Brown was so affected by the story, he tracked him down. His name was James Nottingham and he was working in Oldfield Lane, between Bakewell and Matlock. It turned out that he had no recollection at all of his treatment at Litton Mill, though he vouched that whatever Brown had been told by Blincoe was true: 'I have no distinct recollections of anything that happened to me ... I believe my sufferings was most dreadful, and that I nearly lost my sense.'

Brown states that he went out of his way to gain character references for Nottingham, and also that he had other sources for his story. Indeed, he had sources other than Robert Blincoe for the memoir: 'the testimony not of Blincoe alone, but of many of his former associates, unknown to him, gave similar statements'. Brown's multiple sources are part of the backstory of the *Memoir*: Brown essentially cold-called Robert at his home in 1822, because he had heard stories from other witnesses. In 1828, shortly after the first publication of the *Memoir*, a trade union organiser named John Joseph Betts wrote to the *Lion* newspaper to state that he had worked under Robert as a child, when Robert was finishing his apprenticeship and working as an overlooker in his turn. Betts stated that Robert's account was true, and the treatment grew even worse after he left in 1814, when the apprentices were barely fed at all and had to subsist on what they could find in the woodland. Hearteningly, Betts said that Robert – or 'Parson' as Betts knew him – had never ill-treated anyone: 'he would frequently give part of his allowance of food to those under his care out of mere commiseration, and conceal all significant omissions without a word of reproach.'

Every time someone supplies an account of Robert, the story is invariably about a moment of kindness, if not a moment of bravery. He has an acute sense of fellow-feeling. Where did it come from? It seems he was someone who stood out. A witness statement appended to the 1977 edition of his memoir, dated 1888, recalls him living at a grocer's close to Manchester's High Street: 'a little man in height, his legs being very crooked ... He was well-known in Turner Street at the time I refer to, about 1934 and upwards.' Despite his height, he was a kind of peg around which the strands of a social network were secured. The union organiser, Betts, was another peg. He had heard that Robert was speaking to Brown well before the *Memoir* was published. In his letter to the *Lion*, he recalls discussing the upcoming book with another ex-apprentice who passed the news on to William Woodward, brother of the chief ringleader and psychopath. Woodward turned pale when he learned it was Parson who had spoken: 'He'll give it ma [me].' I admit, I like the idea that his name puts the fear into his old boss. He was not simply kind, he had a streak of righteousness. None of these people were brought to justice, but I want to believe they always lived looking over their shoulders.

The *Memoir* is full of names, as though anticipating the need for a roll call of witnesses. The list of names grew during its long publication history, as the book gained appendices, and acted as a touchstone for the community of activists who worked in the Ten Hour Movement, the first national campaign for a statutory maximum working week. The *Memoir* became a resource, supplying material and witnesses for the parliamentary committee, as well as inspiration and images for the protest marches. Thus, while John Brown is in a sense a conventional lone author, he is also merely one among several collaborators. The text takes shape by borrowing from the campaign against slavery, yet it is not constrained by the form that Brown and Carlile impose upon it. The way that the book expanded to include testimonies, growing with each subsequent publication, means it is also a testament to the emergence of a friendship circle, forged in hardship. The book gives a glimpse of an industrial class as it takes shape. The *Memoir* is populated by people who knew each other well, and never forgot the experience they shared, and which led them to keep up friendships.

John Brown would have been forgotten if it wasn't for the multiple editions of Robert's *Memoir*. Yet the book he produced quickly turned into something more like an open-source text, as Brown's voice is overwhelmed by the clamour of others. The *Memoir* is a story of a hero, but also of the emergence of class in its most immediate sense as a circle of friends. A social milieu.

My brother and I are still trying to make our visit to High Peak. I've cancelled and rebooked our Airbnb apartment three times as, first, I got caught up in a house sale, then Robert got Covid, and finally because of our mother's rescheduled hip replacement. I am trying to keep my research trips to their proper place in the text, in the hope that the book will feel like a journey of discovery.

Or maybe a movie, filmed in sequence out of a stubborn desire to keep the reactions fresh. My mother's hip changes our plans again, but also opens up a new possibility. She has a rota: Robert is first, our sister second, and I am last. Each of us will take a week to see her through the critical early period after the operation. Robert suggests we can dash to Derbyshire the week that our sister is with Mum. I rebook the apartment.

The day my brother arrives at our parents' home, he gets a call that his mother-in-law, Dolly, has died in Wolverhampton. I drive across the country to take his shift, remembering to cancel the Airbnb about an hour into my journey. Robert is on a train, hoping that he can get to Wolverhampton before the funeral. The undertakers have already taken Dolly to the mosque, where Robert's wife is with her.

A week later, I make the drive through the peaks of Derbyshire on my own. Buxton is a strange town, like finding a forgotten city of opera halls and glass palaces in an unexplored land. The road to Litton Mill takes me though villages laid out around idyllic village greens. I soon reach Ellis Needham's estate at Hargate Wall, Wormhill. Today, the clouds seem as tall as skyscrapers, rising to the heavens in steps and pierced by sunlight. I take a road called The Stitch. Needham lost his estate in his lifetime and the new owners built their own baronial hall, with lavish greenhouses and views over the valleys. There are open vistas across the tops on a road called Summer Cross. The clouds shimmer and glower above me. Tideswell has the perfect village collection of fish-and-chip shop, chapel, post office and pub. Only the grey of the tall millstone grit buildings hint at a shadow side. I turn onto the road towards Litton and am surprised by the sight of an enormous church with a sign announcing I have reached the Cathedral of the Peak. Throughout his career as a failing factory owner, Needham was anxious that his money troubles would affect his standing with his fellow church members. I had not realised his church, St John the Baptist Tideswell, was quite so grand: a huge gothic building with all the medieval touches that took the local serfs and tradesmen eighty years to build, interrupted only by the Black Death.

Church Lane leads to Litton, another picture-perfect village on a green. The road descends to the River Wye and after a dogleg turn, Litton Mill is suddenly ahead, beyond two handsome stone gateposts. It's a late Victorian building, like all the mills I grew up with in my childhood in Rochdale. There is nothing left of the mill as Needham abandoned it, after his bankruptcy in 1815.

I take the road out to Chapel-en-le-Frith, the route the original Robert Blincoe took when he finally left Needham's mill. He continued walking to Stalybridge, and over two years made his way to Manchester. I turn off and head to the Dark Peak in Edale, a place that has both the name and the vibe that Fanny Trollope was reaching for. I drive through the eerie windswept landscape of standing stones and peaks: Mam Tor, Kinder Scout and Mount Famine. As I drive towards Jacob's Ladder the weather changes and the clouds broil to sink into the spaces between the hills. That's more like it.

6

DICKENS LOSES THREE FRIENDS: 1816-22

Robert Blincoe's term of apprenticeship ended when he was twenty-one, in 1813, but rather than leave Litton Mill he continued working for another year. He knew no other life and had no money. The wage of four shillings and sixpence was well below the going rate for a journeyman spinner but he did not know this, and he could not move on when he was penniless. Inevitably, the Needhams failed to pay, and after six months of broken promises he left with thirty shillings and his indenture papers in his pocket. He went immediately to consult a fortune-teller in Chapel-en-le-Frith, a haggard and bearded figure named Old Bekka, who told him that his troubles were at an end. Over the next few years, he marched slowly towards Manchester. After working in mills in New Mills and Stalybridge, he finally reached the so-called Cottonopolis, England's 'Shock City'. It was 1815, the year the wars against the French ended. He had a new name, Blincoe for Parson, and a new home. I estimate half my identity is bound up with my odd name and my Northern roots. Destiny is chance in drag.

The end of the French wars marked a change for the Dickens

family, too. The Navy Pay Office recalled John Dickens to London. Elizabeth Dickens had odd bits of family in London. Her twenty-three-year-old brother Thomas Barrow was still at Somerset House in the Navy Pay Office, with rooms on Gerrard Street (now the main thoroughfare of Chinatown). His younger brother, seventeen-year-old John Henry Barrow, was lodging on the Strand and trying to make his way as a poet. The most valuable of her relatives was her namesake, Aunt Elizabeth Charlton (née Culliford), a well-connected businesswoman who owned a 'silvering' factory on Golden Square. A process that involved wrapping a thin wire around a core of another metal or even gut to make high tension piano strings, silvering became outdated by the 1830s with the introduction of cast steel strings and Aunt Elizabeth may already have diversified into property, and bought the lodging house on Berners Street she ran with her husband in the 1820s and 30s. If so, it would explain why the Dickens family took lodgings around the corner, on the upper part of Newman Street, then named Norfolk Street. With most of the Barrow family in hiding on the Isle of Man, Elizabeth and Fanny, now a young widow, would want to be close to their few relatives. The new lodgings at 10 Norfolk Street were above a grocer's shop. It must have been cramped with three adults and two children, along with a couple of servants, all partly paid for through Fanny's navy pension.

Living at the top end of Newman Street also meant that John Dickens was living close to his only family: his older brother and his mother. William had left service when his mother retired, and together they opened a coffee house on Oxford Street. Shortly after setting up shop, William met a woman named Jane Latham and they were wed in the church in Hanover Square where his parents had married thirty years earlier. On the face of it, this little corner of London, between the coffee shop, the lodging house in Berners Street and an uncle in Soho, looks just the place for the Dickens family to put down roots. In the event, they spent less than two years in the city. There's a possible reference by Dickens to his paternal grandmother as 'a grim and unsympathetic old personage of the female gender'. This woman took him to a toy bazaar in Soho Square and told him his present must cost less than half a crown. Stories about John Dickens's mother tend to revolve around money.

Newman Street runs north off Oxford Street. The grocer's shop stood about halfway up the street, where the road marks the border between Marylebone and the sliver of St Pancras that slips down below Euston Road (the district now known as Fitzrovia). There was a workhouse a few doors down from the Dickenses' new home, and its location suggests the border between Marylebone and St Pancras ran through their lodgings. The workhouse belonged to the parish of Covent Garden on land that had been leased from the cash-strapped St Pancras vestry. It was devious to build a workhouse almost a mile outside Covent Garden, keeping the parish paupers at arms' length. This was not the end of Covent Garden's cunning. The workhouse door was positioned so that it opened onto Marylebone – ensuring that Marylebone parish was liable for any foundlings or paupers left at the steps. The design and location of the workhouse reflects the zero-sum war between the parishes as they fought over the urban poor. Anyone who could be dumped somewhere else was one less expense on the local books. The position of the workhouse suggests the Dickenses lived in St Pancras but entered the more upscale Marylebone each time they stepped out of their door.

The proximity of the workhouse to the Dickens family flat

became a feature of a campaign to save the old workhouse building from demolition in 2012. The campaigners argued that it may have been the model for Oliver Twist's workhouse. As Dickens was only four when the family left London, the connection is somewhat strained, though the campaign was effective. The building was saved. The family were off again in late 1816, when John Dickens was posted to Chatham, the inland port on the River Medway. This became Dickens's home until he was eleven and a half – and in many ways, a home for life as he never abandoned his connection to the Medway area. The writer most closely associated with the sprawl of London was always a kind of outsider, a Kentish man undercover. The Medway town of Chatham is bound in a Jekyll-and-Hyde relation with the older Rochester, and these paired towns alongside the surrounding marshes feature in almost all his works. It is also where his lover, Ellen Ternan, was born and raised, and where he bought his grand country mansion in later life, Gad's Hill Place on the road between Rochester and Gravesend. Now a private school, Gad's Hill Place was the official residence of the World's Most Famous Author in the final quarter of his life; his postal address, and the place where his 'people' – namely his sister-in-law Georgina and his daughter Mamie – took care of the administration and correspondence. By this time, Dickens was sharing his life with his secret family, Ellen and her mother, which meant the grand house was to an extent a mere façade of grandeur and respectability. It was a statement. Dickens, the great magician of conviviality, had removed himself from the capital to do his entertaining in the Kentish countryside. His return to the Medway reflects the romantic conservative side of the writer, his sympathy for an older, provincial world before the industrial and political revolutions and the vast migrations from the countryside to the cities. The Kent marshes were a lost idyll. But what was he looking back to? Was it the Rochester side of his inheritance, lampooned as Dullsborough in a sketch of the town in *The Uncommercial Traveller* (1860)? Or the bustling dockside town, Chatham? This is always the paradox of romantic conservatives: are they nostalgic for something simpler and unspoiled, or something dirtier and wilder?

The Medway runs through Dickens's entire career, a touchstone that explained the yin and yang he saw everywhere: beauty and evil, respectability and lawlessness, countryside and marsh. Chatham was where he built the first attachments and friendships that shaped his later life as an entertainer and writer.

Close to the start of *David Copperfield* is a bibliography which sounds plausibly like a list of Dickens's key influences:

> My father had left a small collection of books in a little room upstairs, to which I had access (for it adjoined my own) and which nobody else in our house ever troubled. From that blessed little room, Roderick Random, Peregrine Pickle, Humphrey Clinker, Tom Jones, the Vicar of Wakefield, Don Quixote, Gil Blas, and Robinson Crusoe, came out, a glorious host, to keep me company. They kept alive my fancy, and my hope of something beyond that place and time, – they, and the Arabian Nights, and the Tales of the Genii, – and did me no harm; for whatever harm was in some of them was not there for me; I knew nothing of it. It is astonishing to me now, how I found time, in the midst of my porings and blunderings over heavier themes, to read those books as I did. It is curious to me how I could ever have consoled myself under my small troubles (which were great troubles to me), by impersonating my favourite characters ... I have been Tom Jones (a child's

Tom Jones, a harmless creature) for a week together. I have sustained my own idea of Roderick Random for a month at a stretch, I verily believe. I had a greedy relish for a few volumes of Voyages and Travels – I forget what, now – that were on those shelves; and for days and days I can remember to have gone about my region of our house, armed with the centre-piece out of an old set of boot-trees – the perfect realization of Captain Somebody, of the Royal British Navy, in danger of being beset by savages, and resolved to sell his life at a great price. The Captain never lost dignity, from having his ears boxed with the Latin Grammar. I did; but the Captain was a Captain and a hero, in despite of all the grammars of all the languages in the world, dead or alive.

Forster claims this passage is 'literally true', including it in the 1872 biography because he insisted this was its 'proper place'. Let's take a moment and unpack this claim. Forster doesn't think the passage belongs where we find it, in a universally admired and loved book by one of our greatest writers, but needs to be moved to another book, one written and organised by John Forster. It's a preposterous claim, yet the idea that these books were Dickens's father's library has stuck. *David Copperfield* is a novel about a boy who has lost his father, and these books function as a memorial to a man that Copperfield never knew. It's unlikely Dickens felt like memorialising John Dickens, a man who was ever-present, and annoyed the hell out of him. I doubt John ever owned any of these books. He had a florid and infectious style of speaking, reflecting the soul of a man who wished to be a great companion, a master of the anecdote and epigram: in short, Micawber. He was never a writer, as shown by an inadvertently comical piece he wrote describing a fire in Chatham: 'It is, however, a relief in relating this melancholy accident, to state that no lives were lost on the occasion. One or two persons were, we understand, hurt by the falling of a wall but not dangerously.' His true métier was bar-room oratory. John turned his son into a junior version of himself, teaching Dickens to perform monologues when guests came around, and perform upon a tabletop at the Mitre, Chatham's coaching inn. Did John Dickens actually read? He subscribed to a serialised history from a local bookseller, *The History and Antiquities of Rochester and its Environs*, but as Ackroyd perceptibly says, this 'suggests his urgent need to become a part of whatever environment in which he found himself, to fit in and as it were to aggrandise himself by attaching himself to the grander elements of the reality around him'. It's not the choice of someone who reads for joy.

Dickens was taught to read by his mother, not his father. Elizabeth hoped to become a teacher, and besides teaching him English she also drilled Dickens in the rudiments of Latin. The library reflects Elizabeth's tastes rather than John's, or so I guess. The list is heavily weighted towards the works of Tobias Smollett, even the *Quixote* and *Gil Blas* were his translations. Smollett's great innovation was to make his characters orphans: Roderick Random, Peregrine Pickle et al. You can't go wrong with a hero who has no choice but to rely on his own ingenuity, and acts in the present, with no cumbersome backstory. Fielding's hero Tom Jones is clearly inspired by Smollett's characters; like them he is almost lucky to have escaped the burden of parents. The influence on Dickens is clear, though these novels lack Dickens's heartfelt sense that loneliness is an open wound. In *Copperfield*, the library is presented as the treasure of a lonely seven-year-old, who sublimates his pain in fantasy. This might warn us that Dickens read these books in his later, teenage years, and not as early as David Copperfield (as if a seven-year-old could read such novels). The mood they are supposed to conjure reflects the darker situation of Dickens's return to London. Chatham was a happy childhood.

It is only the last few books in the Copperfield library that may refer to Chatham, a nautical town filled with sailors, marines, shipwrights and naval personnel. The maritime adventures of 'Captain Somebody, of the Royal British Navy' has been taken as Robert Southey's biography of Nelson. But perhaps they also reflect Aunt Fanny's first husband, missing off the coast of South America, or the family's own legends about the miscreant Charles Barrow, who was Nelson's contemporary as an apprentice seaman. Barrow claimed to have been shipwrecked in Madagascar, when he saved himself by walking across the island. This story was apparently passed through the family, but perhaps Dickens also heard it firsthand. Dickens probably did meet his grandfather, certainly after 1824 when the old man broke cover.

Dickens owed his love of reading to his mother but given his ambivalence towards her, he was never keen to give her credit. When did their relationship sour? A new child, Letitia, was born in London in 1816, and another three children were either born or conceived in the Chatham years, bringing the Dickens family to six (passing over Alfred, the child that had died in Portsmouth). Dickens may have felt edged out of his mother's affections. Yet in Chatham he was also able to command the attention of a range of mother-substitutes.

First among these other-mothers was Fanny. His aunt's presence throughout his childhood is perhaps the reason that Dickens always latched on to sisters, essentially seeing them as twofers. (Buy one, get one free.) After he married, he took his wife's younger sister into his home, and when she died he replaced her with another sister, Georgina. His secret Ternan set-up also comprised two sisters, Ellen and yet another girl named Fanny. In his Chatham home, there were two female servants, and one of these, Mary Weller, had a gift for ghost stories. Dickens would go on to fill his novels with female characters; but that does not mean he sees women more clearly than previous male novelists, only that he has curated a far wider number of stereotypes, almost all of whom are stand-ins for absent mothers. They range across the class divide from warm-hearted servants like Peggotty of *David Copperfield*, right up to eccentrics with their own agendas like Betsey Trotwood or Miss Havisham, the saintly and demonic versions of the same woman in *David Copperfield* and *Great Expectations*. In between these extremes are the many young women who first prove their maternal instincts by caring for a man before they become love interests or doomed heroines, with *Oliver Twist* providing examples of both in Rose Maylie and Nancy.

In Chatham, John Dickens rented a house on Ordnance Terrace, the second from the left. It is tall and thin, close enough to the railway that I see it as I emerge from the station. Its place on a hillside means there are sweeping views down to the Medway, and the name suggests it was the site of a gun emplacement that could rake enemy ships on the river below. However, if enemy ships got this far upstream, the dockyards would already have been captured. Chatham is the site of the worst ever naval defeat in the British Isles. For five days in 1667, the Dutch Navy seized Sheerness, razed ships in Chatham and Gillingham, and hijacked the Royal Navy flagship, which they kept. I would guess that Dickens's home on Ordnance Terrace is named because it was built to house clerks from the Board of Ordnance, responsible for stocking and storing the armaments of the Royal Dockyard, which were greatly strengthened after this debacle. The dockyard begins half a mile downstream of the town centre and stretches as far as Gillingham and Brompton.

I plan to start my tour of Chatham at the docks, but I find myself lurking in the station entrance to overhear two transport policemen discuss a man they had detained on my train. The same man is the owner of a husky-cross puppy and twice on my journey Fredo had snapped at the younger dog, once on the platform before we boarded, and a second time in one of the carriages as the man was finding his seat. Both times, the man reacted with smiles and good humour. Then, thirty minutes later, I see him hustled past me by these two policemen. I heard them tell him he would be placed at the end of the train, as far from the incident as possible, to prevent any repetition. Even as he was strong-armed along, the man, a rangy, smiling, open-faced guy in his forties, seemed good humoured. It was difficult to believe that something had kicked off. When I saw the policemen again at the ticket barrier, I strained to hear their conversation with the station master. I heard there had been an argument with a woman. Maybe the man was not as smiley and good-natured to everyone as he was towards dogs, or perhaps the police were jumpy because there had been a serious stabbing the day before; a soldier had been attacked outside Brompton Barracks, opposite Chatham docks. Once I start out towards the river front, walking in the direction of the docks, I notice several off-duty soldiers in uniform, as though in solidarity with their colleague.

By the end of the eighteenth century, Chatham's docks, wharfs and warehouses were a mile long – and this was at a time when Chatham had been eclipsed by Portsmouth, the home of the fleet and the nerve centre for all naval operations during the war with

France. Chatham entered a second life as a shipyard. Most of the navy's ships continued to be built on the Medway and though it is impossible to imagine Chatham being the busy, bustling place it once was, it is still a military town. There is a new museum on the docks, but either side of Dock Road there are zones off-limits to civilians and decorated with signs that warn that the Official Secrets Act is in operation. The military does not seem to bring Chatham wealth or industry. If anything, it contributes to a sense that the town is run-down, ghost-filled and empty. There's been a general election since I made my trip to Portsmouth. The Conservative Party lost both Portsmouth and Chatham, largely because the Reform Party stole their mantle as the party of the military, patriotism and British exceptionalism. (The injured lieutenant will publicly thank the pro-Reform Party presenter Darren Grimes of GB News for setting up a fundraiser after the attack.)

Ordnance Terrace and Chatham Docks represent two different worlds: one a feminine, interior and domestic space; the other a public space of male company. Dickens was old enough to enter this other world, with his father as chaperone, singing comic songs and reciting monologues in pubs, sailing along the river and walking the town. The child had to create his own masculine identity, and his father John is undoubtedly the great role model. However, there are two other important figures, both of them younger men who entered Dickens's life when he was around seven years of age. The first was William Giles, the master of Dickens's first school. He may have been as young as twenty-one when Charles and his sister Fanny began classes at his Baptist church school.

After the docks and a glimpse of the police tape close to yesterday's attack, I turn back to Chatham. I want to see what

I can find of the old school. Fredo is tugging at his lead again. I have to keep him in my left hand because – *dramatic reveal!* – I broke my arm four weeks ago. It's a proximal humerus fracture of the right arm, meaning the top of the bone where it meets the shoulder. I was running in the airport – don't do it! There are three fractures, but I managed to avoid a cast by wearing a sling continuously for three weeks and even sleeping sitting upright so that gravity held the bone in position to line up the breaks. The sling has been off a week, but the pain means I am only sleeping in sixty- to ninety-minute blocks. Today, I travelled with a backpack because I am carrying my heaviest Dickens book, the 700-page-plus Michael Slater biography. It was stupid to bring the book because I can't use my left hand to hold both Fredo and my bag, and I can't really use my right arm. I realise I am going to have to wear the backpack like, well, technically, a backpack. I walk lopsided to try and keep the right-side straps away from the sorest parts of my shoulder.

I am feeling a bit beaten up by the time we reach Chatham's town centre. I take a road that follows an old, now buried stream known as the Brook, then cut through to the High Street. The Brook had become a main sewer during the Dickens family's time in Chatham, so it is a surprise that they moved from Ordnance Terrace to the small grid of streets on the south side of the High Street around Clover Street. It could have been one more attempt to save money, but there was another draw: an energetic Baptist preacher was building a mini-empire in these streets and the family seem to have been sucked in.

The preacher was the schoolteacher's father, and was also named William Giles. He was a West Country man who had started out as an apprentice cobbler but had a Damascene conversion when he saw John Wesley give a sermon. He became a

Methodist and sailed to Sierra Leone among a larger group to establish a mission to the Black Loyalists, the one-time slaves who had fought with the British in the American Revolutionary War. Drawn from veterans living in both Canada and in London, the Black Loyalists had gone to Africa and were in the process of establishing Freetown, alongside more distant settlements, in the hinterland. Giles joined a group intending to start a mission in an isolated settlement three hundred miles from the coast. The project was so badly run it quickly descended into farce. The other missionaries had brought their wives, but the women quickly realised how difficult the journey would be, and refused to go. Within two months, Giles had returned to Britain and abandoned the Methodists for the Baptist Church.

The Dickens family joined his congregation at the height of Giles's building programme in Chatham. While they waited for a new church to be built, the congregation were in temporary accommodation, a five-hundred-seater chapel belonging to the Primitive Baptists, which stood closer to the toxic Brook. The Dickens family were then so enmeshed with Giles and the local Baptists that they took a house next door to this temporary chapel. They were living beside the Giles family, and Charles and his sister Fanny were attending school with the younger Giles children, and taught by an older son, William Giles junior. Dickens drew his first circle of friends from the family and his nostalgia for his schooldays was expressed in memories of rambles across the countryside with the Giles boys, as well as his fondness for a part of the school uniform: a white beaver hat, presumably a kind of top hat, which is mentioned twice in Forster's 'autobiographical fragment'. When the family returned to London, Charles remained in Chatham, lodging with the Giles family for several months to see out the term. In adult life,

Dickens relished male company. This was the rambunctious, and I would say performative, side of his character: his need to embody the essential Dickensian quality of conviviality. He learned to enjoy male company from the Giles boys. His happiness in those days in Chatham contrasts strongly with the chaos he found when he eventually got to London to discover his family was in crisis.

How far did Baptist theology influence Dickens? Chatham was a Baptist town. There had been a chapel there since 1630. His father's decision to join the church might well have been an act of social assimilation, even social climbing. The Baptists were also Dissenters, and Charles would later tend towards supporting Radicals, as did his uncles in the Barrow family. The great attraction of being a Dissenter is telling the establishment where to get off. Instead of accepting the authority handed down to you, a Dissenters' congregation governs itself, like the self-governing rural commune that springs up at the end of *Oliver Twist*. However, the problem is that splitting can become a habit. Shortly after Dickens left Chatham, the local members of the Baptist congregation fell out with the Giles family, who were forced to surrender their church and school and leave town. The family regrouped in the north, where William senior, the schoolteacher William junior, and Dickens's one-time classmate, the even younger brother John Eustace Giles, became significant figures in the church in the northern cities, running Baptist churches in Leeds, Manchester and Liverpool.

Dickens may have been a radical, but it is difficult to see him truly embracing the Baptist Church. A Dissenter bids for power by claiming to have read the big magic book more carefully than anyone, parsed its language more rigorously, and reached conclusions that are more rational and challenging than anyone else. This does not sound much like Dickens, with his dislike of Gradgrindery and his affinity for big, loud, contradictory novels where everyone has a say, even if they damn themselves through their own mouths. He hated the idea of banning pleasures, or policing the sabbath, and similar acts of religious pettiness. But as with his politics, there is always a sense that he is oscillating between opposing positions – romantic and radical, establishment and dissenter. In his own life, he was strongly drawn to the Unitarians, a group which included his best friend, John Forster. He even attended the Unitarian Church, a church so thorough in their biblical readings that they entirely dispensed with the Trinity. When it comes to the Baptist faith, Dickens did absorb one of their conclusions: the rejection of Original Sin. The Baptists provided a justification for his own belief that children are innocent and good, the sentimental heart of so many of his novels. It's their innocence that allows corrupt adults to influence them, but also ensures they can be brought back to goodness if they are lucky enough to be offered that choice.

The home by the Brook, next door to the Primitive Baptist chapel, is gone, buried beneath the Pentagon Shopping Centre. The chapel and the school where William Giles junior mentored Dickens have also gone. The town is full of strange Nonconformist churches – the Nigerian Pentecostal Ona Iwa Mimo Cherubim and Seraphim Church, the Florida-based Jesus Revival Ministries International, or the spiritualist Sanctuary of Healing Church – but there is no straight-ahead Baptist church in the town any more. The Mitre Inn is also gone. This is the hotel that Nelson stayed in when he was down to inspect his ships, and where Dickens first learned the power of entertaining an audience. The site is now a Primark. A pub at the end of the High Street is doing brisk business, with the benches outside the door filled with silent drinkers. What Chatham has left is a tradition of lunchtime drinking. Two young women are sharing a bottle of rosé wine, while pushing a pram and arguing loudly with a group of drunken men.

I show my prejudices when I see a man approach three black children sitting on a bench. He is a hunchback, slow moving, and he has drool hanging from his lip in a twenty-centimetre-long drip. When he stops in front of the children, I fear the worst. He speaks with an impediment, and it takes a moment for the oldest child, a girl, to realise he is only asking if her brother is feeling okay. The youngest child is lying down, feigning sleep in order to annoy his brother and sister by spreading over them. The poor man had taken the child's play-acting seriously. A few minutes later, I run into the man again, shuffling with his head down and the drool still in place. We are both waiting to be seated at the Art Centre Café, where he is greeted like an old friend and shown to his usual table. The women who run the café are all Ukrainian. My waitress notices I am reading a biography of Dickens and asks me which is my favourite of his novels. I decide that it is *Oliver Twist*. And I ask, 'What's yours?'

'I don't know the name in English. In Ukrainian, it is the Pickwick Club. It's very funny.'

When Dickens achieved success with *The Pickwick Papers*, William Giles junior contacted him and sent a snuff box engraved with the words, 'The Inimitable Boz'. Giles was an enthusiastic snuff-taker who introduced the habit to Dickens. He may be responsible for Dickens's lifelong addiction to smoking, which contributed to some of his later illnesses. The real gift was the words, 'The Inimitable'. They fixed an image of Dickens as a one-off, a prodigy. Dickens seized upon the slogan, which swiftly became a part of his personal branding.

It was not simply that William Giles was Dickens's first schoolteacher, but that he recognised there was something special in Dickens and took pleasure in his ability. He was the first-born child in a family of older boys that helped Dickens to practise his father's great skill: 'male bonding'. Perhaps he needed the practice. Anyone reading a biography of Dickens will be struck that there is always something slightly odd about his male friendships. They are never quite equal, they are always slightly transactional, and the fun part of the friendship is excessively based around routines and games. There is always the paradox that a man who is far from lonely seems to feel very much alone, because he is looking to work the angle, find the dramatic pay-off, even sweat his friendships a little. There's always a hustle, at least the effort of always being 'The Inimitable'.

Dickens met James Lamert, his other great friend and role model, through his Aunt Fanny. The family relished the swirl of a military town and, as in Portsmouth, they found entertainment among the officers of Chatham. Fanny met an older widower named Matthew Lamert, a German-Jewish army surgeon whose battalion was stationed in Kent. As she was courted by the forty-two-year-old doctor, the two families blended and Charles grew close to his son, James. Matthew had married his first wife at the Great Synagogue in London, under his Jewish name, Moses, but he and Fanny married in St Mary's Chatham, whose graveyard stands on a promontory above the mud flats of the Medway. The graveyard conjures images of the encounter between Pip and Magwitch in *Great Expectations*, and though that meeting takes place upriver, if you peer between gravestones at the flat river sky, the churchyard has definite Magwitchy vibes.

James had two names, like his father (and, indeed, his new stepmother). He was officially George but always known as James, which might reflect the Hebrew name Haim. Both Matthew and James loved the theatre and included Charles on visits to the Theatre Royal Rochester, where shows were sponsored by the army, and where touring companies played when visiting the town. *The Pickwick Papers* has an episode that draws on the courtship of Aunt Fanny. An army surgeon with the name of Slammer is pursuing a widow at a dance when a travelling actor swoops in with wily charm and quick feet. The name Slammer could not be much closer to Lamert, and the doctor is depicted as a popular figure, lively, full of fun, rotund and bald, but also willing to fight when he feels slighted. Lamert was serving with the Royal Veteran battalions, support units that ran the infrastructure behind the front lines. He had worked in field and ship infirmaries for the Royal Marine battalions throughout the Napoleonic wars, seeing action in Egypt, Spain, Denmark and Holland. When the actor swoops in on the woman Slammer is courting, the doctor issues a challenge, which the actor brushes off as he returns to his lodgings. The next morning, Slammer's second knocks at the lodging-house door and contracts a duel with the wrong man. The mistake and the duel eventually get sorted out with good humour, in part because the actor has been hired to play at the Rochester Theatre in a show put on by another army battalion and no one wants to spoil the entertainment.

James Lamert was a child himself when he met the Dickens family. He was nine years older than Dickens; the pair grew close and remained so for years. James not only loved the theatre, he was an enthusiastic amateur producer-director. Alongside his father, he helped stage full-scale plays in the Ordnance Hospital, which was established in the otherwise redundant Fort Pitt, built for the war against the French but not completed until hostilities were over.

James also enjoyed building toy theatres and staging miniature performances and skits. Dickens joined in, producing his first original work as an eight-year-old – an Arabian Nights-influenced fantasy named *Mishnar*. Dickens's lifelong passion for the theatre can be traced to his childhood in Chatham and his relationship with James, who taught him the breadth of roles that the theatre offers: from writer, to stage manager, producer, director and, of course, actor. During his years with the Ternans, Dickens devoted more time to staging dramas and readings than he did to his novels and magazines, and he always worked across all aspects of the show. He owed this attention to detail to James and spoke about his influence often enough for Forster to know his importance. One might think Dickens's feelings for James would have soured over the years. His aunt died in childbirth shortly after her marriage to Matthew Lamert, and James was responsible for Dickens getting a job in the blacking factory. Yet Dickens always seemed well disposed to both Matthew and James. The depiction of Dr Slammer in *The Pickwick Papers* reads like *bants*; there's an edge to the comedy but nothing is vicious. I hear a Germanic slant to Dr Slammer's lines: his catchphrase, 'Dr Slammer, Dr Slammer of the 97th'. I imagine a Teutonic bark to the qualifications and the battalion. The English were well disposed towards German-speakers, who had arrived in numbers with the run of Hanoverian Georges. The immigrants found success as they brought engineering and manufacturing expertise. This was especially true in the business of pianos and harpsichords. Thomas Culliford employed several Germans: the names Spielspegger and Kaisor have been found inscribed in his pianos. His brother-in-law John Goldsworth formed a short-lived partnership with John Geib, who went on to create the American piano industry. In the early nineteenth century,

English nationalism was not yet tied to the English language. There was no global anglosphere. Australia was only a penal colony, with convicts filling the prison hulks in the Medway as they awaited transportation. South Africa was largely Dutch. English-speaking America was enemy territory, a land of revolution and treason, and Canada was the bit left over. In contrast, the German states had been allies in the war against France. There would be no pushback against the marriage of a German soldier and an English widow.

What about a marriage between a Christian and a Jew? In his life, Dickens journeyed away from the antisemitism of his twenties to something more conciliatory, if patronising, in middle age. This change is often credited to the letter from Eliza Davis, the woman whose purchase of his London home allowed him to buy his country mansion and return to the Medway. Yet the softening of his racism also reflects a more universal story: a changing attitude towards Jews across Britain in these years. Jewish self-assertiveness, seen in the pages of the *Jewish Chronicle*, as well in women like Eliza Davis, and the high profile of Jewish figures like Moses Montefiore, had led to a greater awareness of anti-Jewish racism. Dickens's views changed because everyone's views were changing.

Yet even in his youth in the 1820s and 30s, Dickens's antisemitism was somewhat flexible. He knew the Lamerts were Jewish, and seems not to have cared. Perhaps the transition from one religion to another was more natural or inconsequential then, as the Lamerts moved from Judaism to the Church of England, while the Dickens family switched the C of E for the Baptists. Significantly, Dickens created Fagin just one year after he had caricatured Lamert as Dr Slammer. We can be sure that he would have played up the stereotypes without a second thought, if he had wanted to. There are, again, the weird gradations of Jewishness he chose to explain to Eliza Davis: the Lamerts were too close to being white Europeans to be targeted by racist abuse. But perhaps his complex and variable reactions also reflected his awareness of his own Jewish heritage.

The idea that a reader could see through his words to his secrets would have terrified Dickens. At the same time, he knew people would want to try. In his account of the Copperfield library, he tells us that he read *Tom Jones* as a child and managed to miss all the salacious stuff, but this works both ways: if it is possible for a child to create a 'clean' reading of a book, then someone else can come along and see every spot and blemish. How could he guard against these readers? Dickens burned his private letters in his fifties, which is one way of ensuring your secrets are safe. But what do you do about your books? How do you hide your secrets while pumping out hundreds of thousands of words to a global readership?

The best way for a writer to guard against interpretation is through irony, ensuring that a reader is never sure what should be taken seriously. This is the route taken by Laurence Sterne, whose *Sentimental Journey* is also referenced in the library, and whose influence can be felt in the first chapter of *David Copperfield* headed 'I am Born', which points back to *Tristram Shandy*. Dickens's style develops out of the work of these earlier comic novelists, which he combines with the rhetorical irony of the stage monologuist. In his first novels, you can already hear the voice of the patter merchants who would dominate the emerging music halls and, today, the comedy clubs. If a writer wants to hide behind irony, they have to distribute the 'truth function' across the text in such a way that there is no real code to break: we never know for sure if 'x' is true and 'y' is false, or vice versa. A stand-up like Frank Skinner relies on this, allowing him to be both filthy and respectable at the same time, and so does Dickens. He's cracking wise, cracking jokes, full of fun but always solemn, down with the street, but never risking his place in the parlour. Actor and critic in one.

Once a writer starts playing fast and loose with where they place 'truth', it becomes impossible to go beyond the surface of their work and dig out its 'real' meaning. A text is just the words on a page, not a map of a soul. If this is true of some texts, it raises the possibility that it is true of all texts, including legal documents and the Bible. Indeed, for Dickens only shysters claim to know the literal truth of either a legal judgment or scripture. However, if we can never know what a text is 'really' saying, then this holds true even for the writer themselves. At once, Dickens is back where he started. If he doesn't control his own texts, he cannot prevent people coming to unsettling interpretations. Dickens is his own worst enemy: always anxious, and always feeding his anxiety.

Me too. I have no idea if anyone could look at my books and work out my lifelong obsessions. I wish I knew. I'd like to have some idea where my work has been heading, or what I hoped to achieve, but I have no idea. I can't even read these lines and tell that I've been in constant pain for a month or discern a difference in the pages I typed with my left hand, while high on 30mg codeine tablets. If I cannot read me, how am I supposed to get at the 'real' Dickens? It's one thing to point out the holes in Forster's big story of childhood abandonment, or to tug away at the loose threads left by other biographers. But where I am going with my own notion that his now forgotten friends like Giles and Lamert offer a route into the hidden Dickens?

Janet comes in with some sound advice. She suggests I stick

with the basics. The '5 Ws': Who, What, Where, When and Why. The influence of the schoolmaster William Giles junior helps answer the question, who is Dickens? His family were Baptists, even if only during their stay in Chatham, which means they did not see themselves as privileged, or well-connected, or even interested in looking to the establishment. They were never the 'occluded aristocrats' of Tomalin's reading, but were part of a new political grouping with its power bases in the Nonconformist churches and also in the northern cities. His sister Fanny exemplifies this trend: in the 1830s, she married a Nonconformist and moved to Manchester, the double whammy for English Dissenters. Dickens was a member of an emerging class who preferred to forge their own paths rather than follow their superiors. This also fits with the title that Giles bestowed on him: 'The Inimitable'. If you ask, 'Who is Dickens?' here's the answer: he is the one and only, the incomparable author of his age. Like Forster's story of the blacking factory, it becomes part of the Dickens legend of the lone genius, shaken by the discovery he has no one to rely on but himself.

Focusing on James Lamert's influence offers even more big Ws. He stands at the convergence of three vectors that run through Dickens's life in intriguing and non-obvious ways: Jewishness, the theatre, and the Medway. Lamert appears to be the fulcrum, but also a link in a chain of secret associations. He first took Dickens to the Theatre Royal in Rochester, and the Ternans played this same theatre regularly between 1850 and 1854. Dickens is thought to have met the Ternans through his road manager Alfred Wigan in 1857. In fact, the mother, Frances Ternan, was a close associate of all of Dickens's theatre friends, and we can be sure he had known her since his emergence as a young writer in the 1830s. In the early 1850s, the Ternan girls lived on the High Street with their uncle and his wife (who was also of Jewish heritage). In these years, Dickens was a frequent, even obsessive visitor to Rochester. He went hiking along the Medway, and passed their home often on horse-drawn journeys back and forth to the Kent coast. He would also pass the theatre, festooned with playbills for the Ternans' appearances. He must have noted the girls' performance as the tragic princes in Shakespeare's *Richard III*, a play Dickens had seen in the same theatre with James Lamert. One answer to the questions, 'What was Dickens writing, and what was he writing about?' is that he always cared as much for the theatre as novels, and that he focused on the Medway as much as anything. In important ways, his heart lay there, but it was a heart that was closed off and filled with secrets. Which leads to the other Ws: Where and When. He spent his earliest childhood in Kent, and in later life bought Gad's Hill. Because the purchase of Gad's Hill coincides with his reacquaintance with the Ternans, his late-life return to both the Medway and to the theatre begins to look more complex, more dramatic – and more shameful. His connection to the Ternans not only risked his reputation but, unfortunately for a secretive man, demanded that more and more people were engaged in his conspiracies, which only amplified the risks and anxieties. How could he not think of his grandfather Charles Barrow, the man whose secrets and shame cast such a long shadow over his family? Perhaps Jewishness does not mean Jewishness for Dickens, after all, but instead means what it always means to someone beset by antisemitic prejudices: that is, secrecy, control and outsiderness?

The big question is the 'Why'. Why write? Forster has his answer, but if we don't buy the myth that Dickens is an orphan child, alone and abandoned to a heartless factory system, what could motivate him? Though his childhood was different from the one portrayed by Forster, nevertheless the fate of children was important to him. He populated his novels with vulnerable lonely children. Thinking of children in terms of risks, predators and abuse articulated something for him – and the answer, 'Why?', lies with the final friend he made in Chatham: the family's maid. She was an orphan, taken from the Chatham workhouse in the year before the family moved back to London.

Matthew Lamert was called to Ireland, and Aunt Fanny left with him. The endings to long wars are always periods of political instability as fighting men return home to feelings of disappointment and betrayal. The French wars were no exception. A series of protests in Manchester in 1819 led to the Peterloo Massacre. The rebellious mood in Ireland was stoked by Britain's refusal to lift anti-Catholic laws on an island with a Catholic majority. Lamert's battalion had been disbanded but was revived and sent to Ireland to counter insurrection. When Fanny followed him, she took one of the Chatham servants with her.

With Fanny's marriage, Elizabeth Dickens lost both a sister and the benefits of her widow's pension. The remaining maid – the lover of ghost stories – also left, as she got married. At once, Elizabeth was without any help for her seven children. The finances must have been precarious because the replacement was a parish apprentice, the most low-cost solution to the problem.

Chatham High Street follows the Medway all the way to Rochester. The orphan came from a workhouse located towards the mid-point, built in 1725 opposite an almshouse for old sailors known as the Hawkins Hospital. A directory of English workhouses published by the Society for Promoting Christian Knowledge, 1732 edition, states that the main business of the workhouse was to provide oakum as caulking for the local shipyards. In *David Copperfield* the girl appears under two names, as

Clickett and the Orfling. The first name suggests she is a confident chatterer (Dickens gives us the definition of 'clicketten' as chattering in the novel), while the Orfling suggests an orphan foundling, a girl whose loneliness demands our sympathy. The girl is both, possessing a heart-tugging double-charm, warm yet pathetic. When she reappears as the Marchioness in *The Old Curiosity Shop*, she beguiles Dick Swiveller, the Dickens stand-in, much to his own astonishment. Mrs Micawber, who is based on Elizabeth Dickens, is wise to the girl's sexual allure and is on guard against it. In *David Copperfield*, she castigates her 'vulgar mind'. But in 1821 in Chatham, Elizabeth's fears of the pauper girl's charms are still some years in the future. She or John sign the papers promising to train her up as a maid of all work and in return receive £5. It is an empty contract. By definition, the girl will have no specific skills.

The workhouse system in Chatham expanded hugely after the Poor Law Act of 1834 The string of towns along the river, Rochester, Chatham, Gillingham and Brompton, were bound into a single Medway Poor Law Union, the beginning of a unitary council for the Medway district. In the 1850s, the Union built a new Medway workhouse on Magpie Hall Lane. Neither this workhouse nor the original exists today. I know because I've tramped all over Chatham with a broken arm, a heavy bag and a recalcitrant dog. In the twentieth century, the second workhouse became a hospital. The only survival today is a children's nursery, a low-level redbrick building with a massive municipal crest above the door. The original workhouse is also gone but the almshouses survive. They must be the last eighteenth-century buildings left in Chatham.

I think of John and Elizabeth returning from the workhouse with the Orfling and see the scene from *Oliver!* when the beadle tries to auction off Oliver in the snow. Did the couple march the girl between them? Did she walk a few paces behind? Dickens's feelings for the workhouse orphan girl were warm, sentimental, with the sexualised glimmer of first love. The girl was taken to London, a town where neither she nor Dickens knew anyone, and as they were thrown together, they grew close. Then one day, around the time Dickens and the girl hit puberty, Elizabeth threw her out. How would that affect him? There is a push-and-pull aspect to her expulsion, because if Dickens hadn't somehow alerted his mother to his desires, then she would never have thrown the girl onto the streets. The orphan girl was a charming, chattering, beguiling companion. Janet tells me she had to learn to be charming; if you feel vulnerable then you learn to be a people-pleaser. If Dickens found her sexually alluring, what would he assume other men would want from her?

Almost half a century later, older and feeling both jaded and corrupt, hiding a mistress who was in her teens when they met, Dickens embarks on a mammoth reading tour. He commits to one hundred dates, each performance two hours long, crowned by what would become his most famous performance, the murder of Nancy, a girl betrayed by everyone.

It kills him.

7

RAG TRADE: MANCHESTER, 1819-22

The year that Charles Dickens's Aunt Fanny met her future husband, Robert Blincoe married the love of his life. Martha Simpson was a Yorkshirewoman, born in 1783, which made her eight or nine years older than Robert. She was a spinster, closer to forty than thirty, while he was a small man with bent legs and a head full of scars. On the face of it, this might be the story of two people who clung together because no one else would have them. Photographs of Robert and Martha, taken in the 1850s, do nothing to debunk that idea. Robert is captured in his late fifties, sitting in a tall-backed chair which only emphasises how small he is. He is bald on top but wears his hair long at the sides to hide his battered and deformed ears. His left elbow rests on something out of the frame, to allow his hand to support his face – his head must have been bobbing about too much for the primitive camera. Martha is well into her sixties in her portrait, though her hair is still dark. She is wearing a linen mob cap that frames a plain but strong face. She has a strong jaw, and her expression is set in a slight scowl. Her hands emerge from a thick woollen shawl, and she holds them clasped on her knee. You can tell that neither Robert nor Martha was ever much of a looker. The story of their romance in the *Memoir* can be read in two ways; I find it moving, but from a contemporary perspective it could easily be read as the story of two desperate souls who only come together out of social pressure and loneliness.

Robert and Martha may have known each other already, as they were neighbours in Bank Top, an area now buried beneath Manchester's Piccadilly station. But their romance began on Sunday, 27 June 1819, as they celebrated the christening of a friend's child after a short ceremony in the Old Church, Manchester's parish church. The church is now Manchester Cathedral. It lies on the opposite side of the city, but the christening took place there because there were so few churches in Manchester, and the parish church had what amounted to a monopoly on weddings and christenings. If you went elsewhere, you would still need to buy a licence from the old church, which would mean paying twice for the ceremony. The population of Manchester had risen from 17,000 to over 180,000 in just thirty years, making it the country's second largest urban centre. Like any boom town, it was short of amenities. The oldest part of town was the medieval district between the Old Church and the market square, known as Shambles after an old English term for a display of butchered meat. The square was overlooked by tall half-timbered merchant houses and inns, and it was here Robert's friends continued their celebrations, most likely in the King's Head tavern. The pub still exists under the name it acquired in the mid-nineteenth century, Sinclair's Oyster Bar. Robert was not a drinking man. Shortly after arriving in Manchester, he had been pressured into an expensive round of drinks with his new workmates and the experience had left him hungover and broke. He never drank again, but he was always sociable so when one of the other guests taunted him for being a single man, he took it in good part. The guest was 'a jolly butcher', in Robert's telling, maybe a stallholder in the meat market. After teasing Robert, the guests turned on Martha, the other unmarried guest. It wasn't long before someone had the idea of a wedding between Robert and Martha, so they could pick up the festivities the next day.

In John Brown's account, written three years after the events, Robert says he cocked Martha a sideways look, and replied that if she would take him, he would marry her tomorrow. He wasn't expecting her to say, 'I will.'

Not for the last time in his story, Robert found himself overcome by nerves. But he told her, 'If you'll stick to your word, then I will.'

She said, 'I'll not run from mine, if you don't.'

The story already has the flavour of an anecdote by the time John Brown writes it down. Once Martha and Robert have both given their word, the butcher jumps in with the offer of a leg of mutton if they will get married the next day. Robert vows he will. He picks two companions to accompany him across the square to get a licence from the chaplain of the Old Church, Joshua Brookes. However, once outside the pub, his nerves get the better of him and he returns to Martha with a story that the Reverend Brookes needs Martha there in person. Even when Martha agrees to come too, Robert remains anxious. He asks her for the three shillings and sixpence the licence costs.

She produces the money.

Even after they got their licence, Robert was too nervous to kiss her, or even take her hand. However, he stepped up the next day by hiring a coach to transport Martha, himself and their witnesses to the church. They rattled down the High Street to the Old Church grounds and joined the others who were marrying that day. The Reverend Joshua Brookes had presided over the Old Church since 1790, and had made his name there by conducting mass weddings run with the ruthlessness of a production line. The bride's party would stand in the queue while the groom and his party waited in the pub – and if the groom turned up late, Brookes was prepared to marry a proxy in his place. He was a notable scholar, but an unsophisticated man, short-tempered, acerbic and eccentric. He died shortly afterwards, in 1821, but remained so famous that fifty years later he appeared as a key character in Isabella Banks's novel, *The Manchester Man* (1876). The journalist John Brown had heard of him, of course. He cannot help but interject the words 'the not very reverend' into his description of the recently deceased priest. Despite Brown's authorial asides, there is no doubt that this is an account shaped by Robert's storytelling skills. There is a precision to the details, the flourishes that decorate a well-told tale. The dates are precise: Brown would not have checked that Sunday really did fall on the 27th, nor researched the cathedral records to see if Robert and Martha were married on the 28th. But it did, and they were. These details add veracity, but it is the drama of Robert's nerves that set the tone. He asks Martha twice if she will have him. Even when she confirms, 'I will not run,' his anxiety does not abate, so he twice interrupts the visit to Joshua Brookes with ruses she must surely see through. First he collects Martha, and then he borrows money. Each time he creates a hurdle, Martha shows courage. He keeps faltering, until he doesn't, and finally they are riding from his lodging house in a coach. A man who has every reason to feel insecure has found a wife who is solid and tenacious.

What kind of love story is this? It's not exactly the stuff of rom-coms, which even at their best owe something to fairy stories, with their tales of princesses and valour. The lovers must be special: they have something inside them that makes them noble, perhaps magical, even if that is simply possessing the looks of Hugh Grant. Once they have located this inner spark, it propels them into a hopeless leap of faith. The lover refuses to take 'no' for an answer, culminating in a public declaration or proposal that in real life would probably lead to a restraining order. To win at love is first of all to validate oneself, and only afterwards to think about satisfying a lover.

Martha and Robert's story falls short of the rom-com ideal chiefly because they are not special, except perhaps in the sense that they are even less than ordinary. Even though the story is told by Robert, it manages to suggest two pitiful figures stuck in the last-chance saloon. Not only are they not special, they are not even the agents of their own romance – they are pushed into it by their friends. It could be read as an account of peer-group pressure that sails dangerously close to bullying. The focus on Martha is all about her age. Romantic tales validate the individual, possessed of that inner force, the drive to love and be loved. Robert's story is all about external forces: the unmarried people that must be joined, the group that must be satisfied. It is true that Martha shows some boldness, but it is quiet resilience, always reacting and never proactive. Yet in Robert's eyes, their story is so positive, he wants the world to know it. Rather than seeing an example of undue social pressure, perhaps we should read it as a public event, geared to find the best results for everyone.

In a sense, all of Robert's life was a public event. The flow of apprentices to the north, and the movement of itinerant spinners like Robert across the industrial cities, resulted in social networks bound together by stories, experiences and memories. Robert spent an extra year at Litton Mill as a master spinner, and we know he was respected for his kindness because twenty-five years later a fellow apprentice, John Joseph Betts, could vouch for him. When Robert left Litton Mill, he walked the six miles to New Mills, Derbyshire, and in the first factory he approached, he met parish officials from St Pancras who were bringing a fresh batch of child apprentices from their workhouse. This seems an extraordinary coincidence, but the account has been verified: Robert did arrive at the same moment as a group of nineteen apprentices. When he moved on to Stalybridge, he got a job with one of his old overlookers from Litton named William Gamble. He knew Gamble as a brutal man who dragged children around by their hair, and the job offer was not a favour. Gamble insisted that Robert lodge with him so he could take a cut of his pay packet. Again, Robert did not stay long, but the fact that he knew where to find a man who would give him both a job and a bed shows how thoroughly news circulated.

In fact, Robert did not stay long anywhere. Nobody ever wrote him a reference, so Robert never had proof he was a master spinner. He was dependent on fellow workers vouching for him, and if he was ever given a job, the bosses could set the wages without reference to his skill. He was regarded as a cripple, which made him a charity case and kept him on low wages – something which angered him. He was often employed as a carder, responsible for the process of combing raw cotton to disentangle the threads and clean away impurities. This was an unskilled and poorly paid job, working in a cloud of cotton dust that invariably caused lung disease. In his mid-twenties, after several jobs in mills where the practice was to lock the workers on the shop floor throughout their shifts, Robert began working as a stoker, feeding coal into the steam engines in the mills. This was dirty, back-breaking work – not the kind of work you would expect a man with physical issues to do. But it paid better than other work Robert was being offered, and he was at least able to sleep in the warmth of the engine rooms. Working long hours and saving money on lodgings, he built a little capital. His long-term plan was to start up as a waste cotton dealer. When Robert met Martha, he had completed his second year in this business. He had lost money the first year, but was now doing better. He was now more of a pedlar than a millworker, which had not lifted him far in the social hierarchy.

Robert clearly had enough faith in himself to make long-term plans about his welfare and work, but when it came to the most important decision of his life, he presents his love story as a tale of a weak man who was fearful of rejection, pushed by friends, and only making it to the altar because he had found a woman who was quietly willing to swallow a series of indignities. He wants to tell their story because he sees an exemplary romance. Others might see a catalogue of humiliations. He keeps making dick moves; she has to keep stepping up. Yet there is a real romance there: it clearly means the world to him that Mary stuck with him. He has turned their story into a tale that he keeps telling, because they won through: they ended up happy and married.

You could argue that all romances depend upon a loss of dignity. But in a conventional romantic story, it is only a moment of imbalance, and pride will be restored: Sally's rejection by Harry after they have sex, in *When Harry Met Sally*; Peter Warne seeing Ellie simply as a news story and a meal ticket in *It Happened One Night*. A typical Dickens novel is about individuation and self-actualisation, as a young man proves himself in the world. These novels are not first-and-foremost romances, but

Dickens employs a love story to underscore the hero's journey. In *Great Expectations*, Pip suffers because of Estella's cruelty. (The eighteen-year-old Dickens fell in love with an older girl, Maria Beadnell, who wasn't interested in him.) By emphasising the loss of dignity, he creates a hero who must win back his self-respect. As in modern rom-coms, the value of love is that it proves that you are worthy and good. His two great first-person coming-of-age novels, *David Copperfield* and *Great Expectations*, tell how a hero becomes himself, with the dignity and strength to be loved. They win love almost at the point that they are so secure that they no longer need that validation. David Copperfield gamely copes with having married the wrong woman, who selflessly dies and releases him for another woman. *Great Expectations* was never meant to end with the consummation of the love of Pip and Estella. Dickens changed the ending at the urging of his friend Edward Bulwer-Lytton, and a secure Pip stoops to take the hand of Estella, who has been humbled by sorrow and beaten by experience.

Robert's story is almost the opposite. He is insecure and lonely at the beginning, and he doesn't change: he just meets a woman who will have him anyway. He wants love even though he believes he is not worth it. He is in his late twenties, and Martha in her thirties; neither saw their marriage as a youthful romance. He fears he is the butt of a joke, yet he keeps abandoning a little more of his dignity, until finally he and Martha have none, and they are happy. On the surface, it sounds less romantic than other stories. But the ending is all about love, and nothing else. It's not about proving his intrinsic worth, but only about finding a soul mate. Despite everything, I'd argue that makes Robert's story more romantic than more typical romances.

I first read the *Memoir* when I was around ten years of age.

Each time I return to it, my focus seems to change. Today, the romance seems to be at its centre. Perhaps that's because I am older, and I found Janet in middle age. My first marriage was hobbled by my efforts to make my way in the big city, and prove to myself who I was and what I could achieve. Like a Dickensian hero, I desperately hoped I had an inner story and I kept flailing around as I tried to drag it into the light. Now I'm getting on, I can't say my ambition is extinguished, but at least it's no longer quite such a churning mess. Janet and I met because a mutual friend had talked us up to each other. We arranged to walk our dogs in Hyde Park. Janet's pug, Ken, was a feisty nine-year-old. Fredo was just one. We knew a few people in common, and I was rude about one of them, who turned out to be her closest friend. This was during Covid, which lent a sense of privacy. We felt we were outside normal life, in a span of time suspended from reality. Our marriages had ended long ago, and though we'd both had affairs since then, we had kept them on the downlow. We had learned to be alone, and we didn't want to lose the sense of calm that privacy brings, by becoming the object of scrutiny or gossip. We kept walking around and around the park. Eventually, I asked where she was from.

She said, 'Chadderton.'

Chadderton is a collection of abandoned cotton mills strung along a dual carriageway at the point where Manchester, Oldham and Rochdale meet. It's so small, grim and inconsequential that if I wasn't from Rochdale, I would never have heard of it. She had to be lying. But why choose Chadderton? There are better known dumps.

I gave her a sideways look of such suspicion, she started laughing. She was telling the truth: she really is from Chadderton. We had grown up four miles apart without knowing each other.

Our lives turned out to be far more intertwined than we could have imagined. This made it easier to come out as a couple. The social scaffolding helped. I don't believe the strongest relationships depend on shared references, a common language, mutual friends, or a cultural network. I can see that finding a lover outside the group or tribe can be liberating. No one ever needs the blessing of their family or friends when they choose love. But Janet and I found a romance in emphasising the things we shared. As we got to know each other, it turned out that we shared a lot.

Growing up in small towns on the edge of Manchester we had both looked towards the big city. All the locations in Robert's story are familiar to us, if only as the sites of the nightclubs and bars we went to as kids. We don't remember when the mills produced cotton. The Manchester of our childhood and teenage years was already in long-term decline. That didn't change until the end of the twentieth century with its unlikely revival through popular culture: music, nightclubs and football. Robert's home in Bank Top was close to the Rochdale Canal now home to the gay bars along Canal Street. It's also close to Aytoun Street, once home to the wild Poly Disco, a weekly club night for a young, punkish, queer crowd. We used to frequent a club called Pips based in the maze of cellars beneath the Corn Exchange, accessed through a small door behind Manchester Cathedral. There were five dance floors, including a Bowie Room and a Roxy Room. Janet and I went, but never met.

One of my earliest memories of Manchester is watching the redevelopment of Shambles Square. Sinclair's Oyster Bar and its neighbour, the Old Wellington Inn, were jacked up on stilts so that the square could be rebuilt around them. Twenty-five years later, when the Arndale shopping centre was bombed by the IRA, these two buildings were moved again, painstakingly dismantled and reassembled at the north of the square. The mill where Robert was working when he got drunk and swore off alcohol for the rest of his life was on Water Street, by the River Irwell. This is now the site of a new concert hall, Factory International, whose name references the long-gone heritage of Factory Records. Last year, Janet and I saw Johnny Marr play there, and seven thousand people sang Smiths songs as though they were pouring out their hearts. 'There Is a Light that Never Goes Out' is the great, ambivalent anthem to the possibilities of Manchester's nightlife, the risks and the glorious potential. There's nothing lovelier than singing it beside a Smiths-besotted Manchester girl. The city's nightlife and the fashions and the music that fuelled it were our ticket out of our hometowns. At sixteen, Janet worked in a clothes boutique and modelled for the Vidal Sassoon on King Street, and that opened the way to London. She got a job as a receptionist at the Bond Street salon, took a degree and eventually won a place on the graduate scheme at the BBC. I started art college at sixteen and went clubbing with my new friends. I was even briefly signed to Factory Records. It was a heady, self-conscious world of dreamers and dissidents, filled with pretensions and big concepts, and it became my route out. We aimed to be the heroes of our own stories, just like David Copperfield. A big part of Dickens is the idea that the young have a unique energy that is theirs to exploit. There were other first-person coming-of-age stories before *David Copperfield* and *Great Expectations* (*Jane Eyre* came out a year and a half before *David Copperfield*) but Dickens created a new template. The first novels that Janet and I took to our hearts were everyone's big existential favourites, but aren't Meursault, Holden Caulfield and Stephen Dedalus just versions of David Copperfield with added angst? Dickens created a template for self-conscious young people. I suspect I was a little too self-conscious: like Morrissey, it was all about wanting *my* time to come at last. Janet may have been the bigger Smiths fan, but she knew her trajectory was part of a bigger story, and she shared her enthusiasm with her friends, listening to their suggestions and sparking connections as she seized her chances. Maybe that's our class difference: my individualism, versus her collectivism.

After the concert, we walked back to our hotel with the chants of 'Johnny, Johnny, Johnny Fucking Marr' ringing in our ears. The route took us up Lower Mosley Street to St Peter's Square. Robert and Martha got married just before the Peterloo Massacre. It was intended as a rally in support of parliamentary reform. The crowd was the largest ever seen for a political event in Britain. Estimates vary by wide margins, but in a city of 180,000 and with protesters arriving from across the north, it's likely the crowd was well in excess of 100,000. The urban area that included Salford, Bolton, Blackburn, Rochdale, Oldham, Ashton-under-Lyne and Stockport had a combined population approaching a million. Parliamentary reform seemed urgent when Manchester had no MP, and the whole of Lancashire only had two rural county seats (all the above towns are in Lancashire, with the exception of Stockport, which is in Cheshire). Even before anyone spoke, a wealthy landowner named William Hulton ordered a cavalry charge. Hulton was the sheriff of Lancashire and constable of Lancaster Castle, but in the weeks leading up to Peterloo he had been placed in charge of a new body, the Cheshire and Lancashire Magistrates, with a remit to clamp down on agitators and protesters. On his command, the crowd was charged by the Manchester and Salford Yeomanry, a paramilitary force raised two years earlier specifically to put down popular support for reform. A force made up of shopkeepers, farmers and landowners charged down the huge crowd with drawn sabres, hacking and trampling unarmed civilians.

The main speaker on the day was Henry 'Orator' Hunt who embraced a theory of 'mass pressure'. He expressly believed in bringing out huge crowds with the idea their numbers would force political reform. Hunt was attempting to harness the power of the population boom, just as statisticians like Malthus were warning that the boom would end in chaos and destruction. As the industrialised cities embraced Hunt and his idea that they represented a new political force, a new term emerged to describe their voice. 'Popular'. The popular voice and popular movements were those that existed outside the establishment, understood broadly as the crown and aristocracy; the wealthy merchants and the guilds; and the established church. The rally in St Peter's Field had been organised by a radical newspaper named the *Manchester Observer*, which later coined the description of the events as 'the Peterloo Massacre'. One of the key figures in Robert's story, the Manchester publisher John Doherty, would certainly have been at Peterloo if William Hulton had not already imprisoned him in Lancaster. However, the first publisher of Robert's *Memoir*, the London-based Richard Carlile, was there. He had travelled to Manchester at Hunt's invitation to speak. In the event, he brought the first eyewitness account of the massacre to London, publishing it in his own radical newspaper, *Sherwin's Political Register*. The *Manchester Observer* was a Nonconformist paper, Doherty was a Catholic and Carlile a committed atheist. Clearly, the popular voice was not a single voice. If it was initially recognised in opposition to the establishment, as the voice of protest, that was changing. Popular culture would soon be associated as much with leisure as with protest, and would often be defined by new technology, and by its means of dissemination, rather than any political agenda.

The evolution of the popular space over the next two centuries saw the creation of new spectator sports, mass entertainment, and new stars and celebrities. Beginning with the gaslit stages of Vauxhall Pleasure Gardens, through the steam-driven printing presses that would change the face of newspapers and then novels, and on to photography, recorded music, film, radio and television, to today's socials, pop culture keeps on expanding. Robert Blincoe's *Memoir* is an early attempt to capture a popular voice in print. I don't know if he was at Peterloo, but St Peter's Field is minutes from his home, and everything suggests he was a politically minded man. His story had already become widespread through word of mouth, so well known that a journalist from Bolton would be drawn to his door, with the aim of bringing it to a wider audience.

Our hotel room overlooks St Peter's Square. We have been given the disabled access room and we love the wheelchair-friendly bathroom; not that we have a wheelchair, but we appreciate the sense of space. We are two souls in synch, loving old songs and an outsized bathroom.

We grew up four miles apart, and spent our teenage years nightclubbing in Manchester. We went to two English colleges at the centre of the new wave of critical theory, Janet at Middlesex Polytechnic and me at Warwick University. It was a heady time, and we both relished it; there were big guest lecturers from America and France, and we read lecture notes hot off the fax machines from Parisian universities. One of the big ideas we were introduced to was that nothing is real until it has been transmitted in some form. This idea of the French post-structuralists, articulated by Jacques Derrida (for me), Jean Baudrillard (for her) and others, implies that the repetition of an event, in film or writing or on TV, is needed before it becomes a fact. This is true of the Peterloo Massacre. The events of 16 August 1819 were shaped by their reporting, both by the *Manchester Observer* under the title 'The Peterloo Massacre', and by Richard Carlile's account of 18 August under the headline, 'Horrible Massacre in Manchester'. From our hotel, we can see the latest monument to the dead and injured, designed by the artist Jeremy Deller as a series of steps leading to a speaking platform. The monument has been criticised because unlike our bathroom it is not accessible by wheelchair. It seems designed to mark a particular spot, but I don't know if that's the spot where Orator Hunt stood. Looking out over the square, there's no guide to how the field looked in 1819, where the charge happened or where the injured lay. I could probably find out, but that's almost not important. What is important is that it exists: it was St Peter's Field, but it's now the site of the Peterloo Massacre. That's why it's still a public square, hemmed in by hotels and grand municipal architecture.

In 1822, John Brown travelled to Manchester from his home in Bolton and cold-called Robert at home in Bank Top. He had learned of Robert's story by hearsay, and thought it illuminated a bigger story of the factory system. Inevitably, the dominant voice is Brown's – always editorialising and explaining. But it's Robert's voice that gives the memoir its shape because these are stories he has told before, honing them by repeating them, and keeping them fresh despite the repetition. His experiences have already become known facts, circulated among his friends, and beyond. The *Memoir* is filled with vivid descriptions of horrific scenes. Being forced to stand on a tin as the arm of the machine comes around and knocks him down. Stealing food from the pigs. Or the worst, the account of a girl being caught in a machine and twirled like a mop. But as the end draws near, there's the surprise of a love story. Robert finds Martha.

A wedding may sweeten the end of a tough read, like a Hollywood happy ending before Hollywood existed. It is a relief to learn that Robert has found love. There is something in the way that Robert tells the story of his wedding. You really can tell when someone is telling and retelling their own love story. I know how often I have told the story of my first date with Janet, and the way my voice rose as I gave her the side-eye: 'Chadderton?' Our story is good, but Robert's is at another level. You can hear the way he shaped it, and through that, begin to see an audience emerging as a self-conscious group: the first stirring of the industrial working class.

8

DICKENS ALONE: 1824

The radical Henry 'Orator' Hunt was sentenced to two years' imprisonment following the Peterloo Massacre. He came from a wealthy West Country farming family but after prison he had to rebuild his finances, which he did by inventing the breakfast cereal, roasting and grinding wheat into a powder that was eaten mixed with milk. His bravura concoction was warmly received by his fellow radical Richard Carlile, who recommended it in the pages of his newspaper, renamed *The Republican* after the forced closure of *Sherwin's Political Register* for its reports on Peterloo. In tandem with his fledgling cereal business, Hunt also began to sell blacking, which he packaged in pots with the words 'Equal Laws, Equal Rights, Annual Parliaments, Universal Suffrage, and the Ballot' printed on the label. His delivery trucks doubled as speaking platforms when he appeared at rallies.

Blacking would become a big part of the Dickens legend. After finishing school in Chatham in the summer of 1823, he joined the family in their new home on Bayham Street, Camden Town, and started work at Warren's factory soon after, some six months earlier than Forster believed. In Forster's account, Dickens talks of being forgotten: his sister is about to start at a prestigious music college, while he is reduced to running errands and polishing boots. We see the poor Dickens with his shine-box, hands stained by boot blacking even before he reaches the vile factory. On this account, Dickens continues in this desolate half-state, month after month, mooching and lonely, while the family situation grows worse. Forster's narrative suggests he began work around his twelfth birthday in February 1824, because of his father's money troubles. In fact, he started work at the end of summer or the beginning of autumn, aged just eleven. Initially, the work had nothing to do with his father's bankruptcy. He was sent because it looked like a good deal for his own future. His parents could plausibly argue they were looking out for him.

Blacking is the perfect metaphor for the darkest of experiences because it is so very, very black. Yet in the nineteenth century, blacking was the most everyday of products. It was sold as a hard paste in ceramic jars or as liquid in bottles, and was essential to home life, from keeping the kitchen range rust-free, to protecting the leather and raising a perfect shine on the family's shoes and boots, when streets were still often unpaved, or coated in horse shit, mud and sewage. The rival blacking brands boasted they had proprietary recipes, but their products all contained a mix of grease, commonly tallow, and lampblack. The leading manufacturers, the Coke and Pepsi of blacking, were led by two charismatic entrepreneurs: Charles Day of Day & Martin and Robert Warren, with his eponymous brand. Warren's headquarters at the corner of Villiers Street and the Strand was a combination of mansion, factory and warehouse, a common set-up in the early nineteenth century when even fledgling multinationals were run from the family home. An engraving of the building appears on the labels of his bottles and pots, along with the address: 30 Strand. Warren liked to include comic verses in his adverts, and the verses became a staple of London life. The poems ranged from the story of a cat driven into a rage by its own reflection in a pair of boots, to an epic revisionist account of how the Roman conquest might have fared if only the ancient Britons had access to Warren's blacking. In one of Dickens's earliest sketches of London life, he visits the slum of Seven Dials and discovers one of Warren's poets living in penury in a garret. In *The Pickwick Papers*, the loquacious valet Sam Weller favours Day & Martin, while Sam's father immediately thinks of Warren's when he dismisses poetry as unnatural: 'no man ever talked poetry 'cept a beadle on boxin'-day, or Warren's blackin''. There has been speculation that a young Dickens may have written Warren's poems, owing to a confusion between two different companies, both named Warren's. Dickens's workplace, on Hungerford Stairs, had belonged to Robert Warren's elderly uncle, Jonathan Warren. The story of the Warren family feud reads like an eighteenth-century version of the Adidas/Puma sneaker wars. Warren's Original was founded in the 1790s by two brothers, Jonathan, who came up with the formula, and the shoemaker Thomas Warren, who had a shop on St Martin's Lane. Almost immediately, the brothers fell out, which led to the establishment of rival businesses and an onslaught of legal writs. Jonathan Warren asserted his claim to be the inventor of their 'Real Japan Blacking' in court affidavits – the term 'Japan' was then applied to almost any hard-wearing black surface. Thomas died in 1805, and his son Robert took over the company.

Robert Warren was an energetic salesman who embraced the new art of newspaper and handbill advertising. As his company prospered, his uncle Jonathan struggled. In February 1821, Jonathan Warren hatched a plan to capitalise on his nephew's success. He rented premises on a street parallel to Villiers Street. Hungerford Stairs was a continuation of Hungerford Street, the last buildings above the river piers. There were no more than six buildings on the river stairs, but Jonathan nevertheless chose the number 30 for the factory address. The labels read '30, Hungerford Stairs' (printed in small letters), 'Strand' (in much bigger letters), along with a drawing of an imaginary mansion, strangely similar to Robert Warren's headquarters. Such an ingenious attempt to pass off his product could hardly fail, and yet fail it did. In September 1822, Jonathan Warren put his business up for sale. It was another year before he found a buyer in twenty-five-year-old William Edward Woodd, or 'WEW' as he signed himself. WEW was a young but energetic businessman, recently married to Sophie Lamert, the oldest daughter of Matthew Lamert, Charles Dickens's uncle-by-marriage. Matthew had been called to Ireland to suppress dissent, taking Dickens's aunt with him. WEW also lived there, with business interests that demanded his attention. In his absence, WEW entrusted his new blacking business to twenty-year-old James Lamert. Perhaps wisely, he also retained the services of Jonathan Warren to supervise the manufacture of the blacking, while teaching James Lamert what he knew of the business.

The account of the blacking factory in Forster's biography is a loosely sourced mishmash. We will never know if Forster took the details from an original document; or cobbled together fragments from the novels supplemented by a lifetime of private correspondence; or if he perhaps took notes after private conversations (as he seems to hint). The story of Dickens's time as a child worker is the shock revelation placed at the opening of Forster's book to grab his readers. His account is a character assassination of John and (especially) Elizabeth Dickens, a picture of feckless bankrupts, abandonment, indifference to the long hours and the dirty work, all amounting to child abuse. When the biography appeared in the 1870s, ideas about children and their vulnerability were very different from those in circulation in the 1820s. The view of childhood had been reshaped in large part by popular novels. Forster's readers would see the child Dickens through the lens of the hugely popular factory novels, the genre created by Fanny Trollope's *Michael Armstrong*, as well as via the constellation of saintly child outcasts that followed *Oliver Twist*, such as Hans Christian Andersen's 'Little Match Girl' and Charles Kingsley's *The Water Babies*. The image of Dickens as the abused child worker was fixed for eternity by the frontispiece of Forster's biography with Fred Barnard's illustration of Dickens with blond hair, asleep at a desk worn out from pasting labels.

Young Dickens is portrayed as a pathetic Every-Child, dragged down by the factory system at its most cruel. Forster presents Dickens as a child who is out of place in the factory. John Carey has argued that Dickens is not seeing the world through a worker's eyes, but rather creating and codifying a new middle-class sensibility: the shame at being brought so low. There is something to this: it's always about personal individuation rather than a collective identity. In the text, Dickens claims, 'I held some station at the blacking factory,' and his fellow workers recognise this, always addressing him as 'the young gentleman'. His tragedy is that the longer he spends among the other children, the more the distinction is erased. If he joins the company to learn the business in the autumn of 1823, by the summer of 1824 there is no distinction between him and his closest companion, a boy named Bob Fagin. It falls to Bob to remind another boy of the proper hierarchy. What separates Dickens from the other kids?

Nothing, he admits, as he finds he must work 'from morning to night with common men and boys'.

In Forster's text, Dickens feels he is too good for the blacking factory. Yet Carey's emphasis on social class feels anachronistic, something that is more suited to a world of active trade unions and emerging workers' parties than to the 1820s. The urban fabric was far less settled than it would become, and as Dickens was so young he would not have a conventional grasp of the hierarchies. Dickens is miserable at being treated as factory fodder, true, but the way he talks about his pain, both in *Copperfield* and in Forster's account, is less about social class than about imagination and talent. At heart, he is not insisting that he is posher than the others, but that he has an inner light that makes him superior to them. And, frankly, to almost everybody else in the world. He has 'singular' abilities, a child of genius, reduced to the status of a drudge. The charge against his parents is less that they forced him into factory work than that they pushed him into anonymity, and failed to recognise his talent.

Forster says he learned about the blacking factory in the 1840s, shortly before Dickens began writing *David Copperfield* – the novel which most directly draws on his childhood. By this time, Dickens was still only in his thirties but could already look back on a dozen years of extraordinary success. The proof that he is special – 'the Inimitable' – is all around him. But in recalling his time at the blacking factory, Dickens clearly felt that his life might have been very different. When he works a version of the blacking factory into the new novel – heightened by the addition of dead parents and evil stepfathers – Copperfield's descent is framed as a betrayal, and Dickens addresses it to the class of people who have suffered like him: those who have been traumatised by unhappy childhoods. If we want to place Dickens's account at a historical juncture, it is not the moment when a class is formed, but rather when we begin to see childhood differently, as a time of unique sensitivity, triangulated by a mother–father–child relationship. The full title of *David Copperfield* is *The Personal History and Experience of David Copperfield the Younger*, which could hardly make it plainer: Dickens is interested in characters with personal histories, where what is most personal is a retrieved memory of childhood. In his case, a childhood blighted by parental indifference.

What would his parents John and Elizabeth Dickens have made of this charge?

If we rewind back to the 1820s, we might be more sympathetic to John and Elizabeth. What were they supposed to recognise in their son, exactly? We now know that he began work in the natural way of things, having finished school the previous term. Everything suggests this was always the plan. In London in the 1820s, apprenticeships were still the currency of a child's transition into adulthood. This was especially true in his family, composed of manufacturers and shopkeepers, with Aunt Elizabeth silvering piano wire, and Uncle William running a coffee house. Dickens's start in the blacking factory was essentially a first step in a management trainee scheme. It was a family company, with James Lamert already installed as the general manager, and turnover so healthy that WEW was advertising for better premises. Far from being a source of shame and disgrace, Dickens was entering a flourishing business. He was not even the only junior member of the family to join the firm. John Thomas Lamert, a younger brother of James, is working as a travelling salesman by the summer of 1824 when he is eighteen years old. Two years later, while completing business in Exeter, John Thomas ran into Robert Warren in a hotel. The meeting led to an argument, with Warren accusing Lamert of passing off their product as his. Soon there was yet another court case.

In Forster's text, one of Dickens's big gripes is that he has been forgotten while his sister Fanny pursues her studies. On the face of it, the attention lavished on Fanny seems extraordinary. Would any Georgian family so favour a daughter over a son, sending her to an expensive school while condemning the boy to servitude, glueing labels on blacking jars in a rat-infested factory? We might wonder if the account is too odd to be believable. Scratch a little, and it becomes plain that it didn't happen that way. To begin with, the music college Fanny attended was not nearly as prestigious as it sounds. Forster tells us that she was 'elected as a pupil at the Royal Academy of Music' but the word 'Royal' is out of place: in 1823, the school was a year old, still a start-up, and known only as the Academy of Music. The school's director was a colourful French musician named Nicolas Bochsa. Like Charles Barrow, Bochsa was a criminal and counterfeiter on the run from the law. In 1818, he was convicted in absentia for forging signatures and printing counterfeit bonds, share certificates and letters of exchange to a total value of more than fifty thousand francs, equivalent to £2,000. It took a while for the news to reach England, but when it did, it was explosive. Forging was a state crime. The same year that Bochsa was convicted in Paris, there was a currency crisis in England, with at least one in every twenty bank notes thought to be a forgery and anyone with access to copperplate rolling presses under suspicion, whether artists and printers or sheet music dealers. In 1826, *The Times* reported that a Paris court had sentenced Bochsa to twelve years' hard labour with the letters 'TF', *Travaux Forcés*, to be branded on his shoulder. The board suspended him from the Academy for six months as he protested his innocence, then dismissed him the following year as it became clear the charges were true. The *Harmonicon* music magazine took pleasure in his downfall, railing against 'the indiscriminate encouragement given by a few thoughtless people of fashion to foreign adventurers'. Oddly, in this report, the school is already termed the Royal Academy, though it only won the title in 1830, after strenuous lobbying by the prime minister, Arthur Wellesley, Duke of Wellington – which was rather late for Fanny. She was part of the first or second year's intake, when competition for places could not have been fierce. Later in her college career, she was taught by a significant figure in Ignaz Moscheles, a student of Beethoven and close friend of Mendelssohn, but when she began, Moscheles was not yet a member of the staff. Fanny was at the school because she had family connections – from the redoubtable Aunt Elizabeth, the most likely figure to have obtained her reference from the piano-maker Thomas Tomkison, to the old family friend Muzio Clementi, who sat on the board. Fanny studied the piano and singing. Winning a place at the new Academy of Music makes her sound like a child prodigy, but we should see her as a talented musician attending a version of a trade school and destined for a career in entertainment. In the 1820s, no one could imagine a woman as a member of the larger orchestras or even as part of the ensemble in the respectable theatres. Her work would be confined to private salons, supper concerts and, if she did not succeed at that level, then in the expanding sphere of the popular music halls.

Dickens did not have the talent for music school. As he told Forster, his father 'was proud of me in his way and had a great admiration for the comic singing'. This is faint praise, Dickens would grow to feel he had been underestimated in the most insulting way. But I wonder, how was he supposed to manifest his genius? The problem with being a novelist is that you've got to write novels before anyone takes you seriously. (If then.) The eleven-year-old Dickens would never have felt underestimated in his first few months in the factory; the life was too *convivial*. James Lamert was living as part of the Dickens family, and even when September brought the awful news that Aunt Fanny had died due to complications in her pregnancy, this did not affect the family's relationship with Lamert. Dickens continued sharing his love of the theatre, and theatre models, with the older boy. You can imagine Dickens absolutely devouring the fifty-minute walk to the factory each morning, regaling his favourite cousin with talk of the theatre, the latest popular songs, as well as the stars and celebrities of the London stage.

The initial plan was that Dickens would work with Lamert in the factory office, and receive lessons in their lunch time. Dickens paints a gruesome picture of the tumbledown factory on the river steps. Yet it was close to the fashionable heart of London, including Theatreland. Michael Allen, the most tireless of Dickensians, has gone through the records of the Adelphi Theatre and discovered Lamert appeared on stage on sixty-eight nights over the year 1826–7, in crowd scenes and smaller roles. Lamert was a theatre-struck young man, keeping up a dream while also running a business, and attending court as his company was continually sued. Dickens was also lucky enough to have another theatre-loving young uncle in the neighbourhood: John Henry Barrow had recently registered at Gray's Inn as an aspiring lawyer, while working as a journalist and writer. John Henry made his name as a reporter for his salacious accounts of the Pains and Penalties Bill of 1820, a parliamentary bill that had been staged as a trial, calling a series of witnesses to attest to the infidelity of Caroline of Brunswick, the estranged wife of King

George IV. The young Dickens was working among sympathetic uncles and cousins, ready to talk theatre, alongside all the thrills of the West End, yards away at the top of the street. The blacking factory could not have seemed so horrible, at least at first. So how did it sour so fast?

Things changed around Christmas.

St Pancras finally replaced its flooded and derelict parish church in 1822. The new classically styled building stands on the south side of Euston Road (then New Road). This district, adjacent to Bloomsbury, became the smarter end of St Pancras – soon to be the home of a new Dissenters' university, University College London. The district was sufficiently far away from the brickworks of Somers Town and the dust heaps of Battle Bridge, not to mention the dock workers of Camden Town. Elizabeth Dickens chose this location as the site of a kind of kindergarten – a dame school – and the family moved to 4 Gower Street. Forster presents this as a spur-of-the-moment decision, but given the planning involved it is likely to have been a long-term ambition. A school for children aged between two and five made sense, as three of Elizabeth's six children fell within this age range. By opening a school, the Dickens family could subsidise the care and education of their own children, while enjoying a more fashionable address. Preparations for the school may have begun in Chatham, in anticipation of the move to London, taken in parallel with decisions over the future of Fanny and Charles. In December, the family moved to Gower Street, the two parents and six children along with the maid, their orphan girl. The one person who did not move with them was James Lamert. He finally parted ways with his Dickens in-laws.

Charles Dickens would develop a ferociously jaundiced view of his mother's school – and of his mother, too. The school began to fail immediately but in Elizabeth's defence, there was no money or time to develop a new business and John Dickens was already bankrupt. He was first sent to a sponging house: a kind of halfway house for debtors. The now twelve-year-old Charles was entrusted with carting the family belongings to the pawnbrokers, all the way back to Camden Town – a forty-minute round trip. John Dickens was no closer to settling his debts and was forced to move from the sponging house to the Marshalsea Prison, which is where Elizabeth and the four younger children joined him. Fanny was boarding at the Academy of Music. Somewhere had to be found for Dickens and the orphan maid.

This is when Mrs Roylance re-enters the picture. She was running a lodging house on Royal College Street. Quite how his grandfather's special friend had found her way from Brighton to Camden Town is unclear, but I would guess that the family moved to Bayham Street because the old woman was around the corner and could provide help. Perhaps Charles Barrow was also lurking about. He was certainly being far less discreet about his whereabouts, after ten years on the run. When John Henry Barrow entered Gray's Inn, he described himself in the register as 'the third son of Charles Barrow of Douglas, Isle of Man, Esq.' Charles Barrow would die in 1826. He may already have been ailing and was desperate to regularise his position with the law, at least for the sake of his family. His son Thomas was out of work because of complications following a broken leg. He was laid up in his Gerrard Street apartment for two years, and his leg had to be amputated before he could return to the Navy Pay Office. With John Dickens bankrupt and about to go into prison, the family needed any help that Charles Barrow could supply, even if that was simply turning himself in. At some time between the sponging house and the debtors' prison, thirty-eight-year-old

John Dickens applied for retirement and a pension on grounds of ill health. He had problems with his penis, detailed as his urinary tract on the application. It is possible that he continued working at Somerset House while in prison, though that would entail another fee and the ignominy of being viewed as a prisoner. John was in luck with his employers because the pension was granted. That same April, his mother died. She had altered her will in January to stipulate that his inheritance would be £450. With a guaranteed sum coming from his mother's estate and hopes of a government pension, John Dickens might have felt he could put together a package that would get him out of prison. But the family was not out of the woods yet, and Charles Dickens's situation was only getting worse.

The issues that the future novelist complained of began to bite from late December. The move to Gower Street meant that he lost the regular intimacy with James Lamert, his companion for the daily walk to work. Then the dame school quickly began to unravel, as his mother failed to find any pupils. In February, his father entered the sponging house, and Dickens began pawning the family's goods and furniture. Soon, most of his family disappeared into the Marshalsea Prison. Finally, Dickens finds himself living with Roylance, a woman he actively disliked and whose presence in his life recalled every other time his parents had seemed to abandon him.

The blacking factory on Hungerford Stairs lay below the old and dilapidated Hungerford Market. These were canal-side warehouses, sitting upon wooden pylons sunk into the Thames. The district would be demolished in the early 1830s when new owners attempted to revive the moribund market. The area was demolished all over again to make way for Charing Cross station in the 1860s. Twice in his lifetime, Dickens saw the area he had known as a child razed and rebuilt. This must have confirmed his sense that he knew the area at its nadir. The factory was part of a warren of wood-framed warehouses clinging to the riverbanks below the Strand. The piers were once filled with watermen plying their trade, moving goods and people up and down the river. The area went downhill as the new Westminster and Blackfriars bridges cut into their business, and as the stone quayside of the Adelphi, three hundred yards downstream, replaced the older rickety wooden piers. Although Hungerford Stairs is long gone, Villiers Street still exists: the road leads up from Embankment Underground station to the Strand. The corner where Robert Warren's mansion headquarters stood is now the courtyard in front of Charing Cross station. In Dickens's childhood and youth, this corner of the Strand was dominated by the Golden Cross Inn, a transport hub for stagecoaches running across England. Dickens describes the interchange in *The Pickwick Papers* and *David Copperfield*. As a junior political reporter covering elections in Bristol and Northampton, Dickens had travelled out from the Golden Cross on many occasions, but already these experiences were a part of the past. The railways had made his memories seem dated even before he was out of his twenties. Dickens remained nostalgic about the Golden Cross, but not about Hungerford Stairs. Forster reports him saying that he avoided the place because of its bad associations, yet the address had completely disappeared by the time he was nineteen.

I last walked that way a month ago. I was meeting Janet before we saw *People, Places and Things* at the Trafalgar Theatre. I arrived at our rendezvous at Embankment station a little early. There's an ugly half street below the rail tracks to Hungerford Bridge, but in front of the Tube station the road opens up, with the gardens to the right and Villiers Street looking pretty in the evening sunshine, as office workers come to stroll down to the river. There's Gordon's Wine Bar at the foot of Villiers Street. Anyone who's ever got drunk in London will know the candlelit warren of rooms, but it didn't seem the place to eat before a play about alcoholism. I have my own problems with alcohol. I was thinking about the fast-food shops that dominate the street. I like cheap places that do the things I can't at home: using very hot grills, deep-fat fryers and wood-fired ovens. When Janet appeared in the tiled ticket hall, she looked sunny and colourful, peering round to spot the man waving his arms wildly: me. I suggested Korean buns, filled with breaded fried chicken – and she can't resist chicken.

Hungerford Street – now known as Hungerford Lane – appears on Google Maps, but not IRL. It is marked as running along the western edge of the station, but like the Harry Potter Platform 9¾ it is functionally invisible. Charing Cross station is built on a series of broad brick arches that rise up above the banks of the Thames. One of the arches has been turned into a shopping mall, called The Arches, best known as the location of the nightclub Heaven. After our chicken buns we cut through the mall, feeling the weight of the station through its curved brick ceiling. The Arches follows the central aisle of the old Hungerford Market. It ends in a series of steps that climb to Craven Passage, once known as Craven Court. The hidden Hungerford Lane ought to run in front of these steps. There are service doors either side but they don't seem to lead to a secret lane. The Ship and Shovell pub stands at the top of the steps. It is odd because it is really two pubs, sitting either side of Craven Passage, but the two halves are joined by a subterranean tunnel that connects their cellars. Maybe the only way to get to Hungerford Lane is to organise a team of diggers and break through from the pub's cellars. Sections of the old lane are visible at two points. In the north, at the end of Corner House Street, a few yards of street disappear into a bin store. Then again, between 23 and 25 Craven Street to the south, there's a stretch used as a service road, locked behind a metal gate. I should call my brother so we can break through the gate and explore it thoroughly.

The world of the blacking factory disappeared within Dickens's lifetime. To recall anything of those days would have been an effort: almost literally a work of excavation. In the parts of Forster's biography credited to Dickens, he is always struggling to recall his childhood, pulling up bits and pieces, unsure where it is taking him. In effect, these pages dramatise the act of memory itself. To draw on one's childhood is difficult, the results uncertain. As the first line of *David Copperfield* says, 'Whether I shall turn out to be the hero of my own life, or whether that station will be held by anybody else, these pages must show.' Once you begin to dig, who knows what you will find: perhaps only disappointment? We must do it, because no one else can. There are no other witnesses. Memory is private and internal, guarded by the series of obstacles and barriers we create around them: that is to say, by repression. Repression isn't an obstruction so much as a coded gateway, a part of the memory-making process that gives memories their aura of authenticity, because we have made them hard to reach. In Forster's text, Dickens states, 'That I suffered in secret, and that I suffered exquisitely, no one ever knew but I.' Of course! No one could know, because if they did it would not be a painfully retrieved memory. The act of recalling memories makes us who we are: psychic signatures, etched into our consciousness.

If we're the only ones who can excavate our memories, then no one else can contradict us. As long as we stay in control of selecting and staging our memories, then we can arrange everything in the most flattering light. So what's the risk? Who's going to denounce us, or upstage us? Who else could be the hero of *David Copperfield* but David Copperfield? It's not going to be Jip the dog. The real drama of memory is not the difficulty we face in retrieving them, but rather the idea that things may be forgotten. *We* might be forgotten. Memory tells us that we may mean nothing, absolutely nothing, to anyone else. Everyone dies, of course, but some of us will be obliterated. This is the story of the blacking factory: Dickens is telling us a story about a child who was forgotten.

One night, around eight months into his time at the blacking factory, Dickens decided to tackle his father. He knew he could not claw his way out of the factory, but he wanted to at least protest. Why had they dumped him with Mrs Roylance?

> My rescue I considered quite hopeless. . . . [but] being so cut off from my parents, my brothers, and sisters; and going home to such a miserable blank; . . . *that* I thought might be corrected. One Sunday night I remonstrated with my father on this head, so pathetically and with so many tears, that his kind nature gave way. He began to think it was not quite right. I do believe he had never thought so before, or thought about it.

The tears worked. John Dickens found Charles a new place to live, lodging with a family in Lant Street, a short walk from the Marshalsea Prison, south of the river in Borough. A new period began. This is announced in *David Copperfield* in the scenes where David meets the orphan girl on London Bridge before they go together to breakfast with the family in the prison; in the novel, the family is the Micawbers.

I used to breakfast with them now, in virtue of some arrangement, of which I have forgotten the details. I forget, too, at what hour the gates were opened in the morning, admitting of my going in; but I know that I was often up at six o'clock, and that my favourite lounging-place in the interval was old London Bridge, where I was wont to sit in one of the stone recesses, watching the people going by, or to look over the balustrades at the sun shining in the water, and lighting up the golden flame on the top of the Monument. The Orfling met me here sometimes, to be told some astonishing fictions respecting the wharves and the Tower; of which I can say no more than that I hope I believed them myself.

It would make sense if the bridge was Blackfriars, as this is the bridge that Dickens took to work in the morning. Yet his memory, or the story he wants to tell, insists upon old London Bridge. Here a small spy sits and observes the comings and goings of people, hidden inside a little alcove. Here, too, he makes up stories for the orphan girl who believes his tall tales. The reason for changing the location from Blackfriars to the older and more atmospheric London Bridge can be found in *Oliver Twist*. He had already selected London Bridge as the site where the young villain Noah Claypole spies on Nancy on behalf of Fagin. Claypole finds himself a niche where no one can see him: 'having ascertained with many cautious glances round him that he was again alone, crept slowly from his hiding place'. London Bridge becomes the site where two boys from two different novels merge into one, the over-sexed Claypole and the virginal Copperfield. And as the two boys merge, so do their targets, the two women: the Orfling and Nancy. Nancy has drugged Bill Sikes with laudanum in order to meet Rose Maylie and Mr

Brownlow on the bridge, and when Sikes hears what Claypole has seen and heard, Nancy's fate is sealed. Sikes clubs Nancy to death, then burns the cudgel he has been holding since his first appearance. 'There was human hair upon the end which blazed and shrunk into a light cinder and, caught by the air, whirled up the chimney. Even that frightened him, sturdy as he was.' This awful scene is the one Dickens keeps returning to later in life in theatrical performances, the showstopper that brought down the curtain on his performance, and ultimately also brought down the curtain on his life, such was the strain caused by the drama.

Janet and I make our way through the crowd filling the alley between the two halves of the Ship and Shovell, and through to Northumberland Avenue, joining the queue into the theatre on Whitehall. *People, Places and Things* isn't just about alcoholism, but about the triggers that bring on involuntary memory: (i) people, (ii) places and (iii) things. Which is to say, just about anything. An involuntary memory is a memory we can't fit into our personal narratives. The point of constructing a personal history from our memories is to create a version of ourselves that can't be gainsaid, and that we find personally acceptable. The problem comes when these stories are blown apart – by the things we could never admit, by memories that send us into madness.

In Forster's biography, Dickens reflects on his fear of the places that bring back involuntary memories. He avoids Hungerford Stairs because he wants to avoid recalling his childhood. But he also sets many of his big scenes in places that have been swept away by London's expansion and development, which heightens the sense that painful memories are buried so deep that dredging them up is destructive and damaging. Hungerford Stairs was gone before Dickens turned twenty, as was old London Bridge. In *David Copperfield* he makes clear that he is talking about the old bridge, rather than the new one that opened a hundred feet downstream in 1831. The timeline of *Oliver Twist* is dated by the Poor Law Act, which would mean Nancy's bridge should be the new one. But aside from the Poor Law Act, nothing dates *Oliver Twist* to the 1830s: it is all set in Dickens's childhood and the scene of Nancy's betrayal is clearly the old bridge with its niches and alcoves. The bridges are the same, which creates a link between the girls. And if the girls are the same, then so are the boys. Dickens is both the virtuous David Copperfield, entertaining the girl with stories he makes up, and the furtive Catchpole, spying on a young woman and telling tales that will end in her disappearance.

In *The Old Curiosity Shop*, the Orfling's first appearance, she is a limp rag of a girl who somehow turns into a kind of sexy ingénue through the adoration of her lover Dick Swiveller, in a kind of Dick-led version of *Pygmalion*. (Is there any version of *Pygmalion* that is not dick-led?) It's understandable that Dickens would replay one of the darker moments in his life as a love story where everyone is saved, and they live happily ever after. But one suspects the version that pulls at his conscience is the one where a furtive boy lurks in the shadows and waits for a girl. He wants to charm her and perhaps he does, or perhaps she simply humours him and lets him believe that she is charmed by his fantastic tales. It seems likely that the last time Dickens saw the Orfling it was on the bridge. The great suspicion that his novels keep dredging up – his trigger – is that he did or said something that meant the girl had to go.

Dickens often uses the riverside stairs and bridges as the routes to buried memories, recalling the ferryman Charon who takes us to Hades in classical myth, or Dickens's own watermen of *Our Mutual Friend* who dredge lost bodies out of the water.

These images play with memory, turning triggers into devices for his plots. In Forster's biography, the story of the blacking factory emerges in an entirely unexpected way, outside Dickens's control. Forster produces a witness, setting up a situation in which Dickens is confronted with a memory of his childhood that throws him into a panic.

It begins with John Dickens. Throughout his imprisonment, he had been attempting to sort out his affairs. At some time in May 1824, he put together a deal that satisfied his debtors and allowed the family to leave the Marshalsea. They may have been in prison for less than eight weeks, and though it represented an embarrassing difficulty, perhaps it did not register with the family quite as badly as we might expect. After all, Elizabeth's father and grandfather had both been imprisoned in the Fleet in her childhood. After they were released from the Marshalsea, the family went to live with Mrs Roylance, and they brought Dickens back with them. It seems that things were looking up, yet Dickens continued to work at the blacking factory, though no longer on Hungerford Stairs. WEW had found new premises on Chandos Street, on the Covent Garden side of the Strand. Dickens's job was to package the company's product: he and Bob Fagin were expert with the glue and string and paper used to wrap the pots. Someone – presumably Lamert – decided it would be a great promotional device to set the boys in the shop window where they could be admired, creating the pristine and perfect pots for sale. Dickens sat in the window like a shop display.

There's a scene in *Goodfellas* where Billy Batts, a gangster just out of prison, reminds Tommy – the unpredictable and violent character played by Joe Pesci – that he used to shine his shoes for him. Tommy is now a powerful man, he doesn't want to be reminded he cleaned this guy's shoes, but Batts keeps laughing it off, telling him, 'I'm breaking balls ... I didn't mean to offend you.' There's an intercession, various friends plead for peace, and it looks as though peace has been restored. Then Batts shouts, 'Now go home and get your fucking shine box.' Even if you haven't seen the film, you can guess that the exchange doesn't end well for Batts.

Bear this scene in mind.

One day, John Dickens was walking with a senior figure from the Navy Pay Office named Charles Wentworth Dilke. John was striving to get his retirement approved. He needed to win over figures like Dilke to ensure he got his pension, so he must have been at his most loquacious and charming. Perhaps he chose their route, because he and Dilke ended up on Chandos Street in front of Charles's window. John pointed out his son, and Dilke promptly popped inside the shop and gave Charles a coin, congratulating him on his dexterity. This sounds like the kind of everyday scene that would have been forgotten, but for the fact that Dilke became a confidant of John Forster.

'Now go home and get your fucking shine box.'

Dilke had always kept a literary career going in parallel with his work at Somerset House. He was the owner of Wentworth Place in Hampstead, the most influential of the city's literary salons and the launch pad for Keats, Shelley, Browning and Tennyson. In the late 1820s, Dilke bought the magazine *The Athenaeum*. Shortly after John Dickens's retirement, Dilke also retired on a government pension to dedicate himself to the magazine full time, which he did by turning it into a pedantic and querulous reflection of himself. When the ambitious young John Forster moved to the capital from Newcastle, he became the literary critic of the *Examiner*, a rival magazine owned by Leigh

Hunt, a lifelong friend of Dilke. Everyone in literary London knew that Forster was the best friend of Dickens. This was when Dilke mentioned to Forster that he had met Dickens as a child, and recounted the scene of Dickens pasting pots in the blacking factory window.

In the biography, Forster mentions Dilke to Dickens, which becomes the wellspring from which every other revelation follows. In Forster's telling, Dickens said absolutely nothing. It was only later, in acute distress, that Dickens returned to relieve himself of the burden of his story, his father's bankruptcy and his abandonment by his parents. Forster knew John Dickens well enough to be aware that he was reckless with his family's finances. But the story of the blacking factory was a shock; or, rather, Dickens's distress was a shock. It was not something that Dickens wanted made public. The fact that the story came from a friend of the poets, a *Salonista*, a key figure in literary London, only made it more embarrassing. Dickens told Forster the whole story, but in such a way that it was a confidence that could not be betrayed. What did Forster do?

The moment Dickens died, he turned it into the blockbuster headline of the biography.

In retelling the story, it is Forster who makes the link between Charles Dickens and Oliver Twist. We meet a child whose parents have disappeared, forced to work long hours, a child with no one to turn to, and no one who cares about him. Fred Barnard's illustration for the frontispiece makes the connection even stronger, because the image is based on drawings of Oliver rather than any likeness of Dickens. The connection between Dickens and Oliver has become the founding dogma of Dickens studies, 'the bright pure child in the mouldering house', in John Carey's words, as he merges Charles in the blacking factory with Oliver in Fagin's den.

As we now know, Dickens actually began work in the blacking factory to learn a family business. Dickens's long-standing interest in orphans and abandoned children suggests that he grew to feel that he had been abandoned as his family life deteriorated and he was left alone. Yet as Carey goes on to note, 'after Oliver Twist the child is always a girl.' This should give us pause. Dickens is not really identifying himself with Oliver Twist, and certainly not with the procession of abused girls that follow him. Rather, he is talking about childhood innocence. He tells stories about children in order to talk about his own innocence, and its loss.

Oliver Twist combines Dickens's personal observation with his research reading, which ranges from Robert Blincoe's *Memoir* to the popular *The Newgate Calendar*. These sources are filtered through Dickens's own knowledge of London, from Camden Town to the inner-city slums. *Oliver Twist* also marks the creation of the innocent child, a character that recurs throughout his oeuvre but ever after as a female. Think Little Nell: pathetic yet stoical. In his early novels, the obvious alter egos for Dickens are always aspiring dandies like Dick Swiveller, not saintly waifs. Perhaps Forster would argue that by merging Oliver and Dickens, he has seen through his friend to the inner child, drawing upon the nascent nineteenth-century science of psychology to make a connection that Dickens had not seen himself, and revealing a feminine side of his nature (though he probably wouldn't). Yet a simpler way of looking at Oliver is that he is a straightforward composite of two real-life orphans: Robert Blincoe and the family maid. If he seems feminine, it is because innocence is only innocence because it can be defiled. In Dickens's world, innocence is not always feminine, but defilement is invariably male. There is also shame because wherever Dickens sees innocence, he cannot help but imagine its defilement.

Dickens is a shame-faced master when it comes to dramatising the forces of corruption. Think of Quilp, the tyrannical sex dwarf of *The Old Curiosity Shop* in feverish pursuit of Little Nell. Dickens sexualises the family servant girl as the Marchioness in the same novel, and she is still an object of desire ten years later when he writes *David Copperfield*, the girl described as vulgar, but perhaps only because she's listening to the tall tales of a smutty young boy. Dickens lost his innocence as a child, when his parents were imprisoned. They left him alone with the servant girl, and he developed a crush. If he blames himself for his mother's decision to banish the girl, how does he feel? Like a young boy discovering desire for the first time? Or like a bystander to the killer Sikes, who instead of standing up for his sweetheart, watches her condemned to death?

9

Fleet Street: 1824-28

I broke my arm on our return from a holiday in New York. I saw our suitcase on the airport carousel and ran to pick it up, forgetting that a carousel always comes around again. Two days later we moved house. The removal company arrived with two vans and took us away from Janet's home in Queen's Park. By lunchtime we were in Old Street surrounded by boxes that reached as high as the ceiling. Janet told me she was overwhelmed. Her old house was a handsome Victorian villa on an avenue of cherry blossom trees. She had bought it to keep her children warm and safe after the end of her marriage. She was now in a smaller place, in an area she didn't know, with a one-armed idiot.

Queen's Park is close to the home of the novelist William Harrison Ainsworth, a close friend and ally of Dickens for a short time in the 1830s. In her novel *The Fraud*, Zadie Smith describes the parties Ainsworth threw for Dickens and his circle, before the ruthless younger Dickens dropped Ainsworth, scared that his tales of criminals and outlaws would taint the burgeoning Dickens brand. Zadie also lived in Queen's Park, and we would chat while walking our dogs. In the time we were neighbours, her pug Maud died and so did Janet's pug, Ken. We had both pug deaths and Charles Dickens in common. Zadie had thought she would wait a while before getting a new pug.

'But then I couldn't.'

Mabel appeared six months after Maud's death. Janet was grieving hard for Ken. She held a memorial party with forty mourners and countless eulogies. We were now at the stage of looking at pictures of new pugs but there was a problem. Fredo. When he saw Mabel, he flipped out, as he did every time he saw a fawn-coloured pug. Janet and I had joked that Ken and Fredo were stepbrothers, and his reaction brought it home; Fredo was the kind of stepbrother who couldn't share.

Talking about dogs is easy – you get a dog and become a committed dog-lover. But how do you become a writer? Zadie was finishing *The Fraud* as I was wading into the research for this book, and we were both shell-shocked by the Dickens we had discovered. That he was so controlling, capable of such cruelty, always reordering his life and events to display himself to better advantage. Zadie was certain he was traumatised, though she was also sceptical of the usual blacking-factory account. But if not abandonment, then what? I told her I thought it was the girl, the Orfling.

'That might be it,' Zadie owned. 'What about Urania Cottage?'

For years, Dickens single-handedly funded a home for teenage prostitutes that he named Urania Cottage. As we talked, it became clear that Zadie was still reading letters and stories of Dickens.

'I thought you had finished your book?'

'Yes. But I can't leave him alone,' she said. 'What was his problem?'

'What was it?'

She broadened it out. 'What is it with writers?'

One of the reasons that I write is to feel in control. I hate anything hectic and messy, so I was especially angry that I had broken my arm in such a stupid accident. We moved house on a Tuesday and it was Janet's birthday on the Friday. We had planned to celebrate with twelve of her friends, but were still drowning in unpacked boxes, so had to cancel and eat takeaway. We drafted in her son, my nephew, my brother-in-law and our cleaner, Floran, to help unpack. A low moment was finding the BAFTA statuette Janet had won for a film about Jean-Michel Basquiat was damaged; the bronze mask now leered to the left, with its eyes cast to the floor. She telephoned BAFTA's offices, and was told the statuette could be fixed. The least I could do was take it to be repaired.

I traced the route that Sikes takes when he drags Oliver out of bed in the dark, with the city waking as 'they threaded the streets between Shoreditch and Smithfield...'

> crossing Finsbury square, Mr. Sikes struck, by way of Chiswell Street, into Barbican: thence into Long Lane, and so into Smithfield; from which latter place arose a tumult of discordant sounds that filled Oliver Twist with amazement. It was market-morning. The ground was covered, nearly ankle-deep, with filth and mire; a thick steam, perpetually rising from the reeking bodies of the cattle, and mingling with the fog, which seemed to rest upon the chimney-tops, hung heavily above.

In Dickens's time, the Barbican was a street close to the present-day part of Beech Street that runs beneath the modernist

Barbican estate. I take the high route through the estate so I can (illegally) let Fredo off the lead and get some relief from the weight of the bag and the pulling of the dog on my left arm. We drop back down to street level at Long Lane to walk past Smithfield. The meat market is much smaller even than it was when I moved to London. You could smell cold dripping seeping out of the bricks, and the open refrigeration units cast a blue unearthly light across the market floors. A couple of butchers stand on a street corner, white-coated like doctors, vaping as they hold mugs of tea. The meat market is destined to close for good, and the building will become a food hall and museum.

Charles Dickens famously walked everywhere. It's a habit he picked up when it was the fastest way to get around London, and he stuck with it. Walking plugs into the rhythm of the city, and you notice things in a more granular way. The road dips sharply at the end of the meat market, down the old riverbank to the River Fleet, which lies buried beneath Farringdon. The Fleet Prison, rather than the river, gave the area its name, heard in terms like 'the Liberty of the Fleet', 'Fleet Rules' and 'Fleet Marriages' – all of which refer to the lawless nature of life in the prison's shadow, those serving their sentences or awaiting trial living in limbo, often bailed to houses in the surrounding streets and living by their own anarchic rules.

Oliver and Sikes cross the river on the long-gone Holborn Bridge. For almost all of Dickens's life, the river was an open sewer, spanned by a couple of bridges, Holborn and the broader bridge that supported a market. Every attempt to sanitise the river had required an Act of Parliament, due to the enormous expense, and each one failed. It was finally buried below ground with the construction of Farringdon Road in 1860. As I wait to cross the road, I imagine the river pipe deep below me. It's the hottest day of the year and my head is sweating inside my cap. My sling is damp on the back of my neck. I have the bag with the statuette dangling on my left shoulder, and every time Fredo jerks forward, it slips down my arm to my wrist. I am always fighting two heavy moving objects – dog and bag – pulling my arm in different directions. The lights change. We cross the Fleet, walking up Plumtree Court towards St Andrew's, Holborn, the church which Sikes looks up to and checks the time.

John Brown finished Robert's *Memoir* in 1822 and started to look for a publisher. The obvious man was Richard Carlile, on Fleet Street. Carlile had moved to the area as a journeyman tinsmith from Dorset in 1816. He found work with a company named Matthews and Masterman, specialising in tin packaging and japanning. The company was based beside St Andrew's in a street now lost named Union Court. Carlile was twenty-six and married to a woman named Jane Cousins that he had met three years earlier while working in Gosport. Carlile had been radicalised by reading Tom Paine. Living close to Fleet Street, he was drawn to the publishing industry that was exploding around him. He bought copies of the banned journal *The Black Dwarf* wholesale and sold them himself on London's streets. He moved from wholesaler to publisher when he took over *Sherwin's Register* by assuring its founder he would shield him from imprisonment, going to prison in his place. One of his early coups, in 1817, was publishing Robert Southey's verse play *Wat Tyler*, a radical drama that the now ultra-conservative Southey had repudiated. Carlile moved from publisher to journalist when he reported on Peterloo, and was immediately imprisoned for sedition. The government forced *Sherwin's Register* to close, but this was simply the beginning of his new paper, *The Republican*. It soon garnered a huge circulation, outselling *The Times*, though hobbled by taxes which added fourpence onto a paper that initially sold for a penny. Shortly after getting out of prison over the Peterloo issue, he was arrested again for publishing Thomas Paine's banned works. At his trial, Carlile read transcripts of Paine's *Age of Reason* to put them in the public domain. He received six years in prison which he served in Dorchester, 120 miles from London. His wife, Jane, ran the newspaper until January 1820, when the offices and home at 55 Fleet Street were seized and Jane was also arrested and imprisoned. Carlile's sister continued to run the newspaper, until she too was arrested.

If John Brown approached *The Republic* in 1822, he would have found the paper run by a few juniors, taking orders from the Carlile family in prison. The story of Robert Blincoe seems tailored to Carlile's revolutionary optimism. The final paragraph would appeal to any follower of Thomas Paine:

> Robert has lived to see his tyrannical master brought low to averse fortune, to a state of comparative indigence, and, on his family, the visitation of calamities, so awful, that it looked as if the avenging power of retributive justice had laid its iron hand on him and them. In how short a time Robert's career will verify the prediction of the old sybil of Chapel-a-Frith remains to be seen; but it is in the compass of probability that he may, in the meridian of his life, be carried as high by the wheel of fortune, as in the days of his infancy and his youth he was cast low!

Brown had discovered the Needhams had gone bankrupt, their mill collapsed, their heavily mortgaged estate seized and sold to pay their debts, while Mrs Ellis Needham was scratching a living by running a dame school. Meanwhile, Robert and

Martha Blincoe were beginning to see prosperity. They dealt in waste cotton, the very lowest of surplus products. It is the trade of rag and bone men, but the business was experiencing a boom thanks to the newspaper industry. Until the US Civil War in the 1860s, the only source of raw material for the paper industry was waste cotton. Cheap paper meant cheap newsprint. Robert and Martha were feeding the publishing revolution, part of the same rising tide that enabled Carlile to continuously challenge the establishment.

Before the rise of the British textile industry, almost all cotton came from India and cotton goods were valuable enough to preserve. As a result, the rags that ended with the waste dealers were of the very worst quality; irreparable, often filthy, perhaps bloodied or beshitted. The rag dealers would also buy or collect broken glass, bones, and any other material that could be recycled into new products such as glue, glass or card. Marine stores, the name by which the shops were known, were originally the very lowest of second-hand goods stores, where the objects for sale were rags and rubbish. The name may derive from a time when such stores dealt in ship's rope, or perhaps from the custom of sailors to sell whatever they owned before heading back to sea. By Dickens's day, the marine stores were heavily regulated, under the assumption that they might turn to fencing stolen goods.

As Oliver's journey through the ankle-deep crap of Smithfield shows, Dickens had a horror of dirt. He was disturbed by the idea that anyone could profit through filth. One of his big metaphors is the idea that 'filthy lucre' could literally be ash, shit and garbage. The fortune that is looking for an heir in *Our Mutual Friend* rests on London's refuse collected by the Golden Dustman, a character based on the real-life Henry Dodds. London's city dump sat by the Regent's Canal in St Pancras, now the site of St Martin's art school. In Dodds's day, the ash heap towered a hundred feet high, dwarfing the nearby houses. Dodds had the contract for transporting London's rubbish out to sea on barges. In Bleak House, there is an even more graphic instance of a miser who makes his money through dirt: the misanthropic Krook who runs a marine store behind the Courts of Chancery. Krook deals in rags and bottles and has developed a mania for scrap legal documents. The squalor of Krook's home connects the dots between paper and scrap rags. Dickens is aware they are versions of the same thing.

Bleak House was the first full-length Dickens novel I read. I was already twenty-one and a student at the University of Warwick, which is perhaps a little late. I remember my shock at Krook's end. *Spoiler*: he spontaneously combusts. It's an extraordinary passage. Krook vaporises, leaving the room almost intact except for a smell of burning and a distraught cat, the witch's familiar that signals his satanic nature. The scene feels as though it comes from a different novel entirely, a slice of the lurid penny dreadfuls he had rejected when he ditched poor Ainsworth. Why had he shoehorned Krook's spectacular death into this novel? As spice? A Believe-It-or-Not moment? His readers were so perplexed that Dickens was rattled and felt obliged to put a note at the beginning of later editions defending the possibility of spontaneous combustion. Krook's death sees him damned without hope of salvation, the doors of hell have opened and swallowed him in a single bite.

My guess is that Dickens sees Krook as Jewish. His name reads as a play on the Jewish name 'Kook'. In addition, Dickens appears to be drawing on the idea that Jews are damned because they refuse to accept Christ. The strongest evidence that Krook is Jewish, however, is the fact that Dickens knew the story of

Henry Worms, the Jewish marine store dealer who operated in a similar spot to Krook. The Court of Chancery was regulated by the Master of the Rolls whose historic headquarters stands on Holborn, close to the junction overseen by the Church of St Andrew's, Holborn. To the side of the Master's ornate palace, just off Gray's Inn Road, is Fox Court, where Henry Worms, the great-uncle by marriage of James Lamert, had his store. Though a distant relative, James was close to the Worms family. When he broke with his brother-in-law, William Edward Woodd, Lamert was bankrolled in a new blacking company by Lewis Worms, Henry's nephew and James's cousin. Old Uncle Henry was repeatedly arrested for fencing stolen property and passing bad money and was finally deported to Australia in January 1825, making him a mix of Magwitch and Fagin – as well as a stand-in for Dickens's own grandfather, Charles Barrow, who died the year after Worms was deported.

Fox Court is no longer a slum. There was a large WeWork space there for a while.

Fredo's party trick is to do a handstand when he pisses. At least, I call it a party trick. He gathers a small crowd when he takes a pee in front of St Andrew's. The year Carlile and his wife found lodgings here, the church saw the baptism of twelve-year-old Benjamin Disraeli. Disraeli's life is an example of the fluidity of Jewish and Christian identities at the time, just as Dickens provides us with examples of the prejudice that Jews continued to suffer. Dickens may have felt compromised by his mother's Jewish connections, if he knew about them. I think of Leonard Cohen's 'The Future', with its aside, 'I'm the little Jew who wrote the Bible'. Cohen can taunt the listener, because he recognises that a writer who vents his hate on Jews is also betraying a kind of self-hate. The Bible didn't appear from nowhere. When Dickens conjures up dingy courtyards, filled with people making their living out of rubbish, scrap paper and stolen goods, what is he saying about the writer's trade?

The top of Holborn Hill is absolutely baking in the noon-day sun. The junction of Holborn and Fetter Lane is the gateway to London's legal world. The district spawned the newspaper industry because the law clerks could turn their skills – and shorthand – from trials to news reporting. This was exactly Dickens's route into newspapers. Carlile is unusual in that he started out as a tinsmith, yet from his home by St Andrew's Church, he would see the legal profession around Holborn and Fetter Lane morphing into the hacks of Grub Street. Even more decisively, he would hear the clash of steam printing presses that were beginning to take over the area. The decade from 1816 saw the industrialisation of printing, allowing publishers to exponentially increase their runs. The newspaper business is the ultimate industry for an age of mass production. Watching the presses run off piles of identical newspapers tells us there's a huge and literate audience out there, eager for ideas and news. Or, for the cynical, that there's money to be made in producing salacious dirt for mass consumption. The paper was also undergoing rapid industrialisation. Steam-driven presses and rollers produced stronger and finer paper, while lowering costs.

Robert Blincoe's first year in business as a cotton waste dealer was a failure, but he learned the ropes and built up the contacts necessary for success. Good quality waste could be recycled back into the cotton industry. The unsavoury refuse from the city's hospitals, infirmaries and workhouses, and the rags collected door-to-door, went to the paper manufacturers. Robert would take a cart through the slums of Ancoats, the terraces of

Ardwick, and the larger houses south of the centre, returning by way of Manchester Infirmary, where he could take the bandages, bedclothes and nappies that were past laundering. Once home, he and Martha had the unpleasant job of sorting these rags by colour, essential to the paper industry because the manufacturers were not bleaching the paper. The Blincoes now had a shop in Bank Top, and this would be where the sorting took place – below where the family ate and slept.

Robert and Martha had two daughters by the time John Brown finished the *Memoir*: Ruth born in 1820 and Martha in 1822. With a growing family, Robert decided to try cotton spinning again, this time as a manufacturer rather than a master spinner. He rented space in a mill on Tib Street from an ironmaster named Richard Ormrod who had installed a steam engine in his mill, to offer space and power to small manufacturers. Samuel Crompton's version of the spinning machine – the spinning mule – had never been patented so it was relatively cheap, which led to a growth in the number of freelance spinners. Given Robert's experience as a rag-picker, he may have been spinning his own recycled cotton, which would mean that in addition to Jenny-Mules for spinning, he would need a carding machine. It took him six weeks to kit out his small-scale cotton mill inside Ormrod's building.

Tib Street is well known to everyone from Manchester, despite being a dingy back street. It used to be filled with tropical fish stores, and a joke shop that also sold skateboards. In the 1980s, I would get my hair cut at Tib Street barbers, advertised with a picture of George Best and the slogan, 'Simply the Best'. Janet tells me she remembers the tropical fish stores. And the brothel, of course.

I didn't know about the brothel, but I remember how seedy the

Ancoats end of Tib Street was. The derelict mills provided cover for Manchester's red-light district. Tib Street was filled with the oldest buildings. The joke shop was so tumbledown that the roof was bowed under the weight of its tiles.

My family connection to Tib Street was short-lived and tragic. The day after Robert began spinning, a fire broke out in an adjoining room and spread through the mill. He lost everything. In 1824, John Brown returned to Manchester to speak to Robert and discovered his fortunes had taken a tumble. The news forms a postscript in parentheses at the end of the *Memoir*:

> [In the year 1824, Blincoe had accumulated in business the sum of money he thought would be sufficient to keep his family, with the exception of his cotton waste business; shortly after, he gave up a shop he had occupied for a few years at No. 108, Bank-Top, Manchester, and took a house in Edge-place, Salford. Whilst living there, thought proper to place some of the money he had saved by industry to the purchasing of some machinery for spinning ... the first day it was at work, an adjoining room of the building caught fire and burnt Blincoe's machinery to the ground – not being insured, nearly ruined him. Blincoe declares that he will have nothing to do with the spinning business again – what with the troubles endured when apprentice to it, and the heavy loss sustained by fire, is completely sick of the business altogether.]

Brown's second visit to see Robert, two years after their initial interviews, allowed Robert to read and approve the book. There was more to Brown's delay than his failure to find a publisher: he had suffered a nervous breakdown. His life was extraordinary and varied. He was born in Bolton and at one point was involved in intelligence work at the Swedish court. Alongside the intrigues, there was paranoia. He believed that Home Secretary Robert Peel was out to get him. Was he? The problem of writing a sympathetic account of John Brown is that he was so often unwell, as his friends and colleagues knew. There are periods in his life when he was prolific. He found fascinating stories and championed compelling causes. Yet he also suffered from morbid slumps when he could do nothing. The symptoms suggest he was bipolar, perhaps the most telling being his feelings of persecution. He saw conspiracies everywhere.

He was stronger by 1824, and returned to London. Carlile was released from prison in 1825, and rented new premises at 62 Fleet Street, on the corner of Bouverie Street. The pair seem to have spoken because Carlile learned of the memoir, though he may not have seen an actual copy. Brown had left the manuscript with a moneylender in Manchester as surety for a loan. If there was no evidence of a book, it is difficult to see how Brown hoped to persuade Carlile to publish it. At any rate, Carlile turned him down. Brown remained in the city in poverty. In 1826, or perhaps 1827, he bought a pistol, locked himself in his lodgings and shot himself in the head.

Carlile's memory of meeting Brown echoes through the blunt tribute he later wrote: '[Brown] united, with a strong feeling for the injuries of others, a high sense of injury when it bore upon himself, whether real or imaginary; and a despondency when his prospects were not good. Hence his suicide.'

Fredo and I backtrack from Fetter Lane to look at the corner of Bouverie Street. But I'm too hot to enjoy this kind of research. I am melting. The BAFTA offices are close to the foot of the Strand, off Haymarket. The receptionist points me to the lift, and I travel up to a half landing, where someone finds me turning in dazed circles, and guides me to my destination. A man runs across the office to ask if I want a glass of water. I *do* want a glass of water. I very much want a glass of water. In fact, two, which I drink with a gulp. I realise that I must look wild and ill to these young people. The broken arm doesn't help.

When I broke my arm, I was wearing brand new American sneakers. As I accelerated, they sucked onto the tiled floor like limpets on a ship's hull. I heard a woman laugh as I tumbled over. I didn't blame her. I felt so clumsy, I could see how my fall looked funny. I had got myself into a lather, and in that self-generated chaos I broke my arm. I often feel I am caught in a hectic swirl inside my own head, with too many thoughts, unable to explain myself.

I hate feeling pressured and hectic. It fills me with anger and even a kind of self-hatred. As a child I had a whole catalogue of developmental disorders. These included being late to walk. (I could crawl well enough, once getting to the end of the street before the milkman returned me to the two sleeping twenty-year-olds who were perhaps not yet ready to be parents.) I have never really known my left from my right. I remember my father's frustration that he couldn't teach me to tie my shoelaces: he sat in front of me and showed me the movements, but I couldn't flip his left and right in my mind, to mimic him. At the age of thirty I found a written description for tying a bowtie and customised it to work for shoes.

For a long time, I had difficulty distinguishing certain sounds which meant I was slow to talk. Slow to walk. Slow to talk. A neighbour once took my parents aside and warned them, no matter what, don't let them send him to the special school. My parents hadn't yet realised I might be a candidate for the special school. It stood at the top of the street, in a building that had once been the workhouse.

Even when I started talking, I had a whole basket of speech impediments, because so many phonemes were indistinguishable to me. Not simply indistinguishable but also fluid. So 'd' and 't' were often the same, and so were 'sh' and 's', but sometimes 'th' was 'sh', or 'v', or even 'd' which brought me back to 't'. As I tried to copy the weird unstable gloop that everyone parroted around me, I developed a stammer. When I started primary school at the age of four I was quite the oddity, often surrounded by an excited crowd who tried to make me say all the words I could not pronounce. The kids shouted their suggestions, while prodding and punching me so that I would repeat their words, rather than someone else's. If I wasn't being turned into a comic performance, I was often alone, because I couldn't communicate well enough to make any friends.

Reading was then taught using a system called the 'initial teaching alphabet', or ITA, which aimed to reflect spoken English by increasing the number of phonemes/letters. The difference between these phonemes was often meaningless to me. I couldn't distinguish the sounds anyway, so increasing the number of signs just created a whole new level of arbitrariness. The situation was made worse because there were almost no books written in ITA, so there was no incentive to learn to read. I was given a book in a series of readers, and kept the same one for three years. What would be the point of exchanging it for another book almost identical and equally boring? Naturally my teachers thought I was stupid: it took me three years to read a book of fewer than three hundred words.

I was sent for hearing tests. I had good hearing, so that baffled everyone. I was given speech therapy, which did work, or perhaps my brain finally matured sufficiently that my spoken language began to improve. The moment that changed my life was graduating to books written in the traditional alphabet. I was amazed to find whole libraries filled with vivid, exciting tales. It took another year to realise the full scope of this new world but by the age of eight I was away. I couldn't physically stop reading a book once I opened it. I decided to become a writer the moment I realised it was a job. In a messy world, writing seemed to offer the one thing spoken language never does. The possibility of saying things in the best possible way, swaying people by eloquence, and changing minds by poetry. The fact this almost never happens was a disappointment that came much later in life. I learned that life is messy and hectic and senseless for everyone, not just me.

What is it with writers? Dickens was the spendthrift son of spendthrift parents, selfish and controlling, gambling on each new project, and letting down everyone engaged in the old one. If writers are unusual, odd, even traumatised, do they have to keep flogging that oddness and upping the stakes to continue being writers? To continue making a show of ourselves? Carlile's description of Brown captures the combination of grandiosity and persecution that led to Brown's mania and unhappiness. But what about Carlile's own state of mind? Between 1819 and 1830, he was in prison more often than out. He was fearless in challenging the state, but he also put his family through hell for his courage. He and Jane drew up papers to formally separate in 1819, but Carlile couldn't meet the financial arrangements, so they continued to share a home along with their two sons, named Alfred and Thomas Paine, and presumably made up because Jane gave birth to their last child and only daughter, Hypatia, while she was in prison in 1822. That year, Carlile wrote to Henry Hunt with the ungallant aside that his wife's temper was 'warm'.

If she had been a less angry woman, she may not have stood by him when the state began persecuting him. Her pieces for *The Republican* show that she shared Carlile's politics. In his turn, Carlile was one of the earliest campaigners for equal rights and equal pay for women, the right for women to vote and stand for Parliament, and to have agency over their own bodies through birth control.

In 1827, Carlile took a tour of the north of England. This was his first visit to Manchester since the Peterloo Massacre. The trip proved a stark lesson in how industrialisation was changing the country, and he remembered Robert's memoir. He looked for John Brown and learned that he was dead. He also asked around after Robert, but gave up when he was told Robert was in prison for debt. He was luckier in tracking down the manuscript, which had miraculously remained with the man who had lent Brown money. Carlile took it to London and published it as a five-part serial in 1828 without speaking to either Brown or Blincoe, and with a foreword written without their approval. Without him, it would never have survived.

John Brown's suicide ought to have spelled the end of the story, as the manuscript was standing surety for a loan that could never be repaid. Its survival is a spark of hope. Every writer begins their career with a massive lopsided wager that the amount of work they put into a project will be repaid. The only bit of Milton I can remember well enough to quote is: 'Fame is ... the last infirmity of the noble mind.' There's a bit more to the verse, but I can never get past the word 'infirmity'. It's not as though John Brown is the only writer to suffer from a form of insanity. It often seems like a matter of degree.

10

Publishing Robert's Story: 1828–33

Robert had been in financial trouble since the Tib Street fire. He and Martha had their third and final child in 1826, a son. Robert staved off bankruptcy for a few years, but in 1826 or 1827 he was sent to Lancaster Castle gaol, sixty miles north of Manchester. It put a tremendous burden on Martha, left behind in Manchester. She was a woman in her mid-forties, in poverty, with three children, one of them an infant. Robert was imprisoned during a weavers' strike. The prison filled with the strikers, but the bankrupts lived separately. It was possible to pay for a private room and even hire a servant, a role which someone like Robert might have filled, cleaning, preparing food and running errands.

By 1828, Robert was back in Manchester, and working in the cotton waste trade again, with premises on Turner Street. He only discovered his memoirs had been published when he was handed a copy of Carlile's newspaper, the *Lion*. This was a new venture to replace *The Republican*. Carlile's atheism had become more strident over the years, and the *Lion* was in part a journal dedicated to free critique of religion. But it was also a vehicle for a kind of political travel journalism. Carlile made his tour of the country to reconnect with old comrades from before and during his long imprisonment. The *Lion* presented itself as a report on the state of Radicals across the country. He hoped to rejuvenate this network to build something like a labour party. The third issue of the *Lion*, January 1828, contains Carlile's account of his visit to Manchester, alongside a speech which sets out a series of demands and grievances that he argues represent the 'working classes'. It is one of the very earliest uses of the term, defined as a political identity with a collective voice.

Robert Blincoe's *Memoir* appeared the next week, Issue 4, and ran through to Issue 8.

During his trip to Manchester, Carlile had stayed at the home of a bookseller named James Wroe on Great Ancoats Street, at the end of Tib Street. Wroe features prominently as Carlile's host, interlocutor and opponent – the pair disagree on religion but strengthen their friendship and find common cause in politics. The identity of the moneylender who held Brown's manuscript is not known but it must have been Wroe. He and Carlile were old comrades. Wroe had been one of the organisers of the rally that turned into the Peterloo Massacre, as the publisher of the now defunct *Manchester Observer*. Indeed, Wroe had coined the term 'Peterloo', providing the retrospective origin of the event, as a French post-structuralist might say. Wroe was a publisher and bookseller, and so would have been an obvious call for Brown when he was trying to publish the *Memoir*. Even if Wroe had turned him down, he might nevertheless lend money on it because he recognised its potential. When Robert discovered that his story was being serialised, he immediately went to call on a bookseller known to be a friend of Carlile. Again, Wroe fits the bill.

The *Lion* never reached the circulation of the defunct *Republic*, but Carlile's ambition to produce a newspaper with a national reach succeeded, as the letters published during the serialisation of Robert's story show. Many of the responses came from Lancashire and Derbyshire. The contributions by trade union organiser John Joseph Betts, recalling his time working with Robert in Needham's mill, were published before the serialisation had finished its run. An account of Robert's reaction appears in Issue 11, at the end of March 1828, in a letter from a Manchester bookseller, surely Wroe again. He reports that Blincoe was angry that his life story has been published without his permission but grew happier when he was assured of Carlile's motives and character. Wroe was then involved in parish politics, which would explain why he doesn't give his name in an anti-clerical paper. He does say he gave Robert a copy of his memoir. Robert read it overnight and returned it the next day to correct a couple of typos. Otherwise, he was satisfied, except to say: 'but that the enormities practised in Litton Mill were much greater than those related in the memoir'. Robert shows the wounds he received around the head, and the scars left by the hand vices that had been screwed to his ears. 'And yet, with all these damning proofs of cruel treatment, he says, that he was not so ill-treated as many others at the same mill.'

Carlile replies to the bookseller's letter with a note to advertise the fact that he has republished the whole manuscript in a single volume. This is likely to be the edition that Wroe presented to Robert, though no copies now exist.

Robert returned to his work and rebuilt his life. By 1832, he was also manufacturing cotton wadding, a felt-like material used in quilting and mattresses made from waste cotton. The next publisher was John Doherty. He had been one of the organisers of the weavers' strike that ran concurrently with Robert's time in Lancaster gaol, but the pair only met for the first time in 1832. Doherty visited the Blincoes at their Turner Street address, which was now a grocer's store, a big step up from a marine store. The oldest child, twelve-year-old Ruth, was working alongside her parents in the family business, while Martha junior and Robert junior were at school.

Doherty was responsible for a series of publications, often unstamped in order to evade government taxes. Two years before, he had launched a short-lived national trade union movement modelled after Ireland's mass-membership Catholic Association. At its height, Doherty's union represented 100,000 members across 150 unions, alongside a newspaper, *The People's Voice*. Robert Blincoe subscribed to this newspaper, demonstrating that his politics already aligned with Doherty's. In 1831, Doherty had attended the national conference of the co-operative movement where he was asked to move *The People's Voice* to London, but he was unwilling to relocate his family. By 1832, he was publishing a newspaper entitled *The Poor Man's Advocate*, a vehicle for the Short Time cause, as the head of the local Short Time Committee. His newspaper focused on the hours children were working in the mills. Doherty had personal knowledge of child labour; he had started in Manchester's cotton mills as a seven-year-old immigrant from Ireland. He republished the account of Mary Richards's accident from the *Memoir*, with its graphic image of a girl twirled like a blood-soaked mop. He next decided to print a series of short accounts of industrial lives. This is why he visited Robert. He asked if he would have his portrait done. The artist he had chosen was twenty-five-year-old William Knight Keeling, who would become a significant Victorian artist.

Keeling's woodcut of Robert shows a forty-year-old man holding a top hat in his left hand, as though greeting the viewer. His hair is thinning but grown long to cover his mutilated ears. His eyes are sunken below a bony forehead that appears to be misshapen and bruised, as it also does in his only photograph. Keeling depicts him in a formal frock coat. His right hand is crooked and resting on his coat's cinched waist. The jacket and the pose emphasise that his trunk is far longer than his legs, which are not just stunted but alarmingly bent inwards. Keeling has posed him on a stone pavement with an iron bollard in the foreground which gives a sense of scale. The portrait was used for a series of five lives, with Robert appearing as the second study. The response must have been positive, because Doherty next brought out an edition of the full *Memoir*, which appeared in April 1832. Carlile's postscript to the *Memoir* had described the book as 'a standard work, to which future ages may refer'. Doherty repeated Carlile's judgement and five years later it seemed true. The plight of children had become a lightning rod for considering the ills of society, and the memoir was invariably quoted in all accounts of the Ten Hour Movement. It had become a much-loved book, with its young hero spoken of as 'Bobby'.

The Great Reform Bill, passed in June 1832, extended the vote to anyone living in a property with a rental value of £10. The bill was a disappointment to men like Carlile and Hunt because it tied suffrage to property in the hope that the property-owning class would act as a bulwark against the workers. With the bill made law, Parliament was adjourned. It appeared as though the Ten Hours Bill was lost with the country gearing up to fresh elections. The Short Time Committee in Manchester was determined not to let industrial reform slip away and Doherty called a demonstration for 25 August 1832. The marchers assembled in Ardwick Green where they were handed placards. Doherty had Keeling's five portraits scaled up and affixed to boards, with the words, 'Am I Not a Man and a Brother', borrowed from Josiah Wedgwood's famous anti-slavery medallions. Once again, the campaign for industrial workers drew upon the fight against slavery, echoing Carlile's references to the injustice of 'white infant-slaves' in his preface, which Doherty had retained in his edition.

The parade made its way through the heart of Manchester, the streets lined with well-wishers and supporters who greeted the marchers with calls and chants of support. The images on the placards showed the evils of the factory system. Robert was a well-known figure in Manchester, with his portrait in circulation on the cover of the latest edition of the *Memoir*, as well as in the earlier biographical series in *The Poor Man's Advocate*. The marchers took London Road to Piccadilly, turning along Mosley Street before heading to Deansgate for a rally in Campfield, the site of the present-day Science and Industry Museum. There were many celebrities in the crowd that day, but the leading lights of the Ten Hour Movement were men like Richard Oastler, drawn from the ranks of Tory factory owners and Anglican ministers rather than Radicals. These men were repelled by the brutality of the factory system, but they were also in a political struggle with the Dissenters and Whigs. Robert must have enjoyed a special kind of appreciation, because he was one of them, 'Our Bobby!' Hundreds of images of him could be seen waving in the field. There was a fairground atmosphere on Campfield with families out with their children, as the march organisers had deliberately ensured there were thousands of children present to make the point that the youngest were bearing the brunt of the long hours.

Robert and Martha could enjoy the evening, with their three children alongside them, ranged between six and twelve.

Robert and Doherty grew close. Their friendship was rooted in the campaign for industrial reform, but it was strengthened because Doherty was in trouble, and Robert was determined to help. Doherty had foolishly libelled a Stockport vicar by claiming that he was working with grave robbers to supply medics with practice corpses. The Reverend Martin Gilpin's brother-in-law was a surgeon, and the corpse of an Irishman had been found at his home. Shortly afterwards, there was a grave robbery at Gilpin's own church. Doherty was told by a close friend and activist named Thomas Worsley that Gilpin had organised the theft and Doherty wrote an editorial excoriating Gilpin, who sued. The case was lodged at the Old Bailey in London, and when Doherty failed to appear for a court date, he was arrested and taken to Lancaster gaol. A fundraising campaign in his newspaper covered his costs, but he had to find two men to stand his bail. Robert stepped up, producing one of the forty-pound bonds. Robert was never a wealthy man, but he had the means to help a friend. In the event, Gilpin demanded another £21 for his own costs which delayed Doherty's release for another couple of days. He was back in Manchester but scheduled to appear at Lancaster Assizes just a week later.

Doherty's trial was a national story. It played into the political battle lines of the day: a Catholic working-class radical attacking a Church of England priest. But the key backdrop to the trial was the passing of the Anatomy Act in July which allowed registered surgeons to take the bodies of paupers from workhouses or public hospitals if they lay unclaimed. The act was another sign of the way the poor were dehumanised, treated as commodities to be used and exploited by the privileged. It would have cut deep with Robert, who might easily have landed on a surgeon's slab if his life had turned out differently. Doherty gave a three-hour speech. The heart of his defence was his argument that he had a duty to print widely attested stories when the issue was so serious. The judge was unimpressed and instructed the jury that the only issue was if the libel had appeared in his newspaper. Doherty was ordered to appear in November for sentencing.

Doherty hoped to persuade his friend Worsley to put his original accusation against Gilpin in writing. When Worsley refused, Doherty seems to have finally accepted that the story was unsubstantiated. His wife, Laura, had been distraught with anxiety throughout the trial. She was a Manchester girl, a milliner who had converted to Catholicism to marry Doherty soon after his release from Lancaster gaol in the early 1820s. The couple had four children aged between one and nine years old, named with a slant towards the wisest of the saints: Mary, Ambrose, Agnes and Augustus. Doherty offered Gilpin an apology, which Gilpin declined. In the autumn, Laura fell seriously ill. This was not anxiety, but cholera. The Manchester epidemic had begun in May 1832 and by the end of the year there had been 1,300 reported cases and 700 deaths. The worst affected area was the tightly packed grid where Doherty and Blincoe lived, around the High Street, the area now known as the Northern Quarter. In September, the area saw riots after a surgeon removed the head of an unclaimed four-year-old victim. The horror of human experimentation was still raw after the Anatomy Act and Doherty's trial. But with Laura seriously ill, their children would be alone while Doherty was in prison. It was decided to make a second attempt to ask Gilpin to accept an apology. This time Robert went to speak to the vicar. Doherty had other more powerful and influential friends, and the choice of advocate speaks of Robert's charisma and eloquence. Robert was renting power in a mill in Stockport and visited Gilpin after work. He was kept waiting for hours, and then was told the law must take its course. In November, Doherty was sentenced to one month in gaol and fined £100. The four Doherty children must have been taken in to the Turner Street home by the Blincoe family, while Martha or twelve-year-old Ruth Blincoe stayed in Doherty's Withy Grove home to nurse Laura to recovery.

A weird postscript to the affair is that the youngest child, one-year-old Augustus Doherty, became a property developer in Manchester. In the 1870s he built a grid of roads in Urmston near Manchester that still bear the names he gave them: Gilpin, Blinco (sic) and Allen. The last is that of a character in an 1832 novella entitled *A Manchester Strike*, part of Harriet Martineau's didactic series *Illustrations of Political Economy*. Martineau based the leader of the striking weavers on Doherty, portrayed as an upright and moral man, but essentially simple and deluded. She wrote her novella to popularise the laissez-faire and Malthusian theories that Doherty opposed. In her novel, the strike reduces the Allen family to poverty. Even when it is over, the mill owner refuses to rehire Allen, not because he is an agitator but because the capacity has been reduced by the lay-off. Allen has a daughter, Martha, who is knock-kneed and crippled in just the same way as Robert. Allen breaks her heart by telling her she must get rid of her beloved pet bird, Billy.

Despite the efforts of the Manchester committee, the second push for a Ten Hours Act came to nothing. Parliament remained adjourned until October, then was immediately prorogued with new elections called for December. The electorate had doubled in size and Manchester was represented for the first time. Robert was now a member of that electorate, while in London, even John Dickens was guaranteed a vote.

Following the December 1832 elections, the new Whig

government turned again to factory reform, and yet another royal commission. This time, however, the committee was packed with opponents of the Ten Hours Bill. They were the kind of people that Harriet Martineau represented, the utilitarians, the enthusiasts of laissez-faire economics and the followers of Malthus. Doherty and his Short Time Committee resolved to have nothing to do with the Whigs' new commission. However, Robert Blincoe went the other way. He was more optimistic, or more stubborn, than Doherty and wanted to have his say. In 1833, he appeared before the baroquely titled Employment of Children in Manufactories Committee when it met in Manchester, at the York Hotel on King Street, then a meeting place for Manchester's industrialists and financiers. King Street is the heart of what is still Manchester's financial district, created by demolishing an earlier, Georgian residential district. The York Hotel stood on the site of the family home of the Manchester-born William Ainsworth.

Robert gave his testimony to a doctor, Francis Bisset Hawkins, a high-flying figure in the medical world of the time, only thirty-six years old but a professor at King's College London, a chief examiner for the Royal College of Physicians and head physician of the Western Dispensary, Westminster's free hospital. I wonder how tongue-tied Robert would have felt as he was sworn in on 18 May 1833. He was in a hotel he would never otherwise have visited, though it lay less than ten minutes on foot from his shop door. He was meeting a man younger than him, but who had the confidence and qualifications that would mean he was taken seriously wherever he went in Britain. The first few questions Hawkins asked may have been innocent, but they would have put an inferior in their place. Where was Robert born, who were his parents, what was his name, and what was his age? Robert replied, 'I only know that I came out of St Pancras parish, London... I used to be called, when young, Robert Saint; but when I received my indentures I was called in them Robert Blincoe, and I have gone by that name ever since.... [I am] near upon forty, according to my indentures.'

Robert describes himself as a sheet wadding manufacturer, leaving out the cotton waste business. He tells Hawkins that he rents space in a Stockport mill. He gives a brief account of the accidents he has seen, including the pulverisation of Mary Richards in Lowdham. There is a disturbing quality to Robert's account of an accident in his own factory room, when a young man came to help 'a poor sore cripple' that Robert employed and was killed after being caught up in the strap that acted as the power drive for the machinery. This had taken place only two months earlier, and Robert's tone reads as matter-of-fact. But he had seen many serious accidents in his forty years, so I am not sure what tone I would expect. He tells the panel he was an eyewitness when the industrialist Joseph Bayley had his arms ripped off by the blower in Bridge Street Mill, Stalybridge, in 1814. It must have been a story that Robert had told many times before. How often do you see a rich and powerful man torn in half by the blades of a fan? But the Bayleys were unknown outside of the north-west and the transcript misspells their name as Bailey. A decade later, the family would become notorious when Joseph's son William Bayley reduced his workers' wages, sparking the 1842 General Strike – the backdrop to Benjamin Disraeli's novel *Sybil, or The Two Nations*.

Robert sees mills as dark places. Hawkins is gathering evidence on the employment of children in factories, and Robert testifies that his own children will not follow him into the mills. Thirteen-year-old Ruth works with her mother in the grocery store. The younger children go to good schools – we know they are good because the children must walk two miles. His son will later attend Manchester Grammar. Robert says Ruth is taller than him, and describes the way that working in factories leaves young children stunted and crippled, as the work crippled him. He talks through the damage to his own legs: 'my knees began to bend in when I was fifteen – you see how they are now (*showing them*) ... a very little [exercise] makes me sweat in walking; I have not the strength of those who are straight'. He also talks of other health issues, starting with the heat and dust. Cotton lung was still a long way from being diagnosed but Robert's testimony shows how widely it was understood. He also talks about the effects of the long hours on children, as they fall asleep or lose concentration which leads to them catching and losing fingers or, worse, being dragged into machines.

Robert has fought to be able to make choices over his children, including where they work, and when they begin. There is a strong aspirational trend to his testimony. He does not simply want his children to be healthy and educated, he wants them to be supervised and guided. He talks about the poor morals on the factory floors where hundreds of children are employed together: 'there is such a lot of them together that they learn mischief.' This is how Robert grew up, among children alone, but he does not want to see his own children abandoned in the same way.

Has he moved up a class? He's a small businessman, which gives him choices that others don't have. Yet he remains an activist for working-class rights and industrial reform. This is the birth of the working-class movement and Robert is at its forefront, both as a spokesman and as the subject of almost the sole account of a working-class life. You might say he is *the* working-class voice, as there are so few others in print.

His memoir also powers the nascent working-class movement, not simply as a story, but because it generates profits that both Carlile and Doherty are pumping back into their movements. As Robert gives evidence in Manchester, Carlile founds a new institution in Blackfriars, known as the Rotunda, an educational space as well as the headquarters for the National Union of the Working Classes, perhaps the first political organisation to use the term 'working class'. I often hear people make a distinction between the working-class identity and other, adopted 'political' identities. Yet, as E. P. Thompson famously claimed, the working class were there at the making of their identities and the division between an adopted political identity and one determined by material conditions is far from clear-cut. Robert is speaking as an individual, and as someone whose sense of pride is based on respectability, order, morals, education and hard work. He is also speaking in a personal capacity, as Doherty and his organisation will not cooperate with the commission. But for all that, the idea that Robert has been lifted out of his class would be wrong. His words are as close to the uninflected voice of the working class as one could imagine. It's a voice that is the result of practice; he's a raconteur. He's also lived in a variety of places, with experiences that set him apart. He was born in London, and grew up around people with Nottingham and Derbyshire accents, before landing in Manchester with its highly distinctive mix of Lancashire, Ireland, the West Country and Wales. If there is a voice of the English working class, it would surely be constructed as Robert's voice is, from over-layering and from hours of practice – like a Beach Boys single in glorious twenty-four-track stereo. At a time when fellow-activists like Richard Oastler, the Tory reformer, would speak of working-class children as 'white slaves', Robert offers a real account of an industrial childhood rather than a slave analogy, based on the heat and dust of the factory floor, and the spinning frame that deformed his legs.

Robert has certainly not crossed over to the bosses' side. He sees them in a way that they could never see him. He ends by detailing the scars he has from beatings and from having weights attached to his ears and more. He shows Hawkins the wounds, and talks about being beaten while hung from beams or made to stand in skips. He notes that such treatment is less common now that mills are not isolated in 'country places', but tells Hawkins that children are still beaten by overlookers. He is asked who administered the beatings: the overlookers or the masters? 'The masters have often seen them, and have been assistants in them.' From Robert's point of view, the masters are almost passive: they assist in administering beatings, and are semi-detached from the hurt they cause. This is the great peculiarity of capitalism, that the focus on building wealth lifts you out of reality. The masters pass through, one is even torn apart by a machine, but they are somehow elsewhere, on the other side of a transparent screen that keeps them clean.

Robert ends by telling Hawkins that he has a book 'describing my life and sufferings. I will send it to you.' A footnote to the report notes that the committee has received 'A Memoir of Robert Blincoe'.

11

DICKENS'S LIFT-OFF: 1834-44

Charles Dickens began his career as a writer thanks to his great-aunt Elizabeth Culliford and her husband, Charles Charlton. Charlton was an example of the peculiar intertwining of the bar and the theatre in England. His mother was an actor and his father a theatre manager, while Charlton was a senior clerk at the Doctors' Commons, the court dealing, bizarrely, with wills, divorce and maritime disputes. The plan was for Dickens to get a 'box' at the Doctors' Commons, which would give him the right to record trials as an official court stenographer. But first he had to familiarise himself with the law and, more importantly, learn shorthand. In May 1827, the fifteen-year-old Dickens began work in the offices of a solicitor named Edward Blackmore, who rented rooms from Elizabeth Culliford, in her lodging house on Berners Street.

Between 1827 and 1829, the Dickenses were back in one of their periodic downward spirals into poverty, and lodging in the ramshackle Regency development in Somers Town known as the Polygon. The French priests that came as refugees to this part of London had long ago returned to France, only to be replaced by Spanish refugees from the failed liberal revolution of 1820–3. The memory of the Spanish revolutionaries hanging around the Polygon must have fuelled the writing of A Tale of Two Cities (as well, of course, as the local graveyard. Like Doherty, and everyone else in the country, he was affected by the 1828 trial of Burke and Hare for bodysnatching. Each morning, Dickens passed the waterlogged St Pancras graveyard on his walk to work at the solicitors' office in Gray's Inn). The Polygon was the birthplace of Mary Shelley, which is perhaps why Dickens made it the home of the literary freeloader Harold Skimpole, a character in *Bleak House* that he had based on Leigh Hunt. From the 1840s, Hunt was living on an annuity from Mary Shelley. Dickens is at his slyest in depicting a phoney who cannot live from his writing but has no qualms at making others pay his way. There is a decisive generational break, where Dickens represents a more youthful writer, entertaining a new popular audience. This is the angry side of Dickens, disparaging older writers who depend on inherited wealth or aristocratic patrons, such as Leigh Hunt, and perhaps also Hunt's friend, Charles Dilke, who had pressed a coin into Dickens's hand in the days of the blacking factory.

In 1829, a box became free at Doctors' Commons and Dickens became a court stenographer. Soon after, he also began to freelance for his uncle, transcribing speeches in Parliament. A fellow reporter, James Grant, told Forster that Dickens was the best of the eighty or ninety parliamentary shorthand reporters. It was not easy work. The Thames stank, the boxes were dark and crowded, lit by dripping tallow candles, and the reporters had no desk, but had to write on their knees. The light was so poor that they could barely see their work, let alone the people speaking.

By 1832, the Dickens family was living in Margaret Street, on the border of Marylebone and St Pancras. Charles was still at home, some months shy of his twenty-first birthday and too young to vote even if he had met the property qualification, yet a fully fledged parliamentary reporter. *The Mirror of Parliament* had a reputation for accuracy, publishing debates and speeches in more detail and at greater length than rival papers. For instance, where *Hansard* covered six hundred of Henry Hunt's speeches, *The Mirror* covered more than a thousand. Charles Dickens was regarded as the most reliable member of the reporting team, and would have transcribed many of the speeches relating to the Ten Hours Act and the Great Reform Bill. However, since Parliament had not sat since the summer, there was nothing to report. John Henry Barrow was facing bankruptcy. A saviour came in the form of the Gye family of printers who had bought Vauxhall Pleasure Gardens in 1821. Gye operated out of Fleet Street, not as a newspaper proprietor, but from the headquarters of his London Wine Company at number 141. He also owned the Portugal Hotel, 155/156 Fleet Street, opposite the Carliles' bookshop, the home of the *Lion*.

While they were waiting for Parliament to reopen, Dickens and his uncle went to work writing speeches and campaigning for Charles Tennyson, the prospective parliamentary candidate for Lambeth. This was presumably a quid pro quo to thank Gye for pumping money into their newspaper, because when Tennyson won, he effectively became the MP for Gye's Vauxhall Pleasure Gardens.

During the long break in Parliament, Dickens also began to consider a career in entertainment. He looked to his sister's circle from the Royal Academy, who had graduated to find work in theatre orchestras, and responded by organising his own shows, writing comic songs and adapting favourite operas. One production saw Fanny Dickens sing a song that a century later would become a favourite for Vera Lynn: 'Be it ever so humble, there's no place like home'. By early 1833, his theatrical ambitions led to an audition at Covent Garden. Dickens saw himself as a combination of juvenile lead and patter merchant, a kind of stand-up comic. However, when the day came, he was too nervous to go through with it, claiming an illness, and never rescheduling. If the theatre was his first ambition, he flunked it. Given his chance, it was killed by nerves.

His first published 'sketch', a journalistic short story, appeared in December. Many years later, in the preface to a reprint of *The Pickwick Papers* in 1847, Dickens describes delivering the manuscript, 'dropped stealthily one evening at twilight, with fear and trembling, into a dark letter-box, in a dark office, up a dark court off Fleet Street'. There is no explanation as to why he chose the *Monthly* magazine – he would tell Forster the owner was a military adviser to Simón Bolívar, but not why South American politics attracted him. We are left with the origin myth: Dickens acts mysteriously, always alone, and yet he is immediately successful, as though guided by fate. It is more likely this was the last magazine he tried, having been rejected by all the more popular titles. Working two jobs meant that he was always on the move up and down Fleet Street and the Strand, between his day job at Doctors' Commons and his night-time shift in Parliament. Only his failure to place his story elsewhere could have led him to approach a failing magazine, run by an amateur publisher who never paid his contributors. According to the account in the *Pickwick* preface, he only discovered his story had been published when he was browsing in a bookseller on the Strand on his way to Parliament. He had to buy a copy of the *Monthly* to read his own story.

Dickens's time working and campaigning with John Henry

Barrow meant that he often stayed at his uncle's home in West Norwood. After Parliament reconvened, they shared the stagecoach on the commute to the Whitehall offices of *The Mirror of Parliament*, his uncle acting as both boss and mentor. John Henry Barrow was an unconventional character. He had married young, but the relationship quickly soured. He scraped together the money for a legal separation and now, like his contemporary Richard Carlile, he was living with a common-law wife. As the new session of Parliament got underway, it was clear the next big issue would not be factory reform, now championed by Lord Ashley, nor a further extension of the electorate, but a reorganisation of local government using the new Poor Law to bulldoze through the old parishes and centralise power in Whitehall. Dickens had found a topic that answered the perennial question, 'why now?' A book about parish business hit the mark. He was with his uncle in West Norwood when he wrote to Henry Kolle, outlining his plans for the parish novel that became *Oliver Twist*.

Dickens wanted to write, rather than transcribe. He began looking for a job as a reporter. In 1834, after a few false starts and rejections, he applied to *The Morning Chronicle*. The paper had been running for almost forty years but had recently been bought by Whig politicians with the aim of supporting the new government. Dickens's application to join the parliamentary reporting staff was a reasonable prospect, after more than three years with his uncle's team. His father and uncle weighed in by writing to influential Whigs to lobby the owners. Something worked, because Dickens got the job. He formed a partnership with another young journalist, Tom Beard, the son of a friend of his mother's, the kind of connection that suggests the Dickens family hovered around political and journalistic circles.

The Morning Chronicle had new owners but continued to be

run by the old staff. The most senior were Scottish, including the editor John Black and his old friend and contemporary from Berwickshire, George Hogarth, whom he had made the entertainment critic. In 1835, Hogarth became the editor of a new sister paper, *The Evening Chronicle*. Dickens won over Hogarth when he began courting his daughter, Catherine. Soon, the couple were engaged.

Throughout this period, Dickens was writing sketches for magazines, but rarely getting paid. His standing at *The Morning Chronicle* improved after an assignment with Tom Beard to Scotland, which led to a series of sardonic accounts of Edinburgh celebrations, published in September 1834 under the byline, 'From Our Own Correspondent'. Dickens's sketch voice is already fully formed, built around an easy-going wit that softens his biting sarcasm. The week after the Edinburgh piece, his first standalone sketch is published in *The Morning Chronicle*, under his pseudonym, Boz. Before the end of the year, another four sketches appear, which leads to a more regular spot on Hogarth's *Evening Chronicle*. The audience for his sketches continues to grow, with the twenty-three-year-old Boz recognised as one of the coming men: 'a literary Lion' in the contemporary language. He was soon firm friends with William Ainsworth, who was still not yet thirty but one of the most popular novelists of the day following the success of *Rookwood* – the book that created the legend of Dick Turpin. Ainsworth's publisher was an even younger man, the twenty-six-year-old entrepreneur John Macrone, who raised the funds for his new company from an older woman by promising to marry her, only to ditch her when he experienced success. The traditional story is that Ainsworth introduced Dickens to Macrone, but Macrone had only left his native Isle of Man in 1830 and must have come across the

Barrow family. Dickens's youngest uncle, Robert Irving Barrow, was raised on the Isle of Man and was not only a contemporary of Macrone, but was working in a similar field, exhibiting his illustrations and prints in both London and Liverpool. Macrone was as much a publisher of illustrators as of writers. When he published the anthology *Sketches by Boz* in 1836, a chief selling point was the illustrations of George Cruikshank.

Dickens's fast-paced and funny stories proved perfect for the theatre – by the late 1830s, as many as twenty stage adaptations of his stories could be running simultaneously. Dickens earned nothing from these versions, but he saw his chance to move into the theatre. At this point, George Hogarth did Dickens another favour by introducing him to one of the great figures of the day, the singer John Braham. In 1835, Braham opened his St James's Theatre and was looking for shows. It was planned that Dickens would write the book and libretto for a series of musicals, in collaboration with the up-and-coming composer John Hullah, a close friend and contemporary of Fanny Dickens from the Royal Academy.

This is a breakneck account of Dickens's assault on the world of popular entertainment. It is a story only ever told in retrospect, once Dickens became a famous novelist. What is clear, looking at it from this angle, is that Dickens never actively makes the decision to become a novelist. He had an idea for a novel as early as 1833, but even at that point, his ambitions are vague. He hopes to write sketches, but if he has larger ambitions, they lie in the theatre. It is only once he becomes a novelist that he begins to tell a story that he accomplished everything alone. Why? I think the answer is contained within his attitude to Leigh Hunt. Dickens is not a creature of the snobs, salons and patrons – he recognises that he is a new kind of writer, entertaining a mass audience. Yet, at the same time, he doesn't want to be seen as being *of* the masses, and certainly not representing a class, in the way that Robert Blincoe aims to speak for a class within his memoir or in the few pages of testimony to Hawkins's committee. Dickens stands alone, in the sense that he is not bought or influenced, yet he has a depth of feeling that allows him to speak for all humanity. Dickens begins to construct this character only after he has embraced the life of a novelist. Thanks to Dickens, it's a character that every writer has to try on.

Shortly after the publication of *Sketches by Boz* in Macrone's edition in February 1836, Dickens was approached by William Hall, of Chapman & Hall, to write the text for a series of illustrations by the artist Robert Seymour. It would be the story of a club for sportsmen from the new middle classes – cockneys with cash in their pocket, spending their money on leisure pursuits borrowed from the upper classes. It was an idea Seymour had done before: fat grocers holding on to the necks of galloping horses, or accidentally shooting songbirds in the nets of professional trappers. These were Londoners caught in the countryside, and baffled or terrified to be so far outside their comfort zone. It sounded like a sure-fire hit, but Dickens changed the brief the moment he took the job. It would be a club for explorers, the joke being that they only explored a corner of the south-east of England accessible by stagecoach. Pickwick was their leader, a kind of John Bull character combining irascibility, kindliness and chivalry whose name was taken from a Bristol coaching company (as Magwitch was also, perhaps, taken from a Portsmouth haulier). The shift in storyline meant that the new series could not be confused with anything Seymour had done before. It would be fresh.

The run of Pickwick sketches began in March. Almost

immediately, on 2 April 1836, Dickens was married to Catherine Hogarth. There was a brief honeymoon, then Dickens was back at work. On 20 April, Seymour visited Dickens at home, then returned to his studio to work for a few hours, before taking out a pistol and shooting himself. The day after Seymour's death, someone – Hall or Chapman – had to rifle through the papers on his desk to see what could be salvaged for the project. It was a dark time, with the pressure of producing a magazine leaving no time for grief. It wasn't made easier because Seymour had found Dickens such a tough collaborator. Their relationship was picked over for blame. Seymour's wife wanted Seymour to be credited with the idea. Dickens was adamant that *The Pickwick Papers* owed nothing to him. There never would have been a series without Seymour's original idea, or his popularity – which was a lot higher than Dickens's, despite the success of the *Sketches*. But Dickens had modified every part of the idea until nothing remained that could be definitively claimed as Seymour's input. The next illustrator was handpicked by Dickens and named Phiz, to create a Boz and Phiz partnership.

In June 1836, nothing Dickens has done suggests he is a novelist. He is a sketch writer, he provides comic vignettes in partnership with illustrators, while beginning to explore a career in musical theatre. It is only the death of Seymour that leads him to create a novel, as *The Pickwick Papers* begins to evolve into a deeper and more complex, plot-driven work. The key innovation is the appearance of Sam Weller, who becomes Pickwick's valet.

The series was failing. It needed the boost Sam supplied – with spectacular results. Almost overnight this wise-cracking, fast-talking young Cockney was the sensation of London. The novel becomes the story of the relationship between the bewildered, hapless boss, Pickwick, and the devoted servant Weller.

It was greeted as a version of the partnership of Quixote and Sancho Panza, though Dickens is more likely to be drawing upon characters he had seen in the theatre, rather than Cervantes's novel. Weller and Pickwick are surely drawn from a *commedia dell'arte* idea, a variant on *A Servant of Two Masters* by Carlo Goldoni.

The actor James Corden experienced sudden global success with *One Man, Two Guvnors*, the National Theatre's adaptation of Goldoni's play. Corden played the cockney patter-merchant, in essence a stand-up comedian crossed with a clown. This is Sam Weller to the letter: Goldoni's comic servant translated into a London idiom. The character gives us a glimpse of what Dickens had in mind when he won an audition for Covent Garden. He planned on performing a routine by Charles Mathews, a popular comic actor known for his dexterous multi-character monologues. Mathews is the model for Jingle in *The Pickwick Papers*, and the difference between Jingle and Weller suggests the way that Dickens had planned to perform Mathews's material, turning a wise-guy into a younger, warmer and far less calculating figure. Where Jingle is a clever crook, always one step ahead of the rubes, Weller's fast thinking is more spontaneous and fun-loving – just like the valet in Goldoni's play.

It was once thought that Dickens had rewritten a Goldoni piece as a sixteen-year-old. A version of Goldoni's *Stratagems of Rozanza* signed 'CJH Dickens' was sold several times in the early twentieth century. The document has long been accepted as a fake by most, though Peter Ackroyd continued to view it as authentic juvenilia in his biography. Dickens was familiar with Goldoni: he mentions his work in his Italian travel book. However, in creating Sam Weller, Dickens was not necessarily influenced by any particular play, but rather by the structural nature of *commedia dell'arte* where a sharp young valet lifts and co-ordinates the action. Dickens did not need to be a Goldoni expert to be aware of this character. He could just as easily have come to him through Mozart's *Marriage of Figaro*, a favourite of young musicians in his sister's circle. Mozart's student, Thomas Attwood, taught at the Royal Academy in Fanny Dickens's and John Hullah's day, while their family friend Muzio Clementi had transcribed many of Mozart's pieces, in effect creating the Mozart 'sound' for the modern piano (another example of a retrospective origin).

The Pickwick Papers feels lively and breezy – again, *fresh* – thanks to Sam Weller. The comic alter ego of Dickens transforms the material through force of personality, and thanks to cross-pollination from the theatre. Throughout the publication period of *The Pickwick Papers* – March 1836 to November 1837 – Dickens and his writing partner Hullah were working with John Braham at the St James's Theatre. Their most successful effort was the first, *The Strange Gentleman*, which appeared in September 1836 and ran for fifty performances. This was close to being a straight play but included songs because Braham's new theatre was only licensed for musical performances. In December, *The Village Coquettes* opened, a light operetta which the pair had written first, but held over. John Braham himself played a role. He had been one of the most famous singers of his age, a hugely respected figure, a founder member of the Garrick Club. He was also one of the best-known Jews in English public life, often stereotyped even as the beauty of his singing brought praise. *The Village Coquettes* turned out to be less successful than *The Strange Gentleman*, running for just twenty-seven performances. Braham was in his sixties and his voice was not what it had been. He missed the final few shows, replaced by a much younger singer made up as an old man, another ex-student from the Royal Academy named Henry Burnett, who married Fanny Dickens in September.

Braham commissioned a third piece, entitled *Is She His Wife?*, a thirty-minute farce that was presented as part of a double bill through March 1837. Dickens began all three plays before he set to work on *The Pickwick Papers*, and he was working on them throughout the series' run. The opening of *Is She His Wife?* coincided with the beginning of the serialisation of *Oliver Twist*. Each of his plays with Braham was less successful than the one before. Dickens's next play, entitled *The Lamplighter*, was commissioned by the actor-manager William Macready. It was a rushed, half-baked affair and Macready asked Dickens to withdraw it, presumably so he did not either have to pay the commission or reject it. Dickens did so and remained friendly with Macready all his life. In the mid-1830s, the theatre had seemed to be his main ambition, only for him to abandon it after a few failures and misfires. Yet he was still not fully dedicated to being a novelist.

As always, Dickens relied on his friends and family for promotion and encouragement. Elizabeth Culliford and John Henry Barrow had got him started as a reporter, and now his father-in-law, George Hogarth, played the prime role. He had provided a platform for Dickens's Sketches in the *Evening Chronicle* and introduced him to Braham to kickstart his theatre career. In late 1836, as Catherine was expecting her first child, Hogarth once again acted as Dickens's patron. He introduced Dickens to Richard Bentley as a candidate for editor of a new magazine, *Bentley's Miscellany*. This allowed Dickens to quit the *Morning Chronicle*. The end of his career as a reporter freed up his days and gave him more political freedom as his new novel, *Oliver Twist*, was an attack on the Poor Law Act and the ongoing Whig reform of local government. Dickens's first issue of *Bentley's Miscellany* came in January 1837, as did the birth of his first child, Charley. In February, the magazine began the serialisation of *Oliver Twist*.

As Dickens completes *The Pickwick Papers*, he is staging a full-length musical, starting the new novel, writing another one-act play, and running a newspaper. The reason why he has taken on such a staggering workload is straightforward: money. But in order to pursue so many options, he must continually break every previous contract, and force his partners and publishers to renegotiate. He reneged on his deal with Macrone, who was supposed to be his greatest friend (the year previously, Dickens had asked Macrone to be his best man, until Mrs Macrone forbade it, sensing that Dickens was trouble). He reneged on Chapman & Hall when he signed the Bentley contract. Chapman & Hall decided to take it on the chin, and renegotiate rather than lose Dickens. They got to publish *Nicholas Nickleby* as a serial from March 1838. Dickens did not get a chance to make things good with Macrone, who died of flu in 1837. In 1839, he fell out with Bentley, abandoning the promised *Barnaby Rudge*, and resigning as editor. Given his treatment of every business partnership, his relationship with John Braham must have been equally fraught, especially as the three commissions were only a moderate success. Braham would have been unable to renegotiate terms even if he had wanted to because the St James's Theatre was not making sufficient money to cover the huge debt Braham had taken to build it.

Braham had been the star of Covent Garden for twenty years, and his life story was well known. He was born into poverty, and came up through the singers at the Great Synagogue, winning the sponsorship of the Goldsmid family. His style of singing could be said to be Jewish, in the sense that he was a one-time cantor. More generally, his singing was regarded as being continental in style, because he had been a student of the castrato Venanzio Rauzzini. His singing was often contrasted to the English balladeer, Charles Incledon, and a rivalry was born. The rivalry even inspired a show, *Family Quarrels or The Jew and the Gentile*, which was cobbled together in 1802 as a vehicle for the two men.

The poster for *Family Quarrels* not only emphasised the different vocal styles of Braham and Incledon, but also their facial features. Braham is always described as being small and dark, 'swarthy', with features that were regarded as Jewish. When Dickens met him, Braham was beginning to age. It would be impossible for a small and elderly Jewish man, long regarded as the archetypal Jew, not to see Fagin as a cruel parody. Given the timing of Fagin's appearance in the novel, at the exact moment Braham and Dickens ceased working together, Fagin must be read as a pointed jibe at Braham. Dickens might later tell Eliza Davis that Fagin represented a kind of reportage as there were many Jews working as fences in London at that time, and of course we can find black and Jewish figures in the London underworld. But that doesn't answer the question. If we ask why a Jew has a central role in a book written at that precise time, the answer must be, *spite*. Dickens is monstering his older Jewish collaborator by portraying him as an even older and caricatured Jewish thief.

The years covering the serialisation of *Oliver Twist* not only throw up clues to the life, enmities and ambitions of Dickens, but also his family circumstances. He was newly married but he was also a figure about town, with three plays on in the West

End. It would be easy to feel that he had targeted Catherine for her father's connections, given his appalling treatment of her in later life. There are expressions of impatience and hatred towards her in letters from around this time, such as his 1939 'joke' with Forster: 'The presence of my wife aggravates me. I detest this house. I begin to have thoughts of the Serpentine or the Regent's Canal or the razors upstairs, of poisoning myself, of hanging myself, of abstaining from food to starve myself to death.' Dickens is play-acting a devotion to the young Queen Victoria in this letter, but his attitude towards Catherine feels close to the mark. He had not yet turned on her, but the pressures on the relationship were growing.

In March 1837, shortly after the birth of Charley, Catherine's sister Mary dropped dead at the age of eighteen. Dickens's reaction was bewildering, extravagant and selfish. Catherine was struggling with post-partum depression (judging by the contents of a letter Mary wrote a few months before her death), and now she had lost her sister, yet Dickens reacted as though he was the one who had lost their dearest and closest friend. The death of a teenage girl triggered something terrible inside him. Mary Hogarth is routinely linked to the saintly figure of Rose Maylie in *Oliver Twist*, but it is impossible to think of Rose without pairing her with her 'twin', Nancy, as the two girls both play the role of mother to Oliver. The murder of Nancy is Dickens's reckoning with vulnerability of young women, whether they die unexpectedly, or simply disappear like the family maid.

Between 1837 and 1838, Ellen Ternan's parents were actors in Alfred Bunn's company at Drury Lane. Frances Ternan even appeared in a Royal Command Performance for the teenage Queen Victoria in November 1837. The play was a farce named *Simpson & Co*. In the same season, Thomas Lawless Ternan played Iago opposite Charles Kean. There is a theory that Dickens had an affair with the thirty-six-year-old Frances Ternan in May or June 1838, which would be shortly after the birth of his second child, Mary known as Mamie Dickens, named after his dead sister-in-law. The idea of an affair with Frances Ternan explains away his relationship with Ellen Ternan; she is not his mistress, but his secret daughter. It is fanciful; we know the truth of the affair with Ellen thanks to his third child, Kate, born in October 1839. In later life, Kate gave many interviews to the biographer Gladys Storey, who first revealed the secret. The daughter theory only seems plausible because Dickens clearly knew Frances Ternan; indeed, they knew each other well. One of the benefits of editing *Bentley's Miscellany* was that Dickens had passes to all the great theatres of London. He saw Frances perform at Drury Lane, because she was acting alongside William Macready, his friend and godfather to Kate; Kate's full name is Catherine Elisabeth Macready Dickens. Frances Ternan continued to be part of Macready's company for the next two decades. Frances was known as a beauty, and perhaps Dickens was drawn to her, but he was evidently more smitten by her close friend Priscilla Horton, who was playing Ariel in Macready's *Tempest*. The love poem he wrote to Horton, 'To Ariel', is accompanied by a self-portrait in ink, showing Dickens falling backwards struck by her beauty. Ellen Ternan was born in the same year as Kate, meaning that the woman who would become her de facto 'stepmother' was also her exact contemporary.

When Ellen was seven, her father died of syphilis in the Bethnal Green insane asylum. Frances left her three daughters in Rochester with Thomas's brother, William, and his wife, Catherine Hyman, while she continued to take roles in London and elsewhere. Dickens's friendship with her frequent collaborator Macready, in addition to mutual friends like Horton, means that Dickens must have been aware of her tragic personal story, a woman alone with three daughters. The received version is that they only met when Alfred Wigan, his production manager, hired the Ternans for the Manchester performances of the Wilkie Collins/Charles Dickens play *The Frozen Deep* in the 1850s. The Manchester staging of the play looks like a ruse to help the Ternans without Dickens drawing attention to an act of charity.

Dickens was drawn to vulnerable young women as a protector, but this did not preclude him becoming a predator. He entered the Ternans' life as a paternal figure, but that changed as he pursued eighteen-year-old Ellen. There are clear signs that he tried to normalise this sordid relationship by implicating his friends. As their affair became undeniable, he married his daughter Kate off to the younger brother of Wilkie Collins, and fixed Ellen's sister Fanny up with another old friend, Thomas Trollope.

Thomas Trollope entered Dickens's life in the late 1830s through his mother, Fanny Trollope. In January 1838, Dickens and Hablot Knight Browne – Boz and Phiz – undertook a road trip to the north, with the support of Lord Ashley, who hoped to get the duo to publicise the exploitation of children in factories. Ashley also offered a similar tour to Fanny Trollope, which included a meeting with John Doherty. It is therefore likely that Ashley intended to introduce Dickens to John Doherty, and perhaps to Blincoe, too. Ashley was an associate of Doherty, and so would know that Dickens's ongoing serialisation, *Oliver Twist*, bore a close parallel to Robert Blincoe's memoirs. Dickens was happy to undertake Ashley's tour, and anxious to write about cruelty towards children, but he had no interest in the Factory Bill. He skipped Manchester and instead explored the scam schools in Yorkshire that took unwanted, ailing and illegitimate children off the hands of their parents or guardians – ensuring they were never seen again. This is the heart of the plot of *Nicholas Nickleby*, as Nickleby is sent as a teacher to Wackford Squeers's Yorkshire school. Dickens knew something about the schools: the character of the brutal Snawley is too specific to be an invention; he deals in paint supplies for the fast-moving building industry in Somers Town, exactly the type of man that Dickens would have known from living in the area. Snawley has packed off two boys to Squeers's establishment after marrying their mother.

The complete novel *Oliver Twist* was published in November 1838 in three volumes. This was a full six months before its serialisation in *Bentley's Miscellany* ended. Once the whole novel was out, everyone knew how it ended, including the astonishing scene with Oliver and Fagin in the condemned cell. The serialisation had to continue in a *pro forma* kind of way, but Oliver's adventures were now relegated to the back pages while Ainsworth's new highwayman novel *Jack Shepherd* took pride of place at the front. Dickens was still on friendly terms with Ainsworth. He and Forster (another new friend) had devised a little threesome they called the Cerberus Club, with themselves as the sole members. With *Oliver* finished, Dickens was working solely on *Nickleby* and he had the time to undertake another trip to the north, to see the factory system for himself. He and Browne set off in partnership once again, in October 1838, travelling by stagecoach on the route through the Black Country that Little Nell would later take with her grandfather in *The Old Curiosity Shop*. Dickens wrote to his wife describing what he had seen: 'miles of cinder-paths, and blazing furnaces, and roaring steam engines, and such a mass of dirt, gloom, and misery as I never before witnessed'. In Manchester, he had letters of introduction from both Ainsworth and Ashley to ensure that he met the city's prime movers. Ashley was still hoping that Dickens would support the cause of factory reform, and Dickens still sounded obliging. He wrote to a new friend, the poet Edward Fitzgerald, shortly after the trip, to praise Ashley and his cause: 'With that nobleman's most excellent and benevolent exertions and with the evidence which he has the means of bringing forward I am well acquainted.' He describes the champions of the factory system as 'the enemy' and the children as 'unfortunate creatures'. He continues, 'I mean to strike the heaviest blow in my power for these unfortunate creatures, but whether I shall do so in the *Nickleby*, or wait some other opportunity, I have not yet determined.'

He never returned to the factory children in *Nicholas Nickleby*, even though with ten months still to run he had time to work a factory into the plot. The great problem for Dickens was the appearance of Fanny Trollope's serial, *Michael Armstrong, Factory Boy*. She had sold the idea to the publisher Henry Colburn in late 1838 and the first issue appeared in February 1839. Dickens knew about her proposed series before it appeared. The world of publishing was small, and Ainsworth was also now published by Colburn. Dickens had been introduced to Fanny Trollope, and the pair had expressed mutual admiration, yet Dickens brusquely refused an invitation to dine with her after she sold the outline of the book, a decision which has been interpreted as professional jealousy. In early February, when the first episode was imminent, he wrote to his friend Samuel Laman Blanchard to say: 'If Mrs Trollope were even to adopt Ticholas Tickleby as being a better-sounding name than Michael Armstrong, I don't think it would cost me a wink of sleep, or impair my appetite in the smallest degree.'

It sounds as though Blanchard is asking Dickens to speculate on a novel he has not yet seen. Presumably, he shortly does because he soon writes back to Blanchard to say: 'I will express no further opinion of Mrs Trollope than that I think Mr Trollope must have been an old dog and chosen his wife from the same species.'

It was getting personal.

By the time Trollope started her own tour, sponsored by Ashley, Dickens knew for sure that she was writing a factory book. Her first stop was Manchester. Like Dickens, she travelled with her illustrator, Auguste Hervieu. Dickens seems not to have known that Hervieu was also her lover. She also took Thomas Trollope, who acted as her secretary and researcher. The party left by train on 20 February 1839, after the first two episodes of *Michael Armstrong* had already appeared.

The itinerary mapped out for Trollope overlapped with that of Dickens and Browne. Ashley had friends among both mill owners and union organisers across Lancashire and Yorkshire. By 2 March, the Leeds-based *Northern Star* was reporting, '[Trollope] has introductions to the rich and to the poor; and she seems determined to make herself mistress of the whole question pro and con.' From Hervieu's detailed drawings, it is clear they visited the shop floor of a modern steam-driven weaving mill. Given Ashley's connections, it is likely to have been the calico mill of the Grant brothers, the models for the virtuous and cheerful industrialists the Cheerybles in *Nicholas Nickleby*, who had walked to the city in abject poverty and raised themselves to be great industrialists. The Trollopes also met Doherty and other union organisers, 'men a little raised above factory hands, to the righting of whose wrongs they devoted their lives', as Thomas remembered in his memoirs, written fifty years later.

John Doherty stood out, and not only because of his mother's high church Tory dislike of both the Catholics and the Irish:

> I remember, a Mr. Doherty, a very small bookseller, to whom we were specially recommended by Lord Shaftesbury [Ashley]. He was an Irishman, a Roman Catholic, and a furious Radical, but a *very* clever man. He was thoroughly acquainted with all that had been done, all that it was hoped to do, and with all the means that were being taken for the advancement of those hopes, over the entire district. He came and dined with us at our hotel, but it was, I remember, with much difficulty that we persuaded him to do so, and when at table his excitement in talking was so great and continuous that he could eat next to nothing.

The Trollopes were using the tour to combine research with promotion. As the publicity for *Michael Armstrong* began to mount, Dickens abandoned any plan he may have had to tackle the factory issue. If there is any residual echo of Robert Blincoe's *Memoir* in *Nicholas Nickleby*, it is in the treatment of Smike. Like Robert, he runs away only to be recaptured and face a beating. Squeers takes pleasure in preparing the scene for his punishment, and this is the moment when Nickleby cracks, turning on Squeers. There is one other moment when Dickens refers to the treatment of factory children, an aside in his description of Hampton races. He reflects on the gaiety of the crowds, with even the beggars representing a pre-industrial idyll:

> Even the sunburnt faces of gypsy children, half naked though they be, suggest a drop of comfort. It is a pleasant thing to see that the sun has been there; to know that the air and light

are on them every day; to feel that they *are* children, and lead children's lives; that if their pillows be damp, it is with the dews of Heaven, and not with tears; that the limbs of their girls are free, and that they are not crippled by distortions, imposing an unnatural and horrible penance upon their sex; that their lives are spent, from day to day, at least among the waving trees, and not in the midst of dreadful engines which make young children old before they know what childhood is, and give them the exhaustion and infirmity of age, without, like age, the privilege to die. God send that old nursery tales were true, and that gypsies stole such children by the score!

These are images and ideas found in Robert Blincoe's memoir but pitched in the voice of a romantic conservative, a surprisingly deep streak in him. He chose to travel to Manchester by old-fashioned stagecoach rather than take the new steam train like Trollope's party (they presumably changed at Birmingham, there being no direct line). Yet despite Tory leanings, Dickens is still a Whig. He may have attacked the government's Poor Law in *Oliver Twist*, but he was always on the side of the entrepreneurs. The Grant brothers are his guys, with their abundance of energy and ideas. By coincidence, one of my oldest friends owns a property that once belonged to the Grant brothers: a tower built on a hill above Ramsbottom in 1827. It was once a tourist attraction, a day out for Manchester folk, comprising a tea shop and a steam-driven Ferris wheel. When Fiona and her husband, Gary, bought the tower it was derelict. They have rebuilt it to one storey high, admittedly shorter than in its heyday. The hill has incredible views over the whole of Manchester, a whole city filling a wide shallow basin in the middle distance, hatched through with tall towers and chimneys.

Given his hostility to Fanny Trollope, Dickens may have been pleased at the criticism she received for *Michael Armstrong*. The *Athenaeum* and the *Statesman* both objected to the novel as a piece of rabble-rousing. The *Statesman* described it as a 'mischievous attempt to excite the worst and bitterest feelings against men'. Both magazines argued she deserved to be sent to Chester gaol for sedition, as one of her interviewees had recently been, the Reverend Joseph Rayner Stephens of Stalybridge. Yet the book sold, even if the audience were not Trollope's type of people, as she later admitted. She felt the story had been taken over by the Chartists, the last audience for a Tory like her.

Trollope's surprise and even distaste for her audience reflects a new issue for novelists in the age of mass production. They were writing for a readership way outside any social circle they could recognise. The audience was too large and too distant. There were huge rewards in writing for a mass popular audience, but it was also disorientating. How do you address a people, a community, that you do not know and can't really guess at?

Dickens had intended to remain in Manchester until after the publication of the three-volume *Oliver Twist* in November 1838. Instead, he abruptly broke with Ashley's tour and returned to London. The ostensible reason was to stop publication of a Cruikshank print showing Oliver and his new family – logical if not biological – nestled by a fireplace, in the happy hearth of a home. He abruptly insisted on a religious image. Cruikshank's cosy picture had to be replaced mid-print run with an image of Oliver and Rose Maylie in a church. There was a more significant change, however. Dickens took the opportunity to scrap his professional name 'Boz' and henceforth be known as Charles Dickens.

The name change is surely the real reason he interfered with the print run. He was taking a serious risk. The Boz brand was well known: everything he had written so far had been under the name. The trip to Manchester may have taught him the danger of being viewed as half of a double-act, when he was sharing the limelight with Phiz. The change of name signalled that he no longer identified with sketch writing, nor in being one-half of Boz and Phiz. He was finally, even self-consciously, a novelist. Once he had made the decision, he set about defining the role. We see his jealousy. The bitter attitude towards Trollope, with his barely concealed – and baseless – accusations of plagiarism. He also became estranged from Ainsworth, keeping him at arm's length until Ainsworth realised he had been dropped. Dickens's great power as a novelist is an ability to keep the words buoyant and the plot turns fresh. He didn't want to be associated with Ainsworth, seeing something both sordid and stale in the tone of his books, and the genre he represented.

Dickens rethought the role of the novelist, coming up with answers that are still with us today, in the template we call 'Dickensian'. He embraced the city as the home of the universal 'we', the great abstraction of the Enlightenment, the subject of universal rights and universal dignities. However, it is one thing to recognise our universality in the abstract, quite another to get under everyone's skin, and to feel as everyone feels. The novelist lays claim to the 'human'. It's almost the trade description: we novelists mine human emotions, to tell universal stories. It's the myth the trade is built on, but it's illusory: we can't get inside everyone's skin. Dickens found a way around this, by bringing life to a multi-character terrain, not individuals so much as the interactions of crowds. We can think of him like a theatre manager, setting out a stage. He creates teeming people-scapes, these great dislocated cities, where a crisis has shifted everything off-balance, and fear stalks the alleyways and tenement kitchens. It's a terrain in which everyone appears to get a fair crack of the whip, revealing their inner selves for good or ill, and where the good prevails. But it is never as equal and fair as it appears. Not everyone gets their say. The portrayal of Oliver is one example: how do you get in the head of an orphan when you have parents? It is not simply a matter of subtracting two people in the abstract. A more glaring example is Fagin, where Dickens revives an old prejudice at a new and darker level. *Oliver Twist* shows the big lie: novels are never about everyone; they project a small and powerful spotlight. But a skilful novelist, a Dickens, can use that to create both suspense and fear: beyond this limelight, there are things which are too dark, which must be kept out of sight.

The novel is often pitched as the exemplary art form of the Enlightenment, the attempt to capture the universal 'we', all of us together, believing in the same forms of good and evil, virtue and justice. But before Dickens's generation in the 1830s, no one had written books for this universal audience. In a previous age, the clubbable men like Hunt or Dilke looked to an elite. I half-wonder if Dickens's solution was born out of simple panic. His trip to Manchester would have given him a sense of the breadth of his new audience. In London, he had moved rapidly through an ascending series of circles, filled with talented rivals doing similar things, whether that was newspapers and publishing, music and the theatre, or even politics. In Manchester, he arrived as a public figure. This was a city that on paper might have been made for him, full of self-confident and self-made men who were broadly in tune with his politics and religious faith. The Giles family had moved here, his sister Fanny and her new husband were shortly to make the city their home. In the term coined by Asa Briggs, it was the 'shock city', and the rest of the country already recognised its transformation was unprecedented. In Manchester, he caught a glimpse of this new mass readership, so huge, so unknown and so mysterious. If this was a personal shock, his flight back to London in November 1838 was a decisive response. He would corral and manage his audience by sheer force of personality. He was Charles Fucking Dickens!

The following January, he also resigned as editor of *Bentley's Miscellany*, having served a little over two years in the role. It was galling for Dickens to lead his newspaper with Ainsworth's reheated version of his Dick Turpin book when the very best passages of *Oliver Twist* were tucked away at the back. He recommended Ainsworth as the new editor, which temporarily blinded Ainsworth to the fact that Dickens had dropped him. Shortly afterwards, and true to form, Dickens was reneging on his commitment to deliver to the magazine the novel that became *Barnaby Rudge*. Instead, he launched his own new periodical in partnership with Chapman & Hall with the serialisation of *The Old Curiosity Shop*.

As Dickens's letters show, it was particularly frustrating that *Oliver Twist* was ending its serial run so quietly just as Fanny Trollope was conducting a very public tour of the north and promoting her serial *Michael Armstrong*. The night that Fanny Trollope dined with Doherty, the murder of Nancy was hitting the bookstores. Sikes is stuck on the roof of his hideaway on the Thames, as the streets below fill with police and onlookers. He decides to abseil down the blind, waterside back of the building, fixing a rope around a chimney pot with a noose to hold his body. As he glances backwards, he sees Nancy's staring eyes in the dark and loses his footing. The noose slips tight about his neck, leaving him hanging dead. It's a bravura piece. Dickens even kills the dog: 'A dog, which had lain concealed till now, ran backwards and forwards on the parapet with a dismal howl, and collecting himself for a spring, jumped for the dead man's shoulders. Missing his aim, he fell into the ditch, turning over completely as he went, and striking his head against a stone, dashed out his brains.'

The Trollope party continued their tour with a visit to Richard Oastler in Yorkshire. It was now that the penultimate chapter of *Oliver Twist* came out: 'The Jew's Last Night Alive'. Fagin is in the condemned cell. 'His red hair hung down upon his bloodless face; his beard was torn and hung down in knots; his eyes shone with a terrible light.' Fagin had been attacked by the crowd at his arrest and was terribly beaten. His outward appearance matches his inner state. 'Those dreadful walls of Newgate, which have hidden so much misery and such unspeakable anguish, not only from the eyes but too often and too long from the thoughts of men, never held so dreadful a spectacle as [Fagin]. The few who lingered as they passed and wondered what the man was doing who was to be hung tomorrow, would have slept but ill that night, if they could have seen him then.'

Oliver insists on braving a scene that even adults could not bear. He demands to be taken to the cell to see Fagin. Oliver wants to pray, hoping to save the unbeliever's soul if not his life. Fagin has other ideas. He is now so deranged, he hopes he can follow on behind Oliver and somehow escape the prison, shielded by Oliver's goodness. We see what has been hinted at throughout the book, that Oliver's goodness is Christ-like. Fagin has seen this much, a glimpse of Christ's goodness. When his fingers are prised off Oliver, his screams penetrate the thickest walls and echo in Oliver and Mr Brownlow's ears as they leave the prison. A glimpse of a paradise that is forbidden to a Jew.

Dickens puts himself in the shoes of a man beaten by a violent racist crowd, driven insane and condemned to death. But he is never really extending common human feeling to Fagin. The scene is predicated on the idea of Christian salvation, from which Fagin is excluded. What looks like sympathy is actually condemnation. There's no understanding as to who Fagin is, just what he isn't. Dickens has made every attempt to monster and misunderstand him. His circle in London would know that Fagin closely resembles a man he had been working with a year previously. The scene is dramatic and unforgettable, but it doesn't show a novelist capable of universal feeling, only where this feeling ends.

12

WHITED SEPULCHRES: 1857-68

Robert's dream was to have known his parents. He clung to the possibility that his father had been a priest who had abandoned his pregnant mother. It's not much to boast about, but then the extraordinary happened. Robert's son became a priest. Robert junior won Manchester Grammar's only scholarship to Cambridge in 1844, studying divinity and graduating in 1848. The next year, he became a curate at St George's, Wolverhampton. In 1850, at the minimum age of twenty-four, he was ordained in Lichfield Cathedral. His father must have felt his most outlandish hopes were being fulfilled as he watched his son confirmed as the Reverend Robert Blincoe. The three years Robert junior spent in Wolverhampton coincided with a bad outbreak of cholera, the second in his short life. He must have been brave or diligent in visiting the sick, because his parishioners rewarded him with an inscribed Bible. My brother Robert lives in Wolverhampton, and as we were talking about the coincidence that our ancestor also lived there, we realised we knew the church. After it was deconsecrated, it became the Sainsbury's supermarket where Robert did his family shop. It's now closed, but I once visited it with Rob. I remember, the trolley bay was beneath the heavy neo-classical portico, the old aisles were filled with pasta and cereal, and there were bags of Monster Munch below the old altar.

These were also good years for Charles Dickens, or so he wrote in the preface to the standalone edition of *David Copperfield* in 1850. The two years he spent writing his most autobiographical novel had made him very happy, he said. The novel opens with a paragraph that recalls Sterne's *Tristram Shandy*. In Sterne's day, it was thought that genetic inheritance could be explained by the theory of the *homunculus*, miniature replicas of the father contained in the sperm. Sterne put a twist on this, arguing these little men had to be inducted into life by the parents' 'animal spirit' in the act of lovemaking. Unfortunately for Tristram Shandy, his mother distracts his father by asking if he has wound the clock. The animal spirits scatter, leaving the poor homunculus to its own fate. Shandy is an accident, which makes him responsible for his own character. This appealed to Dickens, who begins *David Copperfield* a moment before Copperfield is born. The midwives tell his mother he will be both lucky and unlucky. He arrives in the world without a father, but he will have the gift of second sight because he was born on a Friday at the stroke of midnight. He also enjoys the protection of a lucky charm, having been born with a caul over his head. In short, Copperfield owes nothing to his parents, and everything to fate. His father has been dead six months, and his child-like mother is an orphan, so in the absence of a family, and with no memory or tradition to draw upon, luck – bad or good – is all he has. He is a lucky-unlucky child, these two fates pulling in two directions in a war for his soul.

Dickens was now in the habit of renting a house in Broadstairs to complete his novels. He needed to get well ahead of the serialisation in the final six months of the run, so the entire work could be prepared for publication as the serialisation ended. He would decamp from London taking his family with him, but that year, 1850, he had also launched yet another new magazine, *Household Words*, and his duties as editor would often take him back to London. The Kent coastline was still a decade away from getting the railway. Dickens would travel back and forth by coach or horse, which ensured his family could never be sure where exactly he was. Between research trips along the Medway, and editorial trips to and from London, he was often passing back and forth through Rochester, the home of the Ternan girls between 1850 and 1854. The girls lived at number 13 High Street, close to the cathedral setting of Dickens's final uncompleted novel, *Edwin Drood*.

Janet and I take a weekend break on the Kent coast. As the high-speed train whizzes us through Rochester, we catch slivers of a handsome town below the castle. An hour later, we reach Broadstairs and check into a dog-friendly bed and breakfast. It is more friendly than we expected, as our hotelier favours short dressing gowns. We are a stone's throw from the place Dickens rented each year above Viking Bay, a solid house with fake castellations along its roof line, surrounded by a flinty wall embedded with folksy statuettes of faces and fishes. It was called Fort House in Dickens's day, and later renamed Bleak House, though Dickens didn't write *Bleak House* there. The house is dour, but its position above the half-moon sandy bay could not be better; it's hard to think of a more perfect English seaside landscape. Dickens disparaged the sunsets in Italy, regarding them as second-best to Broadstairs. We hear children playing in the garden of Bleak House, and catch a glimpse of a yard packed with expensive cars. Until recently, it was a guest house. The novelist Barbara Kingsolver stayed, and was fortunate to meet Charles Dickens in a dream, when he gave her his blessing for her novel, *Demon Copperhead*. I imagine him saying, call it Semen Poppinghead, it won't cost me a wink of sleep, or impair my appetite in the smallest degree.

In 1848, and again in 1849, a toy terrier named Tiny the Wonder killed two hundred rats in an hour in the rat-baiting pit in the cellar of a pub on Bunhill Row, Old Street, called the Blue Anchor. Tiny was so famous, he was still being celebrated in 1852, when the Reverend Robert Blincoe moved into a pair of rooms above a japanner's workshop, one block further up Bunhill Row. I had thought it was a coincidence that my brother did his shopping in the Reverend Robert's old church, but here's a bigger one. I was living in Old Street. In the course of writing a book that I knew would inevitably end with the Reverend Robert Blincoe, I accidentally moved to his parish. You don't have to believe in animal spirits and fate to find that spooky.

The Reverend Robert was twenty-six years old when he became curate at St Luke's, Old Street, beating twenty other candidates to the post. Living above a japanner's could not have been the most desirable spot, although the ovens used to bake the black lacquer would keep his rooms warm. The Blue Anchor, now called the Artillery Arms, was run by a sportsman and dog-fancier named Jemmy Shaw, whose talent as a livestock breeder make him the father of both the toy terrier and the modern lab rat, which he initially bred to supply Tiny with victims.

Robert's duties at St Luke's included visiting the sick and acting as chaplain to the huge workhouse on Shepherdess Walk, City Road, opposite the Eagle pub. The Eagle is still a popular pub but was once much larger, one of the biggest music hall theatres in London ('Up and down the City Road, in and out the Eagle. That's the way the money goes, pop goes the weasel'). All that's left of the workhouse is the imbecile ward, hidden behind a high wall of yellow London brick, and used as student accommodation. The road running across the top of the workhouse was later named Micawber Street in honour of the couple based on John and Elizabeth Dickens. In *David Copperfield*, the Micawbers recruit their maid from St Luke's workhouse. When they do a flit and leave London, Copperfield and the girl are abandoned, two twelve-year-old children standing in the roadway: 'The Orfling and I stood looking vacantly at each other in the middle of the road, and then shook hands and said good-bye; she going back, I suppose, to St. Luke's workhouse, as I went to begin my weary day at Murdstone and Grinby's.' His parents' crime is covered in the most minimal of sentences. In real life, the girl could not return to her hometown workhouse. She had no way of getting back to Chatham.

The Reverend Robert's main role was as a preacher, delivering a weekly educational talk. He was on the evangelical wing of the church, and his talent for public speaking quickly made him a celebrity. In 1855, the *Illustrated London News* wrote a piece on him, describing him as 'an able, energetic and accomplished divine'. In the accompanying portrait, the Reverend Robert has a full beard, a style that had only recently become fashionable. The *Illustrated London News* was the first newspaper to employ a photojournalist, Roger Fenton, and his photographs of bearded soldiers wrapped up against the bleak Crimean landscape inaugurated the beard craze that swept Victorian Britain. The Reverend Robert looks stern yet strong, like a biblical patriarch. The *Illustrated London News* sold autographed copies of his portrait at twelve shillings and sixpence. Our copy was passed through my family. My grandmother kept it in an alcove in her sitting room, above the cutlery canteen.

In 1857, Robert met a local woman, Charlotte Tripp. She was just nineteen years old; he was thirty-one. Her parents were publicans, and she was born and raised over a pub called the Ivey House on Goswell Street. The pub still exists, now named the Old Ivy House, on Goswell Road. I don't know how common it was for ambitious young curates to marry barmaids, but in its way Goswell Street was both dull and respectable. We have Dickens's word for it in *The Pickwick Papers*. The street is so boring that it spurred a retired stockbroker to become an explorer:

> Goswell Street was at his feet, Goswell Street was on his right hand – as far as the eye could reach, Goswell Street extended on his left; and the opposite side of Goswell Street was over the way. 'Such,' thought Mr. Pickwick, 'are the narrow views of those philosophers who, content with examining the things that lie before them, look not to the truths which are hidden beyond. As well might I be content to gaze on Goswell Street for ever, without one effort to penetrate to the hidden countries which on every side surround it.'

The description places Pickwick's lodging at the same spot as the Old Ivy House, halfway along Goswell Street, or a twenty-minute walk to the cab stand at St Martin's Le Grand, where Pickwick begins his life as an explorer. *The Pickwick Papers* is set in 1827 and was written in 1836, while the pub was in my family from the early 1820s through to the 1860s. The Old Ivy House must have been familiar to Dickens, if he made this spot the centre of Pickwick's world. Maybe he stopped by and sampled one of our pies — the records show the pub always had a licence for hot food as well as drink. It still does food, authentic Indian curries. I have lunch there with the musician Oli Burslem, who is a kind of cousin: I share a great-grandfather with his mother. This makes us direct descendants of Charlotte Tripp, though it turns out a genealogical connection to a property is not the same as a legal claim, because the landlady refuses to let me roam around the upstairs rooms, on the grounds her staff live there and some are asleep. She can offer Oli a ration card allowing him to buy a pint of Guinness the next time he orders a drink. This is the great Guinness shortage of 2024 and she is down to her last three barrels. Another instance when Oliver can't get any more, but at least is promised something for the future.

'Are you named after Oliver Twist?' I ask.

'Maybe. I think my mum mentioned it.'

Oli was born in Wolverhampton, and moved to London alone as a teenager, living within view of the spire of St Luke's, which is another example of the animal spirits and strange attractors that affect the movements of my family. Or so I suggest. Oli nods, maybe. We agree the food is good, and the place seems clean. There's no sign the pub ever hosted rat-baiting contests in its cellar.

In the preface to *David Copperfield*, Dickens says no one could believe in a book more than its writer, nor feel a greater sense of separation at finishing it. To stop living inside the book and push it away into a 'shadowy world' is like suppressing a vital part of your identity, because all the people and places and conversations are still teeming inside your head. During the final months of writing *David Copperfield*, as he shuttled back and forth between Broadstairs and London, the journey literally took him back to his childhood, which is also Copperfield's childhood. The road enters

Chatham via a steep hill that leads down to the Brook, where he lived and went to school with the Giles boys, then along the High Street and the pub where his father got him to perform comic songs, and past the workhouse where his parents signed a contract for the Orfling. From Chatham, the road continues to Rochester, where it becomes Rochester High Street at the junction with Star Hill. The Theatre Royal, where James Lamert passed on his passion for the stage, is a three-storey building at the foot of Star Hill. In recent years, the theatre has been a Conservative club, an events space and a nightclub. An old webpage has photographs of the local celebrity, Billy Childish, playing the guitar at the head of his retro-billy band. The building is now closed and appears to be abandoned. I'm retracing the journey with Janet. After looking up at the yellow façade, the colour of old nicotine, we walk around the side to look for signs of life. The side of the theatre rises as a big blank wall over a small car park. Two men cross the car park. I don't see where they came from, but there's a flight of stairs leading to a second-floor door. The door is open. I tell Janet I should explore. She shrugs, okay, and takes Fredo's lead.

The stairs lead to a fire door and a narrow corridor into the back of the theatre. On the left, there is a locked door with its key hanging from a nail inside a box. The key is odd, but I ignore it, walking to the end of the corridor to find a set of stairs leading up to the dress circle, and down to the foyer and bar. There are glass doors on every floor, but each one is locked. No keys. I can only look through. This is a two-hundred-year-old theatre, and I would guess it hasn't seen decorators since the 1970s. I glimpse a bar in disarray. A dust-filled lobby. A large hall with ceiling tiles scattered over the dance floor and a stage at the end. I would get into the building and explore if I could, but I can't find a way. I return through the long corridor and fire escape to the car park.

Janet asks what I saw, and I describe what I have seen, which isn't much. A semi-derelict theatre that seems to have been frozen in time fifty years ago.

She says, 'It's a brothel.'

'This is also a brothel?'

'You saw those two guys earlier. One was adjusting his flies. The other leered at me. He looked dazed and seedy.'

I had seen the men, without noticing what she had noticed. I ask her, 'Did they come out of the theatre?'

'Yes.'

I thought of the mystery door and the key. Is that how the punters get into the building? Later, I wonder if the women can get out.

The theatre was Dickens's only real failure in life. In the 1850s he returned to writing and performing, as though hoping to conquer the stage at a second attempt. He began to act in a company of amateurs, a roll call of his famous friends. In 1851 he staged Bulwer-Lytton's play *Not So Bad as We Seem* to raise money for his latest charity project, a literary fund. He put on a gala performance for the Queen, and its success led Dickens to look for opportunities to stage more charity shows. In the same year, Frances Ternan performed in Bulwer-Lytton's *Richelieu* in Rochester's Theatre Royal, another charity production, this time for herself and her three girls. The choice of play suggests that Dickens and his circle were already stepping in to support Frances, a single mother who was struggling with three daughters in straitened times. The oldest girl, Fanny Ternan, was then aged sixteen, Mary was fourteen, and Ellen just twelve years old, the age when Dickens last saw the family maid.

The serialisation of Dickens's next novel, *Bleak House*, began the following year. After a decade spent working in Broadstairs, he decided on a change of scene and sent his sister-in-law Georgina Hogarth to scout for a house in Boulogne. The boat-train from London to Paris had begun regular services in 1850, via the port at Boulogne, and Dickens had been an early passenger. He must have liked what he saw of the French seaside town. The harbour station no longer exists but I remember it from my childhood. Each June, my family of five, plus my paternal grandmother, would cram into a Cortina estate and take the car ferry to Boulogne for the sleeper to the Mediterranean. I remember the granite walls of the port, the wide low platforms of the station, and the smell of French cigarettes as my father smoked the Gitanes he'd brought duty free on the ferry, to get in the mood for his holiday.

On this earlier visit to Paris, Dickens had begun to make friends among Parisian actors and impresarios, including a young actor named Charles Fechter who had already played a season at the St James's Theatre in London. Dickens and Fechter became business associates and Fechter sent Dickens the astonishing gift of an entire flat-pack Swiss chalet. It now stands in the grounds of Eastgate House on Rochester High Street, a two-storey, two-room wooden house painted a beige cream. In the 1860s, it sat in the grounds of Gad's Hill Place, only three miles away. The chalet is so fragile, we are not allowed inside, though we can get a view of the back from the women's toilets inside Eastgate House. Eastgate House features as Westgate House in *Edwin Drood*. It is an Elizabethan mansion, a little lower down the street from the home of the Ternan girls when they lived in Rochester.

In 1853, and again in 1854, Dickens would shuttle between France and London, while his family were parked in Boulogne. He even placed three of his sons in a boarding school in the town.

In London, he would deal with editorial issues at *Household Words* and catch up with his friends, usually in the company of Wilkie Collins, a lively single man. After 1854, the Ternans moved to London, and moved in Dickens's circles. The two oldest girls acted alongside their mother in Charles Kean's company at the Princess Theatre, where Mrs Ternan played Oberon in *A Midsummer's Night's Dream* in 1857. Ellen had just turned eighteen, and appeared in a burlesque at the Haymarket Theatre, probably *Atalanta*, a vehicle for London's top woman comedian, Martha Oliver. An engraving of a scene from the play, entitled 'The Temple of Hymen', shows the young girls as temple virgins arranged around the stage in their white robes.

Dickens staged charity performances through these years. Although they were technically amateur productions, he employed professional set designers and musicians, and invited London's critics to review them. The cast was composed of famous men and like contemporary TV panel shows, the ability of the participants was less important than their wit and star presence. Dickens staged *The Lighthouse* by Wilkie Collins in 1855, and the next year came up with an idea that would become his biggest theatrical project, *The Frozen Deep*. Though the play was initially written by Collins, the idea came from Dickens, inspired by the Franklin Arctic expedition of 1845 which saw the entire crew lost. A decade later, the explorer John Rae solved the mystery of Franklin's disappearance. He found relics of the expedition, alongside reports from Inuit hunters who had met the crew members. The Inuit reported evidence the crew had resorted to cannibalism before perishing in their turn. Rae gave his report to the Admiralty, who published it, apparently by mistake. Dickens reacted strongly on the grounds that an Englishman would never eat another Englishman, but an Inuit would surely lie about it. The result, *The Frozen Deep*, dramatises the events within a story of rival lovers, ending in the heroic sacrifice of one man for another; in effect, the device that would make *A Tale of Two Cities* so compelling, two years later. The play was performed in Dickens's London home for a week in January 1857, to audiences of ninety. Dickens took the part of the man who lays down his life for the other. He is an antihero tainted by desire and jealousy, but nevertheless proves to have a noble heart at the end.

The Frozen Deep may have remained a domestic piece, but for the news of the Indian Rebellion. The reports arrived in April and May 1857, with lurid descriptions of massacres and rapes in the cities of Meerut and Delhi, including a fabricated story of the rape of forty-eight English children. Dickens would soon have a son in the war; sixteen-year-old Walter was returning from school in Boulogne in June, before shipping to India to join the army. Dickens revived *The Frozen Deep*, feeling that it was even more topical. He staged it as a charity gala for a recently deceased friend, with the profits going to the man's widow. He approached the Gallery of Illustration, a theatre belonging to Priscilla Horton, who had so bewitched him when she played Ariel. Horton staged a royal performance for the Queen. Subsequently, a series of public performances ran in her theatre on the remaining Tuesdays throughout July. The cast were still composed of amateurs, Dickens's famous friends, alongside members of his own household, Georgina Hogarth, Mary Dickens and Kate Dickens. Only when Dickens decided to transfer the show to distant Manchester were these parts taken by Frances Ternan, Fanny and Ellen.

Why Manchester? Dickens had rarely visited the city since bringing his sister home to London to convalesce from tuberculosis; Fanny died in 1848. However, factory novels had become increasingly popular in the years since Trollope's *Michael Armstrong*, and following entries into the genre by the Manchester writer Mrs Gaskell, and Disraeli's own account of the Stalybridge strikes, Dickens published his own northern industrial novel, *Hard Times*, in 1854. Researching the novel brought him back to Manchester, where he spoke at the city's liberal debating club, the Athenaeum. His brother Alfred Lamert Dickens was then living in the city and working as a railway engineer. There were always invitations for Dickens to return to Manchester and so he decided to stage the final performances of *The Frozen Deep* in the Free Trade Hall, a venue capable of holding four thousand people. (Ninety-nine years later, in this venue, Bob Dylan was called 'Judas' for daring to electrify folk music.) The programme was boosted by a two-act farce entitled *Uncle John* about an old man who intends to marry – with hilarious results. Dickens played Uncle John, and Ellen played his intended. The author, J. B. Buckstone, was another old friend, the manager of the Haymarket Theatre who had cast Ellen as a vestal virgin in *Atalanta*.

There's a consensus that Dickens developed a sexual interest in one or other of the Ternan girls, and that his gaze was fixed on Ellen by the end of the run in Manchester. He was forty-five, she was eighteen. We could invoke the idea that the Victorian Age was another time, but I don't think this is true. The year before Claire Tomalin published her biography of Ellen Ternan, fifty-two-year-old Bill Wyman of the Rolling Stones married the eighteen-year-old girl he had been 'dating' since she was just thirteen. Wyman's story was invariably reported in the newspapers as the tale of an old fool, an ambitious mother and a star-struck young girl, which is not so dissimilar to the story that Tomalin tells of Dickens and Ellen's 'love affair'.

Was Dickens's passion for the teenage Ellen an aberration? In his life, he relished the role of chivalrous protector of vulnerable women. Urania Cottage prepared young prostitutes for emigration to the colonies by focusing on their morals; a project haunted by what we would now call victim-blaming. Yet Dickens's treatment of Nancy and the other stand-ins for the Orfling show that his concern for at-risk women was genuine. Dickens could not help micromanaging, but this was true of everything he touched, and it was almost always at a distance. He was an infrequent visitor at Urania Cottage, which was run by his co-director, Angela Burdett-Coutts, and overseen by capable female managers. Yet he would not be the first predator to hide behind a charitable mission. The Victorians were alive to the Janus-faced nature of the white knight. The melodramatic villain of *Michael Armstrong*, Sir Matthew, is charming to his aristocratic friends and brutal to Michael. Dickens plays around with this villain in *The Frozen Deep* and *A Tale of Two Cities* by making an unsympathetic antagonist into an antihero. The most memorable of these good-evil characters in Victorian literature are the psychologically split figures of Dr Jekyll and Dorian Gray, but Dickens had already paved the way for these creations with the villain John Jasper of *Edwin Drood*, the cathedral choirmaster, the opium addict who is secretly obsessed with an orphan girl. Nothing suggests that Dickens used his charitable work to mask abuse, but he was familiar with the psycho-sexual dynamic of a protector obsessing over his ward. As far back as *The Old Curiosity Shop*, his alter-ego Dick Swiveller first saves the orphan girl, then takes her as his wife. As his relationship with the Ternan family became all-consuming, it is notable that he created more of these two-faced characters, good and bad, lucky and unlucky, culminating in John Jasper. Dickens may not have been a lifelong predator, but it seems evident that he knew he had become one in the pursuit of Ellen Ternan. He ceased funding Urania Cottage as his life took a cataclysmic turn, which precipitated the end of his marriage.

The Frozen Deep played over three nights in a long August weekend in 1857 for an audience of thousands. In the weeks that followed, Dickens inveigled his way into the Ternan family. He persuaded Collins to go on a walking holiday, which brought him to Doncaster where the Ternans were appearing in theatre. A partial account of their holiday was published as *The Lazy Tour of Two Idle Apprentices*. The reference to apprentices suggests Dickens had befriended Collins to recapture his youth. It is by no means clear that Ellen surrendered to Dickens that summer. As he continued his pursuit, he wrapped her family in his embrace, offering charity, avuncular bonhomie, and the old conviviality. Dickens set about establishing the Ternans as a second family. A semi-secret family, of course, but not a secret from anyone who mattered, neither his friends nor his family. His daughter Kate told the biographer Gladys Storey that her mother was made to pay a social call on the Ternans. It was a fleeting capitulation: Catherine could not stomach the unhappiness at dealing with these doubles or replacements. In a very quick escalation, Dickens sought a legal separation that provided his wife with a financial settlement but also imposed what we would now call non-disclosure agreements on her family, especially her mother, Georgina, and Catherine's other sisters. Only her younger sister, also named Georgina, remained loyal to Dickens. In retrospect, it looks ominous that Dickens made the real villain of *The Frozen Deep* an old Scottish nurse. The mother, Georgina senior, was Scottish, which looks like the kind of monstering that Dickens had already applied to John Braham with Fagin. The role of

Nurse Esther requires a strong Scottish accent, and was played by Georgina Hogarth junior in the earlier family performances (she was replaced by Frances Ternan in Manchester).

Legal separations were not unusual in the Dickens family. His uncle John Henry Barrow had separated from his wife to live with Lucina Fidelia Arabella Pocock, who became mother to his ten children. Dickens's brother Fred was unhappily married and would also separate from his wife in 1858. Dickens's youngest brother, Augustus, simply moved to America with his mistress, abandoning his wife rather than seeking a separation. Dickens also had the example of his grandfather, who had lived with Mrs Roylance while on the run. The Dickens family was not predisposed to regard marriage as eternal. However, Dickens wanted to be seen as a model father, with or without a wife. He tried to make people believe that Catherine was unhinged, and he fought for the children to remain with him.

The separation broke his family. Kate recalled her father as acting like a mad man. He also destroyed his most important business relations. Dickens wanted the public to believe that his separation was amicable, and any rumours of the involvement of others was a slander. To this end, he produced a 'Personal Statement' – in effect, a press release – that he wanted other magazines to publish. The publishing house behind *Household Words* also owned *Punch*, which was edited by Dickens's friend Mark Lemon, a member of the celebrity company of actors that had performed *The Frozen Deep*. When Lemon refused to print the statement, Dickens ended their friendship and forced the closure of *Household Words*.

Dickens was flailing, yet he kept raising the stakes. It was an act of extraordinary self-righteousness. What did he believe he was doing? Perhaps the best analogy is Woody Allen. Though

Allen's star has dimmed in recent years, he enjoyed respect and even adulation for almost thirty years after seducing the daughter of his long-term partner, Mia Farrow. It once seemed reasonable to give Allen the benefit of the doubt, if you accepted his own account that he believed he had done nothing wrong. Yet even on this account, he had entered Farrow's home and life as her lover, the father of their shared children, an adult carer and protector, only to abruptly rewrite these terms in a spectacularly selfish act of one-sided revision. In the same way, Dickens reframed his relationship with Catherine, his own children, as well as with Frances Ternan and her daughters to suit his own desires and project a blameless sense of self.

Dickens had become a demagogue: the kind of man that had to be obeyed. The lonely child who had to look inside himself to find the moral law had emerged as a tyrant. He projected a vision of the world as frightening, filled with vulnerable women and children, and himself as the protector. Just before the Manchester run of *The Frozen Deep*, he staged a charity book reading in St Martin's Hall, a huge venue operated by another of his old theatrical collaborators, John Hullah. Now, as the fall-out from the Ternan affair grew, he returned to Hullah's hall for a reading on behalf of the Hospital for Sick Children on Great Ormond Street. This one event brought in enough money for the hospital to buy the building next door, effectively doubling its size. Dickens seemed to be saying, if everyone looks to me, I can offer care, meet your needs and provide protection. He was the apotheosis of the Victorian patriarch, the self-made arbiter of the good and the bad, the vulnerable and the powerful. He might claim that his right to command was both natural and traditional, flowing from the father's place in the natural order, since the time of Canaan. But there was nothing natural about it. He was a modern phenomenon: a ubiquitous and insistent moralist whose every opinion was amplified by the steam-driven presses, churning out columns and stories by the score, and making him impossible to escape. It was always his word, which counted for everything, against yours, which counted for nothing. Thus, he was always able to rewrite, reframe, and to believe his own judgements.

The war in India heightened Dickens's slide into demagoguery. When Dickens was born, Britain's war with France was ending and for almost forty years the country had been at peace. It was a strange peace, as life was changing so rapidly under the onslaught of industrialisation and the communications revolution. Yet militarism played little part in Dickens's world. Indeed, old war heroes like the Duke of Wellington, who only died in 1852, seemed to belong to the past, even as he was lauded by Queen Victoria as 'the greatest man this country ever produced'. It didn't seem vain to believe that a rapidly changing world might also be a world that was on the road to improvement. There was broad agreement on what constituted 'civilisation', based on a mix of ideas that felt peculiarly English: popular democracy, reformed Christianity, enlightened self-interest, empirical reasoning and convivial goodwill.

The First Sikh War of 1845–6 was a harbinger of change. Dickens had a direct connection, having sent John Henry Barrow to the Punjab as a war correspondent during his short interlude as editor of a national newspaper, the *Daily News*. Barrow wrote accounts of the battles of Mudki and Ferozeshah, which had taken place before he reached India, and the defeat of the Sikhs at Aliwal. The Crimean War seven years later registered much more deeply – literally changing the face of Britain, as beards were universally adopted by the male population. Dickens grew a beard for his part in *The Frozen Deep* and he never got rid of it. The Dickens that is familiar to us from the photographic portraits and statues is a late invention, Dickens in his imperial blaze as he revived *The Frozen Deep* to whip up patriotic English resolve in the face of the Indian rebellion. Oddly, the character Dickens plays owes a great deal to Mary Shelley's monster who lures Frankenstein onto the ice floes to ensure a harsher and lonelier death. Dickens is the bitter loser in a love triangle, redeemed by his human feeling, yet his capacity for monstrous and otherworldly violence is part of the role. This violence gives the wild speech he delivers at his death its dramatic power. He is more than a man, he is also a divine angel of vengeance.

In the summer of '57, he wrote to Burdett-Coutts on the justice in exterminating the rebels. It would be vengeance, a demonstration of power, and a warning against future treachery:

> I wish I were Commander in Chief of India. The first thing I would do to strike that Oriental race with amazement (not in the least regarding them as if they lived in the Strand, London, or at Camden Town), should be to proclaim to them in their language, that I considered my Holding that appointment by the leave of God, to mean that I should do my utmost to exterminate the Race upon whom the stain of the late cruelties rested; and that I begged them to do me the favour to observe that I was there for that purpose and no other, and was now proceeding, which all convenient dispatch and merciful swiftness of execution, to blot it out of mankind and raze it off the face of the earth.

There is one kind of behaviour appropriate to Camden or the Strand, another to the world of savages, where God's infinite vengeance holds sway. Dickens imagined himself as its sword.

Dickens's faith in genocide as an effective policing strategy was echoed by the Reverend Robert Blincoe, who delivered a sermon full of fire and vengeance, calling for the destruction of the mutineers, just as Dickens was doing privately. His sermon was reported in *The Times* in the first week of October 1857: 'May God grant strength to the sword arm of our troops and iron nerves to withstand the onslaught of infuriated idolaters, to execute, not vengeance, for it is His, but that recompense for their error which is meet.' In these words, he backed the most extreme imperialist programme. Its measures included bringing the entirety of the Indian forces under a unified British command, and the conversion of India by force.

St Luke's was more than a church, it was a social and educational hub. The Reverend Robert's evening sermons were an important part of this outreach, reflecting on political events through the prism of faith. According to *The Times*, his sermon began by describing the causes of the revolt, 'and the efforts to Christianise the idolatrous nations of India'. His congregation rarely numbered less than two thousand, at a time when evangelical churches were growing ever bigger. During his time as curate at St Luke's, the Baptists opened the Metropolitan Tabernacle with space for five thousand worshippers. These new megachurches were a vivid warning to the Church of England. The urban working class felt sidelined or abandoned by the English establishment, and the Reverend Robert's strongly worded sermon appealed both to them and to readers of *The Times*.

The Church of England had always defined itself against the Irish and Catholics. In the age of Empire, it found many more religions and ethnicities to denigrate. The 'National Church' had been supercharged by empire, but preachers were also using ideas of ethnic superiority to appeal to the urban working class, or at least that part that saw itself as different from Irish Catholics and non-white communities. A contemporary work by the radical writer John C. Cobden, entitled *White Slaves of England* (1854), went further than Carlile or Brown in seeing the condition of white workers in England as worse than that of African slaves. The reason being that civilised white workers now had to pay the compensation owed for freeing the barbaric plantation slaves: 'The British government emancipated the negro slaves held under its authority in the West Indies, thereby greatly depreciating the value of the islands, permitting a half-tamed race to fall back into a state of moral and mental darkness, and adding twenty millions to the national debt, to be paid out of the sweat and blood of her own white serfs.'

There is a direct connection between Cobden's work and Fanny Trollope's *Michael Armstrong*. The print on the title page of Cobden's book is pirated from Hervieu's illustration of the shop floor of a cotton mill. The plates are identical, except that Cobden's book substitutes the picture of Michael in rags for a more dynamic picture of an overlooker striking a man with a whip. If the Reverend Robert had seen the book, he may have recognised the picture, because of the direct connection to his father's story. Perhaps it seems unlikely that an evangelical Christian would read a book like John C. Cobden's; nevertheless their politics converged in the idea that the industrial poor were also part of a global elite insofar as they were white and English. The populist view of the English working class was born almost as soon as the class was recognised, and was instrumental in building the idea of a global, imperial Anglosphere.

St Luke's is one of Hawksmoor's most impressive churches. The high white spire rises like an Egyptian obelisk, seeming to hint at occult rites in the temple below. Through the door, you enter a sombre foyer, before a second door opens to reveal a bright hall, the impact all the greater for the narrow entrance. Like St George's, Wolverhampton, it has been deconsecrated, and is now a concert hall for the London Symphony Orchestra. The church was derelict for forty years, and the interior was so badly damaged that it had to be gutted and reconstructed using scaffolding-like structures. The towering wooden pulpit of Robert's day is reflected in two steel spiral staircases that take you up to the new gantry-like balconies. Replacing stone and wood with steel makes the interior feel huge. I once saw a spectacular performance of Julius Eastman's *Three Extended Pieces for Four Pianos* here. The church is so wide that the pianos fitted comfortably together, four concert grands with their sharp bits nestling like pieces of a chocolate orange. Eastman is the great composer of the post-war twentieth century, his pieces as visceral and emotional as the Shangri-Las and as searingly minimal as Steve Reich, with an added take-no-shit political verve, delivered in the most naked and forceful ways.

Eastman was homeless when he died in 1990. How was it so easy for a brilliant queer black composer to be ejected from his home by the NYPD and die starving and sick on the streets? This was a gender-fluid composer, experimenting with pronouns, performing in female costumes, and composing the eternal piano pieces *Evil N-word*, *Gay Guerilla* and *Crazy N-word*. It's not simply that Eastman would be failed or forgotten, and we would lose someone so brilliant. He would be blamed. A modern-day Dickens or Reverend Robert writing for Substack could so easily retell Eastman's story as a version of Fagin's last night: his death the natural fate of a mad, bad outsider.

Up until December 1857, Dickens had only supported the

extermination of the Indian rebels in private. He waited for his annual Christmas story to make his views public. It was a pirate story, influenced by Charles Kingsley's 1855 novel, *Westward Ho!*, one of the first books to popularise the genre. In Kingsley's story, the English navy are fighting a coalition of Spanish Catholics, escaped slaves and people of mixed race. Dickens's story is entitled 'The Perils of Certain English Prisoners', and here, too, the pirates are a veritable Babel of races: 'There were Malays among them, Dutch, Maltese, Greeks, Sambos, Negroes, and Convict Englishmen from the West India Islands; among the last, him with the one eye and the patch across the nose. There were some Portuguese, too, and a few Spaniards.'

The narrator is another foundling child, Gill Davis. The story takes place off the Caribbean coast, a location that recalls the 1813 disappearance of the gunship commanded by his aunt's first husband, Lieutenant Allen. In Dickens's story, the gunship is on a secret mission to exterminate a band of pirates. The local governor, named Pordage, is opposed to the aims and the secrecy. He urges the ship's commander, Captain Carton, to adopt a 'civilised' response to the pirates:

> 'Captain Carton, I give you notice. Government requires you to treat the enemy with great delicacy, consideration, clemency, and forbearance.'
>
> 'Sir,' says Captain Carton, 'I am an English officer, commanding English Men, and I hope I am not likely to disappoint the Government's just expectations. But, I presume you know that these villains under their black flag have despoiled our countrymen of their property, burnt their homes, barbarously murdered them and their little children, and worse than murdered their wives and daughters?'

'Perhaps I do, Captain Carton,' answers Pordage, waving his hand, with dignity; 'perhaps I do not. It is not customary, sir, for Government to commit itself.'

'It matters very little, Mr. Pordage, whether or no. Believing that I hold my commission by the allowance of God, and not that I have received it direct from the Devil, I shall certainly use it, with all avoidance of unnecessary suffering and with all merciful swiftness of execution, to exterminate these people from the face of the earth. Let me recommend you to go home, sir, and to keep out of the night-air.'

As in the Indian Mutiny – as in Gaza – claims of rape and the murder of children furnish the prospectus for a war of extermination. Carton, the instrument of the Lord, dismisses the effete Pordage. If we ever wonder who is right and wrong in a contest between restraint and genocidal violence, we learn in the final paragraph that Carton has saved the narrator from poverty and loneliness by bringing him to live with him and his wife. As in *Oliver Twist*, the story ends with the creation of a new family unit in an English country idyll. It is a vision of England for the elect alone. Failed Englishmen like Pordage are dead.

Gill Davis explains he has no name, only a nickname. He was never baptised because a sacred promise was not kept. His account is so close to the one given by Robert Blincoe that Dickens seems to be recycling the *Memoir*, one last time:

> I was a foundling child, picked up somewhere or another, and I always understood my Christian-name to be Gill. It is true that I was called Gills when employed at Snorridge Bottom betwixt Chatham and Maidstone to frighten birds; but that had nothing to do with the Baptism wherein I was made, &c.,

and wherein a number of things were promised for me by somebody, who let me alone ever afterwards as to performing any of them, and who, I consider, must have been the Beadle. Such name of Gills was entirely owing to my cheeks, or gills, which at that time of my life were of a raspy description.

Gill narrates the story of how a spy – a mixed-race traitor described as a 'Sambo' – sent Carton on a wild chase, which allowed the pirates to attack Gill's settlement and take everyone captive. Gill is one of the heroes of the hour. However, despite his bravery, he disavows England, to the surprise of another captive, a young Englishwoman. When he says that England is nothing to him but a name, she replies: 'No, good friend; you must not say that England is nothing to you. It is to be much to you, yet – everything to you. You have to take back to England the good name you have earned here, and the gratitude and attachment and respect you have won here.'

This might be Rudyard Kipling speaking. Englishness is not a nationality but a destiny that one earns by picking up its burden. Charles Dickens's version of a community of faith makes no claim to be universal. England will be home to 'the elect', alone. Those who mistakenly believe it is their home must be disabused – kicked into exile or killed. Dickens articulates what is subtextual in the Reverend Robert Blincoe's sermon: not everyone is welcome.

The man writing this story is the Dickens we all imagine, with his beard and his books, as he's portrayed in the sculpture in Portsmouth. This mature figure, the ageing writer, was only a short sliver of his life, because he died relatively young. I have outlived him in the process of writing this book. For much of his writing life, he had been the young marvel, the Inimitable, small, feminine-looking, lively and hyper-social, high-maintenance, mercurial and thin-skinned. His early novels reflect the fears and neuroses of a young writer making it on his own, with few resources but his energy. In his novels, the women and children suffer most, whether from gambling addicts like Nell's grandfather, sex addicts like Quilp, or murderers like Sikes. By focusing on the fragility of family life in a fast-changing and topsy-turvy world, Dickens made his own youthful fears feel universal. Like many men, he derived much of his sense of his own goodness from his chivalry, the way that he treated women. True, he seems to have actively disliked his mother and was rude or spiteful about almost all the accomplished women writers who crossed his path, but he was alert to the plight of the vulnerable and the helpless. When he heard the false reports of rape in India, he reacted by trying to drum up a genocide. Perhaps he would always have acted like this, the racism was so hard-wired in him. But the Indian Rebellion came at a tempestuous time in his life. He was no longer a young man living off the fears carried over from his childhood and his hopes for his own family. He had become the ageing destroyer of his own family. The man who had painted monsters like Quilp was now the subject of rumours about his sex life, and whispered to be a monster, too. The very least we can say of Dickens's moral sense is that he knew what a hypocrite is — if he was enraged by the gossips it was because the gossip came close to the truth. From his affair with Ternan onwards, Dickens's stories and novels are filled with people who are not as they appear: Carton in *A Tale of Two Cities* (whose namesake had appeared in the Christmas story), Wardour in *The Frozen Deep*, Jasper in *Edwin Drood*, Magwitch in *Great Expectations*.

In 1857, after five years at Old Street, the Reverend Robert Blincoe was a celebrated preacher and hoping for a great career in the church. His sermon on the Indian Rebellion may have been the high point of his career in London. He was thirty-one years old, newly engaged to a young woman and expecting preferment. He began to apply for new posts, as the chaplain at Dulwich College, and as the rector of St George's Tufnell Park. This required him to collect testimonials from more senior priests. In later life, he pasted these references into a scrapbook, which has been passed down through my uncle's family. They mention his 'superior talents as a preacher', his 'zeal and devotedness'. There are 'few more calculated to spread the Gospel than yourself', he has 'a highly cultivated mind', 'ministerial talent and efficiency'. He also collected newspaper cuttings, full reprints of some of his sermons in the local papers, and notices in larger circulation papers like *The Times* and the *Illustrated London News*. The scrapbook also reflects his view that the church needs reforming. This was a time when the landed aristocracy still held the power to decide who would be the rector of a parish church, and so who would get a 'living', an annual salary that was sufficient to raise a family. The rectorships were bought, sold and dispensed through family connections that could easily exclude curates without connections, from the lower classes. Robert felt the system punished able and popular preachers who could communicate with the urban working classes. He held a particular dislike for the Bishop of London, Archibald Tait, later the Archbishop of Canterbury. Tait was not evangelical, and in one of Robert's testimonials had written that he was 'unable to meet his views' but said 'I know that you have worked acceptably and faithfully', which is damning praise. Robert believed Tait had damaged the church through his failure to reform. When Tait died, Robert stuck his obituary in the scrapbook with a handwritten note: 'He was a wretched time server of no ability himself he hated it in others. He broke many a poor curate's heart.'

Robert's hopes began to recede as he failed to find his own parish, which would allow him to marry. His feeling that his life was souring coincides with his mother's death at the age of seventy-five. He was close to Martha: a newspaper article preserved in the scrapbook tells how he honed his preaching skills in front of her as a child of four. I wonder how much he knew about the life of his parents before he was born. When his mother died in 1859, she and Robert were retired and living with their middle child, also Martha, in comfort in Macclesfield. Martha junior had married a mill owner's son named George Parker, when she was sixteen and he was twenty-one. The Parkers were spinners of waste cotton, and so she might have met her husband as a business associate of her father. An oil painting of Martha, George and their children is reproduced in the 1985 autobiography of George B. Harrison, Martha Parker's grandson, a leading Shakespeare scholar who for many years was the editor of the Penguin editions of the plays. Harrison's autobiography also mentions Robert Blincoe's workhouse story. It is significant that Martha's descendants knew about Robert Blincoe's childhood, because my side of the family, descended from the Reverend Robert, knew nothing. It was only when my father was studying at Manchester University, in the heyday of social history, that another student asked if he was related to the workhouse boy. My father said that he doubted it, but looked at the book anyway, and realised the connection to the vicar whose portrait hung in the alcove above his mother's cutlery canteen. My family, like my cousin Oli Burslem's family, have learned of the connection between our ancestor and Dickens thanks to social historians, not family lore. The Reverend Robert styled himself as a preacher of the people, running evening lectures and even night schools for young men, but it seems that he was ashamed of his own father.

Martha Blincoe was buried in Pott Shrigley, just outside Macclesfield. Robert Blincoe died within the year, aged around sixty-eight, and followed her into the same grave. His wife had been an equal partner with him, she with a grocers' store and he with a cotton waste business. She kept the family together when he was imprisoned. Above all, she stuck her neck out when she decided that she did want to marry Robert in the first place. Robert married Martha without any idea what family life might be. She taught him. Is there something especially moving in the swift death of someone once their love has gone? I think Robert was lost without Martha.

The death of his parents provided the Reverend Robert with the money to purchase a living. He paid £3,000 for one in Swettenham, Cheshire, not far from his sister in Macclesfield. Livings must be sold while the rector is alive, and unfortunately the rector of Swettenham lived for another ten years. However, Robert did marry his girlfriend Charlotte – Charlie – after a seven-year engagement in 1864, soon after the death of her widower father. Charlie could not run her father's pub alone, and so she signed the licence for the Ivey House to the next landlord and moved on. The scrapbook contains her marriage certificate. The Reverend Robert Blincoe's address on Bunhill Row is clear, but I struggle to make out Charlie's new address. There is a moment of disquiet as I recognise the words, Brunswick Place. This is the same street where Janet and I live. Our new house is only yards away from Charlie's lodgings.

I only saw the marriage certificate four months after we moved to Brunswick Place, after I borrowed the scrapbook from my cousin. The Reverend Robert had the bad luck to enter the church at a time when the traditionalists were in the ascendant. His career stalled, and his scrapbook doesn't do much to hide his bitterness. I don't know whether he felt he had stood up for himself, like his father, or been defeated. The testimonials from his parishioners are all positive, and in his scrapbook, there are three preserved drawings. I appreciate a man who can draw. One is of his dog, a retriever (he also preserved his dog licence). Another is of Swettenham Church before he led the drive to restore it. The third is of an Arctic explorer, the astronaut of his day. The explorer is dressed like an Inuit, in sealskin clothes with his rawhide lattice snowshoes leaning on his rifle.

In *Strange Case of Dr Jekyll and Mr Hyde*, the hard-working doctor is also a murderous psychopath and it is this shadow side that is the destructive protagonist of the story. To say someone has two sides is to suggest that the power and the agency lie with the darker side. Dickens understood this, and his late career anti-heroes bring his last stories to their close through destruction and chaos. In real life, it's not like that. Ageing, disappointed men might write of being racked by powerful forces as their worse and better angels fight for moral supremacy but it is a grandiose fantasy. In truth, they rage out of fear and impotence. Rather than indulging these fantasies of moral duality and dark desire, a better image are the 'whited sepulchres' of the Gospels: tombs that glow white on the outside, but are dead and hollow on the inside – there's nothing there but empty and narcissistic nihilism.

The wrath that the Reverend Robert Blincoe poured out from the pulpit, or that Dickens expressed in a Christmas story (of all the blessed places), had real destructive consequences, but there are enough clues to believe their real target was their own failures and disappointment. Reading these jeremiads now, they stand as warnings for my own writing. A writer's trauma and egoism may power great stories, but keep flogging it and you risk hollowing it out and becoming an empty parody of yourself. Rather than focus on one's own trauma, better to reach out and try to understand someone else's pain. Anger can never renew itself. Only hope stays fresh: the hope we will understand each other.

13

UP THE ORPHANS! 1870

In July 2022, the poet Lemn Sissay organised a group photograph of all his friends who had been adopted or spent time in the care system. The picture was published in the *Observer* newspaper, showing fifty-nine people arranged over the broad steps of Coram's Fields Foundling Hospital. I came across the photo as we were moving and reread the piece. Janet is quoted: 'If we spent long enough with each other, we'd probably all start crying. Fortunately, we're all busy people, so we have to rush off.'

Soon after the picture was taken, one of the participants started a film about his search for his birth parents. The film was still unfinished when we saw a preview one evening in October 2024, at Coram's Fields. The audience was largely made up of people who had also been adopted. Lemn was there, the first time Janet had seen him since the day of the photograph. He asked her what she thought of the experience.

She said, 'It was a lovely moment, but I think we all came away traumatised.'

Lemn pulled a guilty look but nodded.

On our walk home, Janet said that everyone who's been adopted feels they lack an identity. I listened, but she might as well have said that cherries taste of vanilla. Her experience is so radically different to mine, I couldn't leap over the gap and see the world as she sees it. If I want to understand her, I can only listen, without being sure that what I heard is what she meant. The photograph of that day contains so many people that the figures are too small to recognise, but there's a key code of each tiny silhouette with a number and the person's names. These include Sophie Willan, Ronnie Archer-Morgan, Stewart Lee, Kriss Akabusi, Jeanette Winterson and Bruce Oldfield. Are they all traumatised?

Robert Blincoe breaks down when he tells John Brown that he wants to do the right thing and honour his parents. He can't, because he doesn't know who they are. He has no idea what family life even means. He feels like a moral outcast because he can't follow something as basic and simple as the Fifth Commandment. No one ever has this problem in a story by Charles Dickens. His heroes have been let down by their parents, but they retain a strong enough sense of family life to improvise or invent their own version and find happiness. His foundlings reflect the fragility of the human experience, but at the end of their stories, the world is healed. It's a false story because Dickens can't imagine the real trauma – a break that can't be repaired.

Even the greatest novelist only picks out a circle on a stage, leaving everything else out of the spotlight. I could tell myself that if I read enough books, by enough different authors, I would grasp the vast tapestry of human experience. In fact, I would simply increase the number of apparent cracks, the spaces between each separate account. The world captured by novelists is made of anxiety, a landscape of unrequited loves, paranoia, jealousy and fear. It's a world that is never healed; we see an endless number of reflections in an infinity of cracked looking glasses.

The year I published my first novel, Jeanette Winterson wrote about collecting books. The piece stayed with me because she described her book dealer, and I realised I knew him; he was my professor at university. She wrote, 'Book collecting is an obsession, an occupation, a disease, an addiction, a fascination, an absurdity, a fate.' It's a classic neurosis. We keep buying books, chasing completeness, a three-hundred-and-sixty-degree picture of creation. And we fail. Rather than total enlightenment, we exponentially increase the sense that all there is, are cracks. But as we are humans, our limited perspective is all we have. Leonard Cohen again: 'There is a crack in everything. That's how the light gets in.'

Keep buying the books. No matter that you are buying them out of a kind of crazy delusion, keep doing it because that's how the light gets in. There are no lone writers any more than there are private languages: every word we use has been used before. To someone who has struggled to be understood, writing is everything. I write because it gives me the ability to master a topic and make it as lucid or dramatic as I wish. Or else complicate it by adding layers of subtext, irony and double meanings, until you have no fucking idea what I am talking about. At my university interview, the man who would later make a fortune from Jeanette Winterson's neuroses asked what I wanted to do. I told him I wanted to write. Despite my poor A level results, he gave me a place.

This is something that Janet often says. 'Books saved me.'

*

No matter how much one claws at the loose edges of Dickens's books and sees his failures, he is a wonderful writer. Perhaps the best metaphor for the world Dickens creates is Miss Havisham's room, a broken palace of embittered memories, yet somehow irresistible. His novels keep circling loneliness, and it must have been his greatest fear because he ensured he was rarely alone. He was proud to be part of a community of writers. He spent all his time with other writers and performers (whether they were as pleased to be bossed around by him is another matter). Above all, he wrote for an audience. When the audience got too big to imagine, he started his mammoth reading tours, going out on the road to maintain that necessary connection. In other circumstances, he might have been an actor, and he never seems certain that he made the right choice. In 1868, he signed a contract with the music publishers Chappell & Co. for a hundred public readings. Chappell & Co. was a familiar name. It had begun life as a piano manufacturer and publisher, and could trace its lineage back through Muzio Clementi's firm, to Longman & Broderip and hence to the pianos that Dickens's own grandfather had once made. Dickens's deal with them would make him £8,000. He had just completed a blockbuster tour of America, and now wanted to connect with his British readers. Touring also suited his secret life. He was responsible for the upkeep of four homes: a London rental by Hyde Park, Gad's Hill in Kent, his ex-wife's place, and a home for the Ternans in Peckham, on the train line to Rochester. If he was always on the road, no one could ever be certain where he was, which allowed him to spend time with Ellen and her mother.

The Chappell tour began on 6 October in the two-thousand-capacity central London venue, St James's Hall, owned by Chappell & Co. These were performances rather than readings.

His act lasted two hours and revolved around a series of set pieces, drawn from his novels but substantially rewritten to work on stage. He lined the upper room of his flatpack Swiss chalet with mirrors to help with his rehearsals. The programme was largely drawn from his earliest works. There was *A Christmas Carol* and two comic extracts from *The Pickwick Papers*, including the scene where Pickwick's Goswell Street landlady believes Pickwick has proposed marriage. The most sensational piece was premiered at St James's Hall on 14 November to a private audience: it was the murder of Nancy from *Oliver Twist*. The performance became the highlight of his show, the thing everyone clamoured to see. However, it was so arduous that Dickens could not manage it every night. He would tell a friend, 'My ordinary pulse is 72, and it runs up under this effort to 112. Besides which it takes me ten or twelve minutes to get my wind back at all: I being in the meantime like the man who has lost the fight.' The halls were so large, and the tickets so cheap, at just a shilling, that fans would attend on multiple nights to catch his enactment of her murder.

Accounts of the performance describe him throwing himself about the stage, physically transformed as the dialogue switches between Sikes and Fagin, and then between the killer and victim. With each line, Dickens is swaggering and whimpering, until he's finally swinging from a rope, hanged by his neck. It was a performance built upon a kind of horrified sympathy for the devil, Bill Sikes. It is extraordinary that of all his work, he chose this piece, but you don't get to be Dickens without having a sense of your public. When he wrote *Oliver Twist*, he denied that he had written a lowly Newgate novel, like his erstwhile friend Ainsworth, but now he was leaning into the genre, showing a murderer racked with guilt, running and returning like a dog running in circles. His performance was a murder ballad made flesh, a horror film where the young girl is always the victim and the sacrifice. Was he pandering to an audience that wanted shocks, or trying to make recompense to the orphan girl abandoned by his family?

He performed in Manchester in March, but stayed in Liverpool to avoid being lionised after the performance. He wasn't feeling well. Nevertheless, he returned to Liverpool in April, before continuing his tour to Blackburn and Bolton. He had completed seventy-four of his readings in just over two hundred days but was struggling with the physical demands. He relied heavily on his new stage manager, George Dolby, yet he came alive in front of an audience. The reviews in the northern newspaper give no clue he was sick, marvelling at his performance of Sikes. He moved on to the Imperial Hotel in Preston, a rest day, and he and Dolby decided to visit Blackpool. He wrote to Georgina Hogarth to tell her he was feeling better, but his description of his symptoms was not good: 'My weakness and deadness are all on the left side, and if I don't look at anything I try to touch with my left hand, I don't know where it is. I am in (secret) consultation with Frank Beard; he recognises, in the exact description I have given him, indisputable evidence of overwork, which he would wish to treat immediately.' Frank Beard was his doctor, and was already on a train to Preston. He had diagnosed a stroke, reporting that Dickens was very close to being paralysed down one side of his body. The Preston show was cancelled.

Over the subsequent year, Dickens had problems with his hands, and his friends often commented on his appearance. He was fifty-seven but looked older. His nerves were straining at his workload. He could not keep up with the tour, nor could he face the number of train journeys it demanded. He had relied on the trains to maintain his secret peripatetic relationship with Ellen Ternan, but three years earlier the couple had been caught in a terrible train crash. They were returning from Boulogne when their train derailed on a viaduct ten miles south of Maidstone. It was a major disaster with ten fatalities and forty injured. Dickens helped care for the injured, bring water to survivors, and protect Ellen and her mother. He tried to keep his identity secret, but he was recognised. Witnesses spoke of seeing him, but it was several days before the reports leaked, by which time Dickens had managed to massage the events to his liking. Since the crash he had found the bumping of the trains affected his nerves. After Beard curtailed the tour, Dickens could not face travelling any more.

He would not return to the stage for almost a year. He arranged with Chappell & Co. to do twelve final shows in St James's Hall. The performances ran weekly from January through to March, with his 'Sikes' spread across the run. The final reading of Sikes came on 8 March, the week before his last ever show on the 15th. In June, he suffered a second, massive stroke at home in Gad's Hill after dining with Georgina and died shortly afterwards.

A dusting of snow lies on the edges of the theatre awnings as we stroll beneath the lights of Shaftesbury Avenue. We are wearing evening dress. Janet has a soft cashmere coat over her pearl satin gown, the bias cut clinging to her body, and pearl pendants in her ears. I am in black tie and patent leather shoes. It's approaching Christmas and we're dressed for the theatre. A new production of *Oliver!* is opening at the Gielgud Theatre.

My grandmother not only circled *Oliver!* in the *TV Times*, she had a complete set of Dickens novels in the nook by the electric fire, where she also kept the novels of Barbara Taylor Bradford, Catherine Cookson and Howard Spring, carrying on the legacy of the first factory novels. In contrast, my father's mother, Rose Blincoe, never read at all. She ran the family paint and gas wholesalers in Rochdale, and thought everything was frippery and nonsense compared to the wonderful world of business. Reading isn't a trustworthy marker of class. Dickens's generation opened up a popular audience for the novel, so reading became something that anyone could do. Or not, in the case of Rose.

Oliver Twist is part of a wave of stories with a social conscience, designed to be consumed in monthly instalments, like the *Memoir of Robert Blincoe* of the previous decade. It's Dickens's first real novel, in part because it is 'issue-led', but also because it is less bitty than *The Pickwick Papers*. However, even if it feels more complete, it is never clear what the central story is. At one level, it's about Oliver and his evil half-brother who orchestrates the campaign to 'disappear' Oliver into the London underworld. Yet when Dickens performed readings of the novel at the end of his life, the focus was on Nancy and Sikes. The audience was gripped by the murder of a young prostitute by her older lover, a kind of brutal king of the criminals. The uncertainty over the key storyline is reflected in *Oliver!* the musical. Lionel Bart adapted Lean's 1948 *Oliver Twist*, itself a streamlined version of the story of a boy who falls among thieves and is on the verge of being corrupted when he is saved by a new, respectable family. But even this is not the story of the musical. At the heart of Bart's version are Fagin and his children. It's the reason we fall in love with the musical when we first see it – and why it can be revived in panto season. Janet and I are not really big on musicals but *Oliver!* is an exception. We have even dressed up.

The musical motors through the early scenes in the workhouse. Lean was old enough to remember the workhouses, and his 1948 film references the Nazi death camps in the spindly metalwork of the workhouse sign, and the pyjamas and shaved heads of the inmates, all still fresh horrors only three years after the liberation. Roman Polanski's 2005 version does the same. Polanski was the only member of his family to escape the camps. He spent the war alone while still a child, and lost his mother, who was killed in Auschwitz. It's part of the vision of both Lean and Polanski's films that the brutality of the workhouse was a precursor to the death camps, because they criminalised and isolated everyone the state considered undesirable. The night-vision scene in *The Zone of Interest* recalls the account of children foraging in the pig troughs in Robert's memoir and Michael Armstrong because the link feels real, not simply a metaphor.

We're all waiting for our first glimpse of Fagin.

We are in the circle of the Gielgud Theatre, looking down on a sea of families and first-time children. The excitement catches with the first big street scene, 'Consider Yourself', complete with its chorus line of costermongers and fishwives. The Artful Dodger is seventeen-year-old Billy Jenkins, who has already played the part in one of the TV spin-offs. He is good, but Fagin is the star. He is played by Simon Lipkin, rather young at thirty-eight for a Fagin who is worried that the years are catching up with him. Lipkin is Jewish, which is the only possible decision for a role originated by Ron Moody. His Fagin turned the tables on Dickens. Moody never doubted the role was antisemitic and it's only the force of his personality that flipped the switch and made Fagin a hero. Lipkin brings a forceful muscular swagger to the role, which perhaps owes something to Captain Hook in Christmas pantomimes of *Peter Pan*. Lipkin is also happy to break the fourth wall, which brings the audience over, helping us to invest in his performance as something we share a part in.

A book about a foundling child has become a musical about an unrepentant Jewish thief, who refuses to go gently into his night. This Fagin has roots in Yiddish theatre. *Oliver Twist* was translated into Yiddish at the height of the late nineteenth-century Russian pogroms. It might seem improbable that the story was immediately embraced by a Jewish audience. Yet Odessa, the centre of Yiddish literature and theatre, already had many stories of Jewish gangsters, thieves and Robin Hoods. When every character is Jewish and speaks Yiddish, Fagin's Jewishness becomes almost invisible. One of Dickens's greatest fans was the author of *Fiddler on the Roof*, Sholem Aleichem (a pseudonym, equivalent to the Arabic *as-salamu alaykum*). Aleichem even wrote his own version of Oliver Twist, *Motl Peysi, the Cantor's Son: the memoirs of an orphan boy*. The musical *Oliver!* is twice removed from Dickens's novel, first in being a remake of the Lean film, and secondly in drawing on Jewish influences from music hall, popular songs and Yiddish literature. Fagin is the heart of the musical, because he's an Everyman in a world that is essentially a reflection of him.

Where Dickens's Fagin is an Arab-Jew, the Fagin of the musical is a refugee from the Russian shtetl. However, in this production, Lipkin seems to be leaning into the colour and excitement that Georgian England saw in the Ottoman Near East, playing Fagin as a strutting peacock. As a young man, Dickens embraced the fashion for all things Oriental, wearing his hair long in oiled curls, and dressing in colourful velvet as he lounged in salons led by the Duke D'Orsay. This is where he met Ainsworth, Bulwer-Lytton... and Benjamin Disraeli. As I wrote this book, I often found myself wondering why Dickens was not friendlier with Disraeli. They exchanged some short and formal messages which never suggest they knew each other personally. Perhaps the problem was Fagin, as Disraeli recognised an attack on John Braham was an attack on all English Jews.

The song by Bill Sikes, 'My Name', catches me by surprise. Janet doesn't know it either. It was dropped from the film by Carol Reed because his Sikes, Oliver Reed, couldn't sing. Oliver was Carol's nephew, and while everyone denied the casting was nepotism, a tone-deaf man doesn't win a major role in a musical every day. Reed was not their real name. Carol was the illegitimate son of the great Victorian impresario Herbert Beerbohm Tree. His mother, Beerbohm's long-term mistress, chose the name in a high-flying piece of passive aggression. She said, 'Beside the great Tree, I am a broken Reed.' The Tree family had been timber merchants in the Russian empire, which led to rumours they were Jewish refugees. Hostile gossip was still swirling in the 1960s, as the broadcaster Malcolm Muggeridge declared that Max Beerbohm, Carol's uncle, was 'Jewish and Gay and in denial about both'. Oliver Reed feels as though he is in a different film from everyone else, yet he brings a sense of threat that has never been equalled. If I could have put into words the effect he had on me, when I first saw the film, I would have kept it secret. I had enough sense to know it would be a tricky conversation. The thrill was not very different from the effect of Sophia Loren, though more frightening because Reed looks so brutal – and leaves the world devastated in his wake. It's the idea that the Devil may have the best tunes, even if they're murder ballads. Even if Oliver Reed can't sing. In Charles Dickens's dramatic readings, the Oliver Reed role was the star turn.

But not in the musical.

'Reviewing the Situation' is the song most clearly derived from Yiddish theatre. If it appeared in *Fiddler on the Roof*, would anyone bat an eye? True, it's an ode to villainy – asking why anyone should conform to a world that humiliates and exploits him. Moody weighs the straight life against the criminal, and sings frankly that he's decided to choose crime. But crucially Fagin doesn't want to hurt anyone. He even asks Dodger to look after Oliver. He doesn't orchestrate the murder of Nancy, as the original Fagin does. This is Fagin with a good heart, sentimental, yet funny and transgressive. The audience gets the ending we want as Fagin and Dodger dance off together to commit fresh crimes – and keep alive the Fagin and Dodger cinematic universe.

Lionel Bart's musical isn't really *Oliver Twist* any more than Percival Everett's *James* is *Huckleberry Finn*. They are route maps out of the worlds of older writers who, for all their talent, can't imagine the people they write about. Yet there's undoubtedly a richness to *Oliver Twist* that allows it to be turned into so many different stories. Perhaps because Dickens found he couldn't do much with Oliver, so he had to give room to so many other characters. Oliver is so good and so innocent that he lacks almost all agency. Dickens struggles with any motivation that isn't powered by weakness, cruelty or greed. At the end of his life, only the antiheroes, running on love and hate, achieve anything.

I once worried that the angrier or disappointed sides of my character would become baked into my personality. I'd risk becoming another of those old white sepulchres. But I found Janet, so I was lucky. Dickens was unlucky. I don't say this to dismiss his books, but you can't read him without looking for the route out. As Janet and I do, in the Christmas air of London in December, where the smell of roast chestnuts and the silvery lights seem to capture a world that is quintessentially Dickens. But we know we are going home together, and we don't have the shame and the secrets that marred his too short final years.

I tell Janet, 'I'm lucky.'

Janet says, 'Up the Orphans!'

SOURCES

When I was doing the research for this book, the British Library closed its doors following a cyber-attack. I had seen myself pottering among original copies of nineteenth-century memoirs and novels, and discovering old periodicals as well as the latest research papers. The ransomware demand killed these fantasies. My alarm turned to anger as the library remained shut. There is a class of jobs in English public life – running museums, university colleges and libraries – that seem to be regarded as sinecures to mark the end of big careers. I was concerned the management team was out of its depth. I couldn't delay the book so I had to find a workaround. This is when I discovered how much work had been digitised by the giant tech companies, as well as universities, charities and foundations. The same scraping of world literature that has enabled a leap-forward in AI provided me with a way to research this book. I'm not saying that's an adequate trade-off, but only noting that something profound has shifted.

Working from home meant I saw some unusual works. I used an obscure collection to read the Kolle letters, simply because it was online, but it came with a frontispiece of Dickens's flirtatious message to Priscilla Horton – an unexpected bonus. Edmund Wilson notes that the scholarship on Dickens is so often personal. Dickens's memory is safeguarded by people who love his work, and many influential figures are essentially self-taught historians. The Dickens Fellowship runs the museum and the magazine, and it still has connections to the Dickens family. I felt like an interloper, but not a hostile intruder. The warmth and fervour of Dickens scholarship keeps the field alive as other nineteenth-century figures fade away. Dickens and Forster curated the Dickens biography to an unusual and powerful degree but the willingness of researchers to explore every corner of Dickens's life means the official story is always trembling – at times it is reduced to absurdity. Ellen Ternan was certainly Dickens's mistress, not his protégée, charity case or daughter. Exploring his secrets reveals just how long Dickens must have known the Ternans. His need to adopt a secret family means the relationship was always incestuous and abusive, yet I never felt Dickens was a monster. He is haunted. The parish orphan is always with him, not Robert but the unnamed Orfling.

This work has been shaped by the closure of the British Library. Yet the end result reflects my choices – I wanted to write about my girlfriend, my dog, my travails and my broken arm. I've chosen to make these notes low key: no numbers, nothing to direct anyone here, but offering explanations to anyone who cares to look. As my research has been almost entirely online, it can be retraced by anyone using a search engine. I used multiple versions of Dickens's works and letters, across different editions, so giving page numbers is pointless. I have given chapter headings, but it's easy to find my quotes by searching the texts on Google Books or Project Gutenberg. As to Dickens's biography, I have drawn on the timeline of events left to us by Dickens/Forster and drawn upon recent histories, especially the one by Michael Slater, which puts the official history under a microscope. That leaves a shadow field: the secret world of Dickens. What has been suppressed, and how significant are the omissions? I have supplied sources only where I have strayed away from the Slater or other histories. Similarly, I have relied on John Waller's biography of Robert Blincoe, and only supplied notes where there is original research – or where I have gone to sources other than Waller.

Introduction

His memoir was one of only seven working-class memoirs published in the 1820s: Robert told his story to the author John Brown in 1822 and the text was revised in 1824. The figure of seven autobiographies comes from the critical bibliography by John Burnett, David Vincent and David Mayall. The literary historian Cassandra Falke cites this bibliography, making the point that Robert ought to be seen as the co-author of his own story. Robert's story is also different in being overtly political where other memoirs have an evangelical thrust. I have several copies of the memoir beginning with the 1966 edition by the Derbyshire Archaeological Society, the first one I read. My favourite copy is a gift from my grandmother Rose: Brown, John. *A memoir of Robert Blincoe*. Caliban Books, 1977. See, Burnett, John; Vincent, David; and Mayall, D. *The Autobiography of the Working Class: 1790-1900*. Harvester, 1984. And, Falke, Cassandra. *Literature by the Working Class: English Autobiographies, 1820–1848*. Cambria Press, 2013.

I invented it ... Mrs Mann. We name our fondlings in alphabetical order: Dickens, Charles. *Oliver Twist*, chapter 2.

His first sketches of London appeared that December, and he adopted his pen name, Boz, a corruption of Moses, the most famous foundling in religious myth: The story given by Dickens is that he adopted a nickname he had already bestowed on his younger brother Augustus. 'Boz' is baby-talk for Moses. The name comes in turn from the character of Moses in a favourite novel, Goldsmith's *The*

Vicar of Wakefield. The fact that Dickens borrows a name from a favourite book, and then takes it on as his own shows the depth of personal meaning the name had for him, alone.

In 1836, in the run-up to the serialisation of Oliver Twist, *Dickens wrote a short autobiographical piece drawn from his Camden childhood*: Dickens, Charles. *Sketches by Boz. First of May*, chapter 20. This story also reflects Robert Blincoe's story that he wished to be a sweep, unlike Oliver, who resisted. Another sign that Dickens knew Blincoe's account.

The story of Dickens's miserable childhood: Forster, John. *The Life of Charles Dickens*. Available from Project Gutenberg, though the relevant extracts – chapters 1 & 2 – appear as an appendix in Dickens, Charles and Tambling, Jeremy. *David Copperfield*. Revised edition. Penguin Classics, 2014.

Dickens's whole career was an attempt to digest these early shocks and hardships: Wilson, Edmund. 'The Two Scrooges', p. 8, in *The Wound and the Bow*. Houghton Mifflin, 1941.

The blacking factory permanently wounded Dickens's mind: Carey, John. *The Violent Effigy: A Study of Dickens' Imagination*. Faber & Faber, 2008. pp. 148–9.

In official records, from court documents to civil registers, James is only ever known as 'George': All the bureaucratic excavation cited here is by Michael Allen. See Allen, Michael. *Charles Dickens and the Blacking Factory*. Oxford-Stockley, 2011.

always in some sense the solitary observer: Ackroyd, Peter. *Dickens, A Memoir of Middle Age*. Vintage, 2012. p. xii (Prologue).

No words can express the secret agony of my soul: Forster, chapter 2.

The Two Workhouses: 1790s/1830s

It would be a novel based on his parish, St Pancras: The letter is undated but gives the address of Bentinck Street, which became the family home in December 1833. The letter is given a date of 1834 in the collection I used, but has been credited to the previous year by others. Dickens had been staying in Norwood with his uncle regularly since Parliament ended in August 1833. Parliament didn't reconvene until February 1834, and Dickens was looking for new ideas during the six months he was not reporting from Parliament. See Smith, Harry. *The Dickens-Kolle Letters*. The Bibliophile Society, Boston, 1910. The idea that the parish novel becomes *Oliver Twist* was raised by Kathleen Tillotson – and obviously I agree. See Tillotson, Kathleen. Introduction. *Oliver Twist*. Clarendon Press, 1966. Also Tillotson, Kathleen, chapter 12, *Oliver Twist: Essays and Studies*, 1959.

one of the most, perhaps THE most, important member of the local administration: Dickens, Charles. *Sketches by Boz*, chapter 1.

The parish board acquired it in the 1770s on a short-term lease but kept it for thirty years: See https://www.workhouses.org.uk/StPancras/

In 1791, an abandoned child was found 'dropt at a Gentleman's Door in John Street, Tottenham Court Road': The report was discovered by Australian historian John Waller for the in-depth biography of *Robert Blincoe: The Real Oliver Twist*. Icon, 2005. This was an invaluable resource, and my book could be said to be standing on its shoulders. My family participated in Waller's biography, loaning him research material and providing interviews. Waller placed Blincoe in his age, making it a social history, whereas I wanted to look at questions of voice and ownership as a writer, but also the creation of a collective voice. In retrospect, I wanted to answer the question, 'Who are we?', by looking at the moment that this question begins to make sense.

The famous Foundling Hospital at Coram's Field was also in the parish of St Pancras: The hospital had an open-door policy until 1760, when admissions became much tighter. Aside from contributions, admissions were also judged on the basis of morality, which effectively disqualified foundlings as there was no way to judge their mother's morals. See, Outhwaite, R. B. '"Objects of Charity": Petitions to the London Foundling Hospital, 1768-72.' *Eighteenth-Century Studies*, vol. 32, no. 4, 1999, pp. 497–510. The vast majority of children accepted were the children of domestic servants, as the records by the nineteenth-century administrator John Brownlow show. Brownlow was presumably the source for Mr Brownlow of *Oliver Twist*. See https://www.historyhamper.com/john-brownlow/

London was fast becoming a city of children, a development propelled in part by new brick homes: see Razzell, Peter. 'The Growth of Population in Eighteenth-Century England: A Critical Reappraisal.' *The Journal of Economic History*, vol. 53, no. 4, 1993, pp. 743–71.

When the friends, relatives, parents of other [workhouse] children: Brown/Blincoe, chapter 2.

So are the coffins: Oliver Twist, chapter 4.

Boys is wery obstinit, and wery lazy: Oliver Twist, chapter 3.

When Robert Blincoe lived in the workhouse, there was a brickmakers' field almost opposite the Mother Black Cap: There is a map at https://theundergroundmap.substack.com/p/the-camden-town-of-the-year-1800. This is based on the maps of Christopher & John Greenwood: 'Map of London: made from an actual survey in the years 1824, 1825, & 1826' (1829), See also the extraordinary print by Cruikshank, 'London going out of town – or – the march of bricks and mortar!' (1829). The view is from Somers Town looking up Camden High Street towards Hampstead. In the British Museum.

The Polygon and the rest of Somers Town became home to several thousand French priests: see 'Note on French Catholics in London after 1789', compiled by Scott, Helen from W. Douglas Newton's book *Catholic London* (1950). Kelly, Debra, and Cornick, Martyn, editors. *A History of the French in London: Liberty, Equality, Opportunity*. University of London Press, 2013.

Two Families: Dickens and Barrows, 1790–1801.

the figures who influenced him most are found on the father's side of the family: Ackroyd, p. 4.

when submerged, bobs up to the surface again, none the worse for the dip: This is a great line, often quoted (Ackroyd, p. 8, for instance). I would assume the source is a letter but I have not found it. Ackroyd seems to recognise it may be dubious, as he provides a source for a similar quote: 'He is just one of the careless, good-for-nothing, happy fellows, who float, cork-like, on the surface, for the world to play at hockey with: knocked here, and there, and everywhere: now to the right, then to the left, again up in the air, and anon to the bottom, but always reappearing and bounding with the stream buoyantly and merrily along.' The Broker's Man. *Sketches by Boz*.

Maria Catherina Haeck de Jong: I am grateful to Richard Coles for identifying Lady Blandford for me. I was stumped.

It took Claire Tomalin to make the connection explicit: Tomalin, Claire. *Charles Dickens: A Life*. Penguin, 2011. p. 5.

Charles Barrow was only in his forties but had already led a colourful life: See Carlton, William. *Links with Dickens in the Isle of Man*. Reprinted in 1941 in the *Journal of the Manx Museum*. Available at http://www.isle-of-man.com/manxnotebook/jmmuseum/n75p042.htm. No one seems to have followed up Carlton's original research, which appeared exclusively in *The Dickensian*, the journal of the Dickens Society. Carlton was also a historian of shorthand, which isn't a bad qualification to research the Dickens and Barrow family.

Her family were picture-framers and gilders whose escape from the Spain of the Inquisition had taken them first to the Netherlands: See

Musgrove, Theresa. *The Dickensian*. No. 510, vol.116, 2020, part 1. It is easy enough to follow the family's history on modern genealogy sites, and I have added my own very speculative suggestion there was an elopement.

In the mid-1780s: Charles Barrow found work with a music company based in Cheapside, opposite the church of St Mary Le Bow. His story is told in: Lancaster, Geoffrey. *Culliford, Rolfe and Barrow: A Tale of Ten Pianos*. UWA Publishing, 2017. See also accounts of the competitive world of eighteenth-century piano manufacturers in Bozarth, George; Debenham, Margaret; and Cripps, David. 'Piano Wars: The Legal Machinations of London Pianoforte Makers, 1795–1806'. *Royal Musical Association Research Chronicle*, 42(1), 2009, pp. 45–108. Margaret Debenham kindly provided advice and encouragement. A quick overview of Culliford & Co. and its heirs can be found online at: https://boalch.org/instruments/makerprofile/164.

the famous Vauxhall Pleasure Gardens: See Coke, David and Borg, Alan. *Vauxhall Gardens: A History*. Paul Mellon Centre for Studies in British Art, 2011. For the general temperature of London's racy nightlife, see: Cruickshank, Dan. *The Secret History of Georgian London: How the Wages of Sin Shaped the Capital*. Windmill, 2010.

I have to show her a YouTube clip of Robert Lindsay in Me and My Girl: Lindsay played Bill Snibson in the West End and on Broadway 1985/86.

Factory Boy, 1799–1803

As Noah Claypole tells Oliver, his mother was 'a regular right down bad 'un': *Oliver Twist*, chapter 5.

There were 150 inmates in the workhouse throughout the 1780s, but the number grew rapidly over the next decade: Waller, John. Chapter 2, p.34.

parishes also began to look for ways to get rid of boys in bulk: The Virginia project was relatively short-lived but an important first step in using joint stock companies to underwrite British imperial ambitions. Apprenticeships were used both to supply workers to the colonies, as capital, and girls as wives for the colonisers. See Reiner, Martha Louise, *Women In The Records Of The Virginia Company Of London*. MA thesis, College of William & Mary, 2023. Pauper and parish apprenticeships became institutionalised and widespread in America, making unpaid labour a foundational part of the colonial project – arguably accustoming America to slavery. Doggett, Barbara Lynn, *Parish apprenticeship in colonial Virginia: A study of Northumberland County, 1680–1695 and 1750–1765*. MA thesis, College of William & Mary, 1981. The London Guilds turned their attention from Virginia to Derry – where their involvement was longer lived. The practice of sending apprentices provides the background to the semi-mythical actions of the Loyalist apprentice boys: the Siege of Derry in 1689 was retold and largely invented in 1814, with the idea that an apprentice from each of the guilds shut the city's gates – a founding myth. The Royal Navy was hungry for recruits, especially in war time. The merchant Jonas Hanway created the Marine Society Charity in 1756, initially to supply children for the navy during the Seven Years' War, recruited thousands of children for the navy – 4,000 between 1770 and 1780 alone. At least half came from London. See. Payne, Dianne. *Children of the poor in London, 1700–1780*. PhD thesis, University of Hertfordshire, 2008. Also, Taylor, James Stephen. *Jonas Hanway, Founder of the Marine Society: Charity and Policy in Eighteenth-Century England*. Scolar Press, 1985, chapter 8.

Between the 1790s and the 1820s, workhouses across London looked to the industrial cities of the north to unload their children: Throughout this book, I am reading Blincoe's memoir in conjunction with Waller's biography. Where I have taken other sources, I will mention them in these notes. But as a broader look at the issue, I would recommend, Honeyman, Katrina. *Child Workers in England,*

1780–1820: Parish Apprentices and the Making of the Early Industrial Labour Force. Aldershot, 2007. Honeyman looks at the organising networks and methods of resistance used by the apprentices, which is a particular interest of this book, as I am claiming that the voice of Robert Blincoe is already a kind of collective voice, in that his stories are shared and circulated – which is how John Brown heard of him.

A variation for the piano was published by Culliford & Co., and distributed by Charles Barrow through his circulating library: See the Petrucci Music Library, IMSLP. The website is https://imslp.org/wiki/File:PMLP1236401-haigh_g.443.b.-23.-_roast_beef_of_old_england_rondo.pdf.

On the train to Nottingham, I had read the novel James *by Percival Everett*: Everett, Percival. *James: A Novel*. Pan Macmillan UK, 2024. For the original slave memoir: Smith, Venture, *A Narrative of the Life and Adventures of Venture, a Native of Africa, But Resident of USA: A Journey from Africa to Freedom: A Gripping Slave Narrative*. Project Gutenberg.

Portsmouth: 1805–14

Claire Tomalin speculates that, 'as daughters often do', Elizabeth Barrow was drawn to the echoes of her father: Tomalin, p. 7.

He was good-looking, but he was also physically imposing: See Phiz's picture that accompanies the text of chapter 36. Micawber is clearly a big man, in Dickens's description in the same chapter: 'Mr Micawber walked so erect before his fellow man ... that his chest looked half as broad again', i.e. he was broad to start off with.

might drive me into gaol, strip my family of what little furniture, clothes or other resources they may possess: Alexander, Doris. 'In Defence of John Dickens'. *Dickens Quarterly*, vol. 9, no. 1, 1992, pp. 3–7.

He had his own problems as a director of the Bristol Dock Company: The company was set up by the Society of Merchant Venturers in 1807 but immediately ran into problems. Barrow was a senior officer of the society from 1808 to the 1820s (followed by his son Robert Gay Barrow from the 1830s to the 1860s). The cost of building a floating harbour in 1807 was 'grossly underestimated', but was recapitalised and completed in 1809. Latimer, John. *The History of the Society of Merchant Venturers of the city of Bristol*. Arrowsmith, 1904. p. 252.

Madgwick has been described as 'one of the most localised names in the country': Pointon, Tony. 'Madgwick or Magwitch?' *The Dickensian*. Vol. 99, Issue 460, 2003. Also see: https://www.portsmouth.co.uk/news/crime/portsmouth-councillor-little-scroats-who-brazenly-stole-ps500-worth-of-vapes-should-be-willing-to-take-a-beating-4477683

Aunt Fanny's new husband was lost with his ship off the coast of Brazil in 1813: There seems some confusion over where the ship was lost. Though last seen off the coast of Brazil, the Naval loss lists says it was lost off Nova Scotia between October and December 1813.

The news that he had been hiding out in Brighton with Elizabeth Roylance only emerged in 1872: The Roylance granddaughter got her husband, a Mr Wood, to write the letter shortly after Forster published his biography in 1872. Alexander, Doris, pp. 3–7.

It was not then widely known that Charles Barrow had been a fugitive: Not until Kate Dickens (Perugini) told Gladys Storey, and the story was published in the 1930s. Storey, Gladys. *Dickens and Daughter*. Haskell House Publishers, 1971. P. 37.

Speaking of memory one day, [Dickens] said the memory of children was prodigious: Fields, James T. *Yesterdays With Authors*. Bod Third Party Titles, 2020. P. 233.

It seems more likely that Fanny is amazed at the two-year-old Dickens's recollection of Roylance's Brighton home: The relevant section is Dickens, Charles. *Dombey and Son*. 1848, chapter 8.

'I hope you will like Mrs Pipchin's establishment. It is from the life and I was there – I don't suppose I was eight years': Letter, 4 November 1846.

An essay by Robert L. Patten from 2012, written in the light of the doubts over Forster's account: Patten, Robert L. 'Whitewashing the Blacking Factory'. *Dickens Studies Annual*, vol. 46, 2015.

The archive editor of The Times *found a story of a black criminal, Henry Murphy*: *The Times*, 3 December 2011.

He may also have read the 1836 book, London and The Londoners: This connection was presented by the researcher Eva-Charlotta Mebius in *The Dickensian*, though I read about her research in the *Guardian*, 22 December 2019. I can't find the passage she cites in the book, but it is a stodgy, unreadable work. Mudie, Robert. *London and Londoners: Or, a Second Judgment of Babylon the Great*. HardPress, 2012.

Fagin I fear admits of only one interpretation: Davis wrote in 1863, and Dickens replied in a letter dated 10 July 1863.

He is both feminine and masculine, both cooing mother and proud father: Something I haven't written about in the body of the work is the idea that Fagin might be a paedophile, a groomer and pimp. There is certainly an idea he has groomed Nancy, who was once one of his children. Did he simply introduce her to crime, or did he also pimp her out for sex work? One cannot say, but the hint is there – it is supposed to be a possibility in the text. Is Fagin also a homosexual paedophile? He is an Arab-Jew, cooking Arabic coffee and what I assume are merguez-style lamb sausages, which is all quite specific and suggests that Dickens had a model in mind, a particular kind of Jewish figure or stereotype. The use of 'feminine' language ('my dear') is not feminine in the original, but simply translations from

Arabic – although Arabic customs were seen as soft and effeminate in Britain as Christianity was promoted as masculine and muscular – an idea coined by Charles Kingsley (see also, Edward Said, *Orientalism* [Pantheon, 1978]). The argument that Fagin is homosexual has leant on the Yiddish word 'feygele', which means little bird/gay man. I would raise several issues. Firstly, did Dickens know enough Yiddish to make the connection? If he did, why name him Fagin and give a source (Bob Fagin)? Fagin can be a Jewish name, a corruption of 'Afghan', meaning someone with Persian/Farsi/Indian roots. If he meant Fagin to be read as Feygele, why not just call him Feygele, Feigel, or similar? It's also worth pointing out that an Arab-Jew would not have spoken Yiddish. Finally, did feygele mean homosexual in the early nineteenth century? Most experts seem to think it had not yet acquired the modern derogatory meaning. I don't think Dickens has planted hints that Fagin is fucking his boys. The fact that he is offering an extremely offensive caricature suggests that he would have dropped these hints, if he had wanted to.

The High Peak: 1804–14

In November 1803, the children of Lowdham Mill were loaded once more onto covered wagons: Brown/Blincoe, chapter 4.

In Fanny Trollope's novel The Life and Adventures of Michael Armstrong, *Ellis Needham has become Elgood Sharpton*: The panegyric to Sharpton starts on p. 119 in Trollope, Frances. *The Life and Adventures of Michael Armstrong, The Factory Boy*. Henry Colburn, 1840. I started off using a first edition but I hated reading it and ended up using the version on Project Gutenberg.

the Jonathan Glazer film The Zone of Interest: Based on Martin Amis's novel, of course. The film is faithful to Amis's devastating idea, that the eyes of the protagonists are turned away from the horror. The idea that there are uses and abuses of the Holocaust has become a political issue. We talk about 'Never Again' but often at cross-purposes: to some, it means there should be no more genocides, while to others it means only that there will never be another Jewish Holocaust. These aren't mutually exclusive but Glazer's Oscars speech, citing the dehumanisation that has led to the horror of Gaza, resulted in a letter of condemnation signed by 1,200 Jewish film professionals. Amis wrote two Holocaust novels: *Time's Arrow* (1991) and *Zone of Interest* (2014). He clearly felt this was a subject he ought to tackle, yet both times produced a work that I feel fails. What can one say about the Holocaust? The Holocaust must be compared to other atrocities, not to relativise it (whatever that is supposed to mean) but to locate it within a historical continuum. The transatlantic slave trade was a holocaust. The British, American, South African and Australian colonial projects were not accidentally or inadvertently genocidal, they were genocidal at their core. But if these racial projects were genocidal, what about the workhouse, and the spin-off pauper and parish apprenticeships? You can see that, even if these institutions are different from racialised genocides, much of the relevant machinery is there. The death camps were built as slave labour camps; the industrial murder of Europe's Jews was made palatable in increments because we'd already accepted the idea of reducing our Jewish neighbours to slaves. Both David Lean and Roman Polanski make the comparison between the workhouses and the death camps explicit in their versions of *Oliver Twist*. Perhaps Lean was motivated by a visual analogy having seen the pictures coming out of Europe. But Polanski was actually there: he is a survivor.

The reference throws into relief the story of a girl named Phebe Rag: This story and the later one about Blackey are both in Brown/Blincoe, chapter 5.

In 1828, shortly after the first publication of the Memoir, *a trade union organiser named John Joseph Betts wrote to the* Lion: Appended to the Doherty edition and all subsequent editions.

As an adult in the 1830s, a quarter of a century later, Robert gave evidence to a parliamentary committee: The 1833 Royal Commission. Blincoe's evidence is appended to the Caliban edition (1977), and to the edition that appears in the anthology, Simmons, James R., Carlisle, Janice. *Factory Lives, Four Nineteenth-Century Working-Class Autobiographies*. Broadview, 2007.

Dickens Loses Three Friends, 1816–22

John Henry Barrow, was lodging on the Strand: Though only seventeen, he had been in the capital for at least a year because he had sent a poetry submission from the Strand address to the Drury Lane Theatre, which was running a competition for a speech to be given at their re-opening following a fire. See the indefatigable William Carlton. Carlton, William J. 'Dickens's Literary Mentor'. *Dickens Studies*, vol. 1, no. 2, 1965, pp. 54–64.

The most valuable of her relatives was her namesake, Aunt Elizabeth Charlton (née Culliford): See Kent, Marie E. *Exposing the London Piano Industry Workforce (c1765–1914)*. London Metropolitan University (2013). Elizabeth Culliford Charlton is mentioned on p. 96 and in the footnote. Kent notes that Elizabeth is a contemporary of Mary Lukey, who is also a silverer, which suggests that it was a trade linked to women. (Lukey's father-in-law had also been in partnership with Elizabeth's father in the 1780s.)

Their new lodgings at 10 Norfolk Street were above a grocer's shop: Richardson has a lot on life at the Norfolk Street address. Richardson, Ruth. *Dickens and the Workhouse: Oliver Twist and the London Poor*. OUP, 2012. This is a solid book by a talented historian. I disagree with its thesis that the Cleveland Street workhouse was ever especially important to the three-year-old Dickens. But the picture of workhouses and the London poor, and the Dickens family movements is all spot on.

A grim and unsympathetic old personage of the female gender: Dickens is writing a characteristically over-egged seasonal piece for his magazine. In *Household Words*, New Year's Day, 1859.

Rochester side of his inheritance, lampooned as Dullsborough: Published in a series, 'The Uncommercial Traveller', for his latest magazine, *All the Year Round*, September 1860.

My father had left a small collection of books: David Copperfield, chapter 4.

It is, however, a relief in relating this melancholy accident, to state that no lives were lost on the occasion: *The Times*, 4 March 1820.

Did John Dickens actually read?: Ackroyd, p. 17.

Barrow claimed to have been shipwrecked in Madagascar: Carlton, William. 'The Barrows of Bristol'. *The Dickensian*, vol. 46, January 1950, 33.

my heaviest Dickens book, the 700-page-plus Michael Slater biography: Slater, Michael. *Charles Dickens*. Yale University Press, 2009. If any historical fact lacks a reference, assume the source is Slater.

The preacher was the schoolteacher's father, and was also named William Giles: I got all my information from a fascinating family blog. See, Piggott, Chris, blog: 'The Pigott Family of Queen's County, Ireland; Some Ancestral Connections'. 22 July 2013.

Alongside his father, he helped stage full-scale plays in the Ordnance Hospital: Langton, Robert. *The Childhood and Youth of Charles Dickens*. Hutchinson & Company, 1891. Although this was written seventy years after the events, Langton did have access to the Dickens family, who he thanks. p. 53. 'Young Lamert not only took Charles to the theatre at Rochester, but himself got up some private theatricals in the spacious buildings of the Ordnance Hospital, not far from the dockyard, and his father. Dr. Lamert, sometimes took a part in these performances. Dr. Lamert and Dr. Slammer (of Pickwick) are of course the same person.'

the high profile of Jewish figures like Moses Montefiore: The death of Montefiore in 1885 (at the age of a hundred) was a national event. He had lived in Ramsgate for around fifty years, so was practically a neighbour of Dickens. His wife died in 1867, which was contemporaneous with the Dickens/Davies correspondence. Dickens subsequently donated to the Judith Montefiore Fund, a charity whose aims included creating and supporting a Jewish community in Palestine. The rise of Christian-Zionism was the biggest driver of change in the average English person's reaction to Jews.

Dickens is thought to have met the Ternans through his road manager Alfred Wigan in 1857: Until recently, there were only two books on the Ternans, and both accepted the story that Dickens met the family through the tour manager Alfred Wigan. See Nisbet, Ada. *Dickens & Ellen Ternan*. University of California Press, 1952. This has a foreword by Edmund Wilson and used the new development of infrared photography to find excised references to Ternan in Dickens's own hand, but is only a monograph recounting accepted events. Then forty years later, a book initially presented as a novel: Tomalin, Claire. *The Invisible Woman: The Story of Nelly Ternan and Charles Dickens*. Penguin, 1991.

He would also pass the theatre, festooned with playbills for the Ternans' appearances: The initial meeting between Dickens and the Ternans was questioned only recently. There is every reason to believe he knew of the family and their plight from the death of Ellen's father onwards: because the London theatre world in the late 1830s was so small, just when Dickens was in its midst as playwright, celebrity and fanboy; because the home of the Ternans and the theatre where they worked lay on the route Dickens took when travelling to the Kent seaside; because the family were indebted to Macready and Bulwer-Lytton for support; and because they moved to London at the moment Dickens renewed his theatre ambitions. I drew upon the work of two researchers. Kelly, Helena. 'Ellen Ternan's Connections with Rochester: Some New Material'. *Dickens*

Quarterly, vol. 38 no. 1, 2021, pp. 83–7. This is a precursor to her book suggesting Dickens is untrustworthy on every point in his life, and may have had more children with Ternan. Ruck, Brian. 'Illegitimacy in Dickens, and the Riddle of Ellen Ternan.' *The Dickensian*. Winter 2022. pp. 319–34. Ruck's research has resulted in a book, which is not yet out as I write these lines. Ruck goes the other way to Kelly, arguing Dickens was honourable in supporting an illegitimate child (aside from the initial infidelity with Frances Ternan) and her family.

Rag Trade: Manchester 1819–22

Photographs of Robert and Martha, taken in the 1850s, do nothing to debunk that idea: The photographs are in my father's possession, but as they were reproduced in Waller, they can be found on the internet quite easily.

Not for the last time in his story, Robert found himself overcome by nerves: Brown/Blincoe, chapter 6 – in fact, the last couple of pages of the *Memoir*.

in Isabella Banks's novel, The Manchester Man *(1876)*: Banks, Isabella. (writing as Mrs G. Linnaeus Banks) *The Manchester Man. [A Novel.]*. Hurst & Blackett, 1876. p. 38.

This seems an extraordinary coincidence, but the account has been verified: Robert did arrive at the same moment as a group of nineteen apprentices: See Waller. pp. 207–8.

Sally's rejection by Harry after they have sex: Reiner, Rob. *When Harry Met Sally*. (1989). Capra, Frank. *It Happened One Night*. (1934).

I was even briefly signed to Factory Records: Meat Mouth, *Meat Mouth is Murder*. FAC 196.

Sources

There were other first-person coming-of-age stories before David Copperfield: Brontë, Charlotte. *Jane Eyre*. Smith & Elder. 1947. *David Copperfield* was serialised from May 1849 to November 1850.

Meursault, Holden Caulfield and Stephen Dedalus: I chose three novels I read between the ages of fourteen and eighteen. (The characters from Camus, Albert. *The Stranger*; Salinger, J. D., *The Catcher in the Rye*; Joyce, James. *Ulysses*.)

Richard Carlile, was there: From Conway Hall's website, a piece to commemorate the two hundredth anniversary of the massacre. 'Whilst most journalists present were arrested in an attempt to prevent the event from being widely reported, Richard Carlile, a radical journalist and publisher who had intended to speak at the gathering, managed to escape to safety. He went on to publish an eyewitness account of the atrocity in his newspaper *Sherwin's Political Register* under the title "Horrid Massacres at Manchester". The article described how the cavalry had charged unarmed civilians and openly criticised the government for its role in the incident. The authorities raided Carlile's Fleet Street shop, confiscated his stock and closed down his newspaper. But Carlile merely changed the name to *The Republican* and continued to use it as a vehicle to demand that "the massacre [. . .] should be the daily theme of the Press until the murderers are brought to justice."' Carlile also commissioned a famous print of the events, a copy of which is in the British Museum. This was a donation from the dealer Andrew Edmunds. I was touched when I saw this. I knew Edmunds, and always thought he was the loveliest of men.

nothing is real until it has been transmitted in some form: Janet read this and pointed out that she also knew the relevant essays from Derrida's 'Writing and Difference'. I was also thinking of Baudrillard's text on the Gulf War, which we'd spoken about. His argument is that the war didn't happen, because what we are talking about under that designation is something that had already been mediated, and there is no original. The post-war French thinkers had known the Nazi occupation and French collaboration (Derrida was an Arab-Jew attending school in Algiers during the war). These thinkers were keen on a critique of the idea of an 'origin', its absence or its impossibility, at least because Fascism always appeals to an original unmediated experience that must be reclaimed – such as 'whiteness' or 'womanhood', gender or race or faith. Derrida, Jacques. *Writing and Difference*. University of Chicago Press, 1978. Baudrillard, Jean. *The Gulf War Did Not Take Place*. Indiana University Press, 1995.

Dickens Alone: 1824

His bravura concoction was warmly received by his fellow radical Richard Carlile: There's a fascinating account of the history of Chartist breakfast powders online. Carlile neutralised his praise for Hunt's breakfast by stating he had made a drink from hay that he preferred. https://www.chartistancestors.co.uk/chartist-beverages-and-breakfast-powders/.

If we rewind back to the 1820s, we might be more sympathetic to John and Elizabeth: My primary source for this account is: Allen, Michael. *Charles Dickens and the Blacking Factory*. Oxford-Stockley, 2011.

In The Pickwick Papers, *the loquacious valet Sam Weller favours Day & Martin*: Dickens, Charles. *The Pickwick Papers*, chapter 10.

The school's director was a colourful French musician named Nicolas Bochsa: Robert-Nicolas-Charles Bochsa (1789–1856) an accomplished harpist, multi-instrumentalist, composer and forger. He lived in France until 1817, when he was compelled to flee the country. He lived in England until 1839, holding positions at the Royal Academy of Music and the King's Theatre. In 1818, he was tried in Paris in absentia and condemned to twelve years' imprisonment and a fine of 4,000 francs. He left England in 1839 with his mistress, Anna Bishop, wife of Henry Bishop, the composer of 'Home! Sweet Home!' the song that Fanny Dickens would later sing in the Dickens-produced domestic show. Bochsa and Bishop's whereabouts for the next several years are unknown, but he taught in New York and left via San Francisco in 1855, bound for Sydney, Australia, where he died in 1856. Source Grove Music online.

The Harmonicon *music magazine took pleasure in his downfall*: See Johnson-Hill, Erin. 'Miscellany and Collegiality in the British Periodical Press: The Harmonicon'. *Nineteenth Century Music Review*. 1823–33. The article states that editor William Ayrton was frequently rude about Bochsa, who he detested.

Lamert appeared on stage on sixty-eight nights over the year 1826–7: Allen, Michael, chapter 6.

Perhaps Charles Barrow was also lurking about: Charles Barrow was still publishing music, as he produced a set of Manx airs in 1820, published in Douglas and London, as *Mona Airs*, 1820. Charles Barrow supplied the music while his son John Henry provided the lyrics. A copy is available online from Manx Music with an essay by Robert Corteen Carswell. Carswell noted that the patronage of a local grandee, Catherine St George, led to a dedication to the Duchess of Kent, the mother of the future Queen Victoria. https://www.manxmusic.com/

I was meeting Janet before we saw People, Places and Things *at the Trafalgar Theatre*: Macmillan, Duncan. *People, Places and Things*. Dir. Jeremy Herrin. Starring Denise Gough.

My rescue I considered quite hopeless: Forster, chapter 2.

I used to breakfast with them now: *David Copperfield*, chapter 11. The scene with the Orfling on the bridge is in the same chapter.

having ascertained with many cautious glances round him that he was again alone, crept slowly from his hiding place: Claypole spies on Nancy. *Oliver Twist*, chapter 47.

In The Old Curiosity Shop, *the Orfling's first appearance, she is a limp rag of a girl*: The Old Curiosity Shop, chapter 35. She becomes the Marchioness in chapter 57.

There's a scene in Goodfellas: Scorsese, Martin. Goodfellas. (1990).

Yet as Carey goes on to note, 'after Oliver Twist the child is always a girl': Carey, pp. 149-150.

Dilke had always kept a literary career going in parallel with his work at Somerset House: The fact that there's so little written about Dilke is a sign of his standing. However, I found a PhD treatise from 1958 useful. See below. The author, Garrett, gives a detailed account of the work of Dickens, Dilke and Forster to reform the Royal Literary Fund. This is ten years after the date Forster gives to his blacking-factory anecdote. I wonder if Dickens hoped to keep his secrets buried by wrapping Dilke in an embrace as a valued collaborator on a project of national importance? Garrett, William. *Charles Wentworth Dilke as a literary critic.* University of Florida, 1958. https://ia601307.us.archive.org/20/items/charleswentworthoogarrrich/charleswentworthoogarrrich.pdf.

the popular The Newgate Calendar: Knapp, Andrew, and Baldwin, William. *The Newgate Calendar: Comprising Interesting Memoirs of the Most Notorious Characters who Have Been Convicted of Outrages on the Laws of England Since the Commencement of the Eighteenth Century: with Occasional Anecdotes and Observations, Speeches, Confessions, and the Last Exclamations of Suffers.* J. Robins and Company, 1824.

Fleet Street: 1824–28

Smith, Zadie. *The Fraud.* Hamish Hamilton, 2023.

Mr. Sikes struck, by way of Chiswell Street: Oliver Twist, chapter 21.

He spontaneously combusts: Bleak House, chapter 32.

Dickens knew the story of Henry Worms, the Jewish marine store dealer who operated in a similar spot to Krook: In Allen, Michael, chapter 6. See also the family trees in the appendices.

The obvious man was Richard Carlile, on Fleet Street: Carlile's influence is everywhere, from the accounts and prints of Peterloo, to the birth of labour politics, and terms like 'working class', and even *The Black Dwarf*, which was revived as a radical student magazine in 1968 by Tariq Ali and other activists. The downside when it comes to lionising Carlile is that he was in some awkward sense a complete lunatic. He moved from radical atheism and collectivism to spiritualism – but this makes his ideas on free thought all the more interesting (if not always either lucid or comfortable). Information about Carlile is all over the internet, like the Spartacus site. But there are very few biographies. I was grateful for: Wiener, Joel H., *Radicalism and Freethought in Nineteenth-Century Britain: The Life of Richard Carlile*. Bloomsbury, 1983.

Until the US Civil War in the 1860s, the only source of raw material for the paper industry was waste cotton. An eighteenth-century rhyme states: 'Rags make paper, Paper makes money, Money makes banks, Banks make loans, Loans make beggars, Beggars make Rags.' (from Schwartzott, Carol. *A Short History of Paper*. Self-published art book, 2001). For the transition from rags to wood pulp, see Kurlansky, Mark. *Paper: Paging Through History*. Norton, 2016.

I'm the little Jew who wrote the Bible: Cohen, Leonard. 'The Future'. 1992.

Carlile was released from prison in 1825, and rented new premises at 62 Fleet Street, on the corner of Bouverie Street: See, 'Number 62 Fleet Street', https://www.fleetstreetheritage.co.uk/104.pdf.

Carlile's memory of meeting Brown echoes through the blunt tribute: In Carlile's introduction to the *Memoir*, available in all the subsequent editions.

The only bit of Milton I can remember well enough to quote: Fame is the spur that the clear spirit doth raise / (That last infirmity of noble mind) / To scorn delights and live laborious days. See https://www.poetryfoundation.org/poems/44733/lycidas.

Publishing Robert's Story: 1828–33

The Lion *presented itself as a report on the state of Radicals across the country*: The newspaper is entirely digitised, available and searchable on Google Books. *The Lion*. R. Carlile, 1828.

The third issue of the Lion, *January 1828*: His conclusion states: 'In conclusion, the working class of Manchester beg leave to suggest to your majesty that the only hope which they have towards obtaining a full remedy for these manifold and extensive grievances is in such measure as shall lead to a full representation of the people in parliament.'

Wroe features prominently as Carlile's host, interlocutor and opponent: He says, 'In Manchester I was received as a lodger in the home of Mr Wroe, the bookseller.' He goes on to mordantly mock Wroe's Christianity, whose founder, 'Jesus Christ, is made a radical reformer of a bad government and a bad priesthood thus making him to answer the double purpose of a religious and a political saviour'.

Many of the responses came from Lancashire and Derbyshire: These letters are included as appendices in Blincoe 1977 and in *Factory Lives*, 2007.

By 1832, he was publishing a newspaper entitled The Poor Man's Advocate, *a vehicle for the Short Time cause*: For the full text of Poor Man's Advocate 1–50 see, *Poor Man's Advocate*, Greenwood Reprint Corporation, 1969 (digitised).

It had become a much-loved book, with its young hero spoken of as 'Bobby': Cited in Waller. The testimony comes from *Manchester*

Notes and Queries, 16 June 1888, which elicited a flurry of replies about 'Our Bobby': 23 June, 30 June, 7 July, 14 July, pp. 208–22.

Doherty's trial was a national story: The account of Doherty in Waller is drawn from the older biography of Doherty. Kirby, Raymond George, and Musson, Albert Edward. *The Voice of the People: John Doherty, 1798-1854: Trade Unionist, Radical and Factory Reformer*. Manchester University Press, 1975. The first edition of Blincoe's *Memoir* I saw was published in 1966 by the Derbyshire Historical Society with an essay by Albert Musson.

The Reverend Martin Gilpin's brother-in-law was a surgeon, and the corpse of an Irishman had been found at his home: The brother-in-law was Edward Lacy. In his obituary it states: 'It was while in Manchester that he became embroiled in 1832 in a law suit concerning grave-robbing. The Rev Gilpin of Stockport was successful with a libel case against an activist and publisher, Mr Doherty, who had stated that a body was removed from the graveyard attached to the church to the dissecting room of the surgeon Mr Lacy, who happened to be the Rev Gilpin's brother-in-law. The case featured strongly in the local and London newspapers, and must have been very embarrassing both professionally and personally for Edward.' See Plarr's 'Lives of the Fellows', Royal College of Surgeons of England (website).

Richard Oastler, the Tory reformer, would speak of working-class children as 'white slaves': The analogy comes from a letter to the *Yorkshire Mercury* dated 29 September 1830. 'Thousands of little children, both male and female, but principally female, from seven to fourteen years of age, are daily compelled to labour from six o'clock in the morning to seven in the evening, with only— Britons, blush while you read it!— with only thirty minutes allowed for eating and recreation. Poor infants! ye are indeed sacrificed at the shrine of avarice, without even the solace of the n***o slave.' The solace of the slave being that their master needs them to stay alive, while the systemic abuse of children does not require it.

Dickens's Lift-off: 1834–44

Charlton was an example of the peculiar intertwining of the bar and the theatre in England: See, Long, William F. 'Dickens, Macready and the Theatrical Charltons'. *Dickens Quarterly*, vol. 30, no. 4, 2013, pp. 299–309.

The memory of the Spanish revolutionaries hanging around the Polygon: Bleak House, chapter 63. '[Skimpole] lived in a place called the Polygon, in Somers Town, where there were at that time a number of poor Spanish refugees walking about in cloaks, smoking little paper cigars.'

A fellow reporter, James Grant, told Forster that Dickens was the best of the eighty or ninety parliamentary shorthand reporters: This was some forty years later. But Grant had earlier praised Dickens as an excellent writer in 1836. See Chittick, Kathryn. 'Dickens and Parliamentary Reporting in the 1830s.' *Victorian Periodicals Review*, vol. 21, no. 4, 1988, pp. 151–60.

The Mirror of Parliament had a reputation for accuracy, publishing debates and speeches in more detail and at greater length than rival papers: See Slater.

This was presumably a quid pro quo to thank Gye for pumping money into their newspaper: The idea that Barrow and Dickens helped Tennyson's campaign at Gye's behest is guesswork. But why on earth would they do it? Tennyson wasn't a friend, they didn't live in Vauxhall, and they no longer had any relatives in Lambeth. Gye lost a considerable amount of money with Barrow. See, Salmon, Philip. https://victoriancommons.wordpress.com/2017/11/17/reporting-parliament-a-view-from-the-victorian-commons/.

According to the account in the Pickwick *preface*: The 1847 preface to the so-called 'Cheap Edition'. Dickens, Charles. *The Pickwick Papers* (1847).

He was with his uncle in West Norwood when he wrote to Henry Kolle: Or had left shortly after. See Tillotson, Kathleen, chapter 12, *Oliver Twist: Essays and Studies*.

Dickens's sketch voice is already fully formed, built around an easy-going wit that softens his biting sarcasm: Patten, Robert L. 'Characterizing Boz (1834–1837): Sketches by Boz.' *Charles Dickens and 'Boz': The Birth of the Industrial-Age Author*. Cambridge University Press, 2012. Pp. 47–77.

Macrone had only left his native Isle of Man in 1830 and must have come across the Barrow family: My guesswork. However, Macrone has been described as being Scottish. See Grader, Daniel's introduction to *The Life of Sir Walter Scott by John Macrone: Edited with an Introduction by Daniel Grader*. Edinburgh, 2013.

Dickens's fast-paced and funny stories proved perfect for the theatre – by the late 1830s, as many as twenty stage adaptations of his stories could be running simultaneously: The 'Boz Cascade' and 'Dickens Deluge' according to Fawcett, Frank Dubrez. *Dickens the Dramatist, on Stage, Screen, and Radio*. Allen, 1952. See also, Harvey, P. D. A. 'Charles Dickens as Playwright'. *The British Museum Quarterly*, vol. 24, no. 1/2, 1961, pp. 22–5.

It was planned that Dickens would write the book and libretto for a series of musicals, in collaboration with the up-and-coming composer John Hullah: According to Hullah, he went with Hogarth, Dickens's future father-in-law, to see Braham (without Dickens). A fascinating account appears in: Hullah, Frances Rosser. *Life of John Hullah, by his wife*. Longmans, Green, 1886. 'This year (1836) the opera was completed. The title of "The Gondolier" was abandoned, and an original subject having presented itself to Mr. Dickens, it was, after many consultations, put forward as "The Village Coquettes," of which certain songs, duets, and concerted pieces soon formed constituent parts. These, accompanied by Mr. Hogarth, I took one morning to Mr. Braham, then living at a house no longer existing, The Grange, at Brompton. This interview was, of course, to me an important and a trying one. At no time was I ever a skilful pianist; to sing at any time in the presence of Mr. Braham was a serious matter, and what would be the end of the presentation I knew not. A very few moments swept away the nervousness with which I began. It is needless to say that Mr. Braham was an admirable musician. His once unparalleled gifts of voice were then, though a little failing, still considerable. He almost immediately took his position near the pianoforte, and in spite of the unfamiliar handwriting of the manuscript read bar after bar as though he had known it all his life, accompanying the performance with kind words, never to be forgotten. Some half dozen friends strayed in, and the audience was completed by Mrs. Braham, Miss Braham, and others of the family. A long morning, during which I heard nothing but praise, brought this session to a close, and I left The Grange with a sort of understanding that my opera was accepted, and would be put in rehearsal at the earliest possible moment. Not for many months, however, did this moment arrive: not till December 6, 1836, was "The Village Coquettes" played for the first time. The performers were Miss Rainforth, then a debutante, Miss Julia Smith, Messrs. John Parry, Morris Barrett, James Bennett, Strickland, Gardner, Sidney Harley, and Mr. Braham.'

Mathews is the model for Jingle in The Pickwick Papers: See the excellent essay by Earle Davis that traces Mathews' style, through a stock character called Goldfinch. 'It seems fair to say that all the comic characters of Dickens retain some of this early influence, an influence which lasted into the days when Dickens read publicly and acted out his many characters who provoked laughter by their mannerisms.' Davis, Earle R. 'Dickens and the Evolution of Caricature.' *PMLA*, vol. 55, no. 1, 1940, pp. 231–40.

Goldoni's Stratagems of Rozanza *signed 'CJH Dickens'*: It was sold most recently on 13 December 2022 at Bonhams in New York. Lot 119 is cited as 'Dickens Juvenilia?'. The text pretty much admits it isn't.

He [Braham] was also one of the best-known Jews in English public life: David Conway says, 'As the most famous English Jew of this period he became a significant incarnation of "the Jew" in the British consciousness.' The article contains all the available autobiographical information of Braham's early life, before opening theatres. It also has a reproduction of the poster with Incledon. Conway, David. 'John Braham – from Meshorrer to Tenor.' *Jewish Historical Studies*, vol. 41, 2007, pp. 37–61.

The love poem he wrote to Horton, 'To Ariel', is accompanied by a self-portrait in ink: Reproduced as the frontispiece to *The Dickens-Kolle Letters*, Smith, and elsewhere.

The received version is that they only met when Alfred Wigan, his production manager, hired the Ternans: The source for this is Gladys Storey.

Ashley also offered a similar tour to Fanny Trollope, which included a meeting with John Doherty: See Waller. Also Thomas Trollope's memoirs. 'My mother neglected no means of making the facts stated in her book authentic and accurate, and the *mise en scène* of her story graphic and truthful. Of course I was the companion of her journey, and was more or less useful to her in searching for and collecting facts in some places where it would have been difficult for her to look for them. We carried with us a number of introductions from Lord Shaftesbury to a rather strange assortment of persons, whom his lordship had found useful both as collectors of trustworthy information, and energetic agitators in favour of legislation.' Trollope, Thomas Adolphus. *What I Remember*. Cambridge University Press, 2010.

Ticholas Tickleby: For the rejection to Fanny Trollope, p. 499. Disparaging the plot of Michael Armstrong as a copy of his work, p. 640. The two letters to Blanchard: pp. 506–7. Dickens, Charles. *The Letters of Charles Dickens: 1820-1839*. Clarendon Press, 1965. There's a mystery here because Trollope is not copying Nicholas Nickleby, so why is Dickens angry? Perhaps because he must rework Nickleby to avoid factory stories. But Elsie Michie has another explanation: Nickleby copies aspects of Trollope's earlier anti-slavery novel. Michie, Elsie B. 'Morbidity in Fairyland: Frances Trollope, Charles Dickens, and the Rhetoric of Abolition.' *Partial Answers: Journal of Literature and the History of Ideas*, vol. 9 no. 2, 2011, p. 233–251.

Dickens seems not to have known that Hervieu was also her lover: Or perhaps Hervieu was not her lover. Even Frances Trollope's biographer is circumspect about it, only saying that Hervieu was dedicated to her, and adopted her family. Contemporary newspapers go out of their way to hint that he was her lover, however. See *The Edinburgh Review*, 1832. 'No Mr Trollope … who should appear but her friend "H".' Quoted in Ransom, Teresa. *Fanny Trollope: A Remarkable Life*. Alan Sutton, 1996, p.77.

Even the sunburnt faces of gypsy children: *Nicholas Nickleby*, chapter 50.

In the term coined by Asa Briggs, it was the 'shock city': In Briggs, Asa. *Victorian Cities*. Odhams Books, 1963.

A dog, which had lain concealed till now: *Oliver Twist*, chapter 50.

Those dreadful walls of Newgate, which have hidden so much misery: *Oliver Twist*, chapter 52.

Whited Sepulchres: 1857–68

Robert junior won Manchester Grammar's only scholarship to Cambridge in 1844, studying divinity and graduating in 1848: His potted life is available on the database of Cambridge alumni. His name was misspelled when he received his MA in 1858 – which we know angered Robert because we have his letter of complaint in the scrapbook handed down through the family.

Blinco, Robert.
Adm. sizar at QUEENS', May 1, 1844.

Matric. Michs. 1844; B.A. 1848; M.A. 1858.
Incorp. at Oxford, Dec. 3, 1857 (*sic*). Ord. deacon (Lichfield) 1849; priest (Rochester for Lichfield) 1850; C. of Wolverhampton, 1849–52.
C. of St Luke's, Old Street, London, 1852-69.
Hon. Chaplain of St Luke's Workhouse, City Road, 1853–69.
R. of Swettenham, Cheshire, 1869–78.
R. of All Saints', Bolton, 1878–80.
Disappears from *Crockford*, 1881.
(*Al. Oxon.*)

The novelist Barbara Kingsolver stayed, and was fortunate to meet Charles Dickens in a dream: See slate.com/culture/2023/08/book-charles-dickens-inspired-barbara-kingsolvers-demon-copperhead.html. Also see, Kingsolver, Barbara. *Demon Copperhead: A Novel*. HarperCollins, 2022.

In 1848, and again in 1849, a Toy Terrier named Tiny the Wonder killed two hundred rats: See Museum of London for the painting and details. https://www.londonmuseum.org.uk/collections/v/object-102061/rat-catching-at-the-blue-anchor-tavern-bunhill-row-finsbury/.

The Orfling and I stood looking vacantly at each other in the middle of the road: *David Copperfield*, chapter 12.

Are you named after Oliver Twist?: We later established that Oli is named after either Oliver Reed, or a family cat.

In the preface to David Copperfield: The 1850 edition. He reiterated this in the preface to the 1869 edition, when he also claimed it as his favourite.

In the same year, Frances Ternan performed in Bulwer-Lytton's Richelieu in Rochester's Theatre Royal: See Kelly, Helena. Also https://www.kent-maps.online/19c/19c-ternan-biography

An engraving of a scene from the play, entitled 'The Temple of Hymen': See Bridgeman Images. 'The Temple of Hymen', from the New Classic Story of Atalanta, or, The Three Golden Apples.

The result, The Frozen Deep, dramatises the events within a story of rival lovers, ending in the heroic sacrifice of one man for another: The complete play is available: https://www.bottecilindro.it/bottecilindro/wp-content/uploads/2011/01/The-frozen-deep0001.pdf.

Kate recalled her father as acting like a mad man: In Storey, p.94. She goes on to say: 'This affair brought out all that was worst – all that was weakest in him. He did not care a damn what happened to any of us.'

Even as he was lauded by Queen Victoria as 'the greatest man this country ever produced': In a letter to her uncle Leopold on Wellington's death in 1852.

This violence gives the wild speech he delivers at his death its dramatic power: Dickens's character takes two pages to die, monologuing in a hallucinatory daze that includes the confession he planned to murder Frank, then changes his mind for the sake of Clara. 'I took him away alone – away with me over the waste of snow – he on one side and the tempter on the other, and I between them, marching, marching, till the night fell and the camp fire was all aflame. If you can't kill him, leave him when he sleeps – the tempter whispered to me – leave him when he sleeps!' pp 158–59. https://www.bottecilindro.it/bottecilindro/wp-content/uploads/2011/01/The-frozen-deep0001.pdf

he wrote to Burdett-Coutts on the justice in exterminating the rebels: Letter, 4 October 1857. See Peters, Laura L., *Dickens and Race*. Manchester University Press, 2013, chapter 4.

According to The Times, his sermon began by describing the causes of the revolt: Written in the same week as Dickens's letter. The clipping is in his scrapbook in the possession of my family.

A contemporary work by the radical writer John C. Cobden entitled White Slaves of England: Cobden, John C., *The White Slaves of England: Comp. from Official Documents. With Twelve Spirited Illustrations*. Derby and Miller, 1853, chapter 10.

influenced by Charles Kingsley's 1855 novel, Westward Ho!: Kingsley, Charles. *Westward Ho!* CreateSpace Independent Publishing Platform, 2017.

There were Malays among them, Dutch, Maltese, Greeks, Sambos, Negroes, and Convict Englishmen: Dickens, Charles. *The Perils of Certain Englishmen. Household Words* [1857], chapter 1. n.b. There are only three chapters and Dickens only wrote the first and last.

Up the Orphans! 1870

In July 2022, the poet Lemn Sissay organised a group photograph of all his friends who had been adopted or spent time in the care system: https://www.theguardian.com/society/2022/jul/24/portrait-care-leavers-lemn-sissay-foundling-museum.

Book collecting is an obsession, an occupation, a disease, an addiction, a fascination, an absurdity, a fate: https://www.independent.co.uk/lifestyle/my-hardback-heaven-1619336.html.

Leonard Cohen again: 'There is a crack in everything. That's how the light gets in': Cohen, Leonard. 'Anthem'. 1992.

My weakness and deadness are all on the left side, and if I don't look at anything I try to touch with my left hand: To Georgina Hogarth, Wednesday, 21 April 1869.

A new production of Oliver! *is opening at the Gielgud Theatre*: Bart, Lionel. *Oliver!* It will be running still when this book is published, and possibly for years after.

The broadcaster Malcolm Muggeridge declared that Max Beerbohm, Carol's uncle, was 'Jewish and Gay and in denial about both': In his review of Cecil's biography of Beerbohm. Cecil, David. *Max: A Biography*. Atheneum, 1985.

In the Christmas air of London in December, where the smell of roast chestnuts and the silvery lights seem to capture a world that is quintessentially Dickens: We didn't see *Oliver!* at the Gielgud at Christmas. We saw it at the Chichester Festival Theatre the previous June. A Dickens story needs a Dickensian scene, I feel, so I created one.

Acknowledgements

I must extend credit and thanks to the chief sources for this book: John Waller, Michael Slater, William Carlton, Michael Allen, Margaret Debenham, Geoffrey Lancaster, and also Janice Carlisle, James R. Simmons, Albert Musson, Ruth Richardson, Peter Ackroyd and Claire Tomalin.

I owe the greatest debt to my editor Sameer Rahim, who has been everything one could ask for in a wise collaborator. To Janet Lee, who has been overwhelmingly helpful and kind in reading and commenting on the book, and providing a sounding board for my ideas. I also owe so much to my family: I got companionship and support from Robert, and huge help from my father, Edward, my cousin Christopher, and support and encouragement and comments from Lucy, and from Jen, my mum.

I want to thank Matthew Hamilton, the warmest of agents, and Nithya Rae, my philosophical project editor. I want to thank the Dickens world, too. I have been quietly swimming along with Dickens readers and fans for the past few years and they really do embody the warmth and conviviality that Dickens has come to stand for (even if the man himself sometimes fell short).

INDEX

Ackroyd, Peter, 9, 37–9, 117, 219
Act for the Health and Morals of Apprentices, 71
Adelphi Theatre, 50, 163
adoption, 35–6
Ainsworth, William Harrison, 179, 205, 215, 227–8, 233, 235, 273, 278
Akabusi, Kris, 270
Aleichem, Sholem, 278
Ali, Tariq, 303
Allen, Lieutenant Thomas, 82–3, 260
Allen, Michael, 163
Allen, Woody, 253–4
American Civil War, 185
American Revolution, 43
Amis, Martin, 293–4
Anatomy Act, 202–3
Andersen, Hans Christian, 158
apprenticeships, 6, 27, 42, 55–7, 107, 111, 160, 289
Arabian Nights, 125, 129
Archbishop's Park, 49
Archer-Morgan, Ronnie, 270
Arches, The, 168
Arkwright, Richard, 10, 94–5
Artful Dodger TV series, 15, 277
Ashley (later Shaftesbury), Lord, 5, 214, 226, 228–30, 232, 309
Atalanta, 248, 250
Athenaeum, The, 175, 232
Attwood, Thomas, 220
Austen, Jane, 48
Australia, 130, 187

baby farms, 25, 27
Bacon, Sir Francis, 41
Baker, Mr, 66
Banks, Isabella, 141
Baptists, 123–5, 130, 133, 257
Barbican, 181–2
Barnaby Rudge, 34, 53, 89, 222, 235
Barrow, Ann, 43
Barrow, Charles (CD's grandfather), 42–9, 51–2, 55, 58, 73, 75–6, 78–9, 84–5, 87–90, 118, 134, 161, 165, 187, 253, 272, 291, 301
Barrow, Edward, 6, 45
Barrow, John, 76
Barrow, John Henry, 37, 45, 112, 163, 165, 212–14, 221, 253, 255, 301

Barrow, Mary (CD's Aunt Fanny), 82–4, 118, 127, 129, 135, 138, 163
Barrow, Mary Culliford (CD's grandmother), 43, 75, 82, 88
Barrow, Robert, 45, 216, 291
Barrow, Thomas, 42, 79, 112, 165
Barrow, William, 42–3
Bart, Lionel, 89, 102, 276, 280
Basquiat, Jean-Michel, 181
Battle Bridge, 26, 164
Baudrillard, Jean, 151, 299
Bayley, Joseph, 206
Bayley, William, 206
Beard, Frank, 274–5
Beard, Tom, 214–15
Beerbohm, Max, 279
Beethoven, Ludwig van, 162
Bentley, Richard, 221–2
Bentley's Miscellany, 221–2, 227, 235
Bernard, Fred, 158, 176
Best, George, 189
Betts, John Joseph, 106–7, 143, 198
Bible, 132, 187
Bishop, Anna, 300
Bishop Waltham, 84
Bishopsgate workhouse, 57
Black Death, 110
Black Dwarf, The, 183, 303
Black, John, 215
'Black Loyalists', 123
Blackfriars Bridge, 49, 167, 171
Blackmore Edward, 210
Blanchard, Samuel Laman, 228–9
Blandford, Maria Catherina Haeck de Jong, Lady, 40
Blandford, William Godolphin, Marquess of, 40
Bleak House, 186, 211, 240, 247
Blincoe, Edward, 59
Blincoe, Martha (née Simpson), 138–45, 149, 153, 185, 189, 196, 199, 201, 204, 265
Blincoe, Martha (daughter), 189, 199, 265
Blincoe, Robert, 2–5, 9–11, 14–15, 19–28, 30–5, 48, 177, 226, 238, 265, 270, 276
  apprenticeship, 53–5, 57–71, 94–5, 99–102, 104–8, 110–11
  his death, 266
  and Gilpin affair, 203–4
  imprisonment, 196, 199
  and industrial reform campaign, 199–202, 205–9, 217
  kindness, 107
  known as 'Saint' and 'Parson', 27, 33, 69–70, 107, 111, 206
  marriage, 138–45, 149
  and *Nicholas Nickleby*, 230–1
  and Peterloo, 150–1
  his portrait, 199–201
  publication of his *Memoir*, 189–91, 195, 197–9
  working life, 142–4, 147–8, 152–3, 184–5, 188–90, 198
Blincoe, Rev. Robert, 196, 199, 207, 238, 241–3, 257–9, 262–7
Blincoe, Robert (author's brother), 58–72, 108–9
Blincoe, Rose, 276
Blincoe, Ruth, 189, 204, 206–7
Blue Anchor pub, 241
Board of Ordnance, 119–20
Bochsa, Nicolas, 161, 300
Bolívar, Simón, 213
Boston Tea Party, 43
Boulogne, 247, 249, 275
Bradford, Barbara Taylor, 275
Braham, John, 216, 221–3, 252, 278, 307–8

Briggs, Asa, 234
Brighton, 79, 84–6, 165
Bristol Dock Company, 76, 291
Broadstairs, 239–40, 244, 247
Brompton Barracks, 120
Brontë, Charlotte, *Jane Eyre*, 148
Brookes, Rev. Joshua, 140–1
Brown, John, 27, 30, 36, 60–1, 95, 100, 102–3, 106–8, 140–1, 152, 183–4, 190–1, 194–5, 197, 258, 270
Browne, Hablot Knight (Phiz), 73–4, 218, 226–7, 233
Browning, Robert, 175
Buckstone, J. B., 250
Bulwer-Lytton, Edward, 145, 246, 278, 297
Bunn, Alfred, 224
Burdett-Coutts, Angela, 251, 256
Burke and Hare, 211
Burnett, Henry, 221
Burslem, Oli, 244, 265
Burton Joyce, 69

Camden Palace, 32–3
Camden Town, 3, 6, 18–22, 27, 30–3, 48, 57, 68, 84, 154, 164–5, 177, 256
Carey, John, 7, 158–9, 176–7
Carlile, Alfred 194
Carlile, Hypatia, 194
Carlile, Jane (née Cousins), 183–4, 187, 194–5
Carlile, Richard, 102, 108, 150, 152, 154, 183–5, 187–8, 194–8, 200–1, 208, 212, 214, 258, 299–300, 303
Carlile, Thomas Paine, 194
Casteels, Ann, 43
Catherine of Brunswick, 163

Catholic Association, 199
Catholics, 33, 135, 150, 199, 202–3, 230, 257–8, 260
Cerberus Club, 227
Chadderton, 146, 153
Chapman & Hall, 217–18, 235
Chappell & Co., 48, 272, 275
Charlton, Charles, 210
Charlton, Elizabeth (née Culliford) (CD's great-aunt), 112, 160, 162, 210, 221
Chartists, 232, 300
Chatham, 114–19, 136, 154, 164, 242, 245
Chatham workhouse, 10, 135–6
Childish, Billy, 245
chimney sweeps, 29–31
Christian-Zionism, 297
Christmas Carol, A, 273
Church of England, 130, 202, 257
City of London, 57
Clementi, Muzio, 48, 162, 272
Cobden, John C., 258
Cohen, Leonard, 187, 271
Colburn, Henry, 228
Collier, Fanny and Mary, 70–1
Collins, Wilkie, 226, 252
commedia dell'arte, 220
Cookson, Catherine, 275
Corden, James, 219
cotton industry, 4, 10, 67, 71, 94–6, 102, 185, 188–90, 206–7
Covent Garden Theatre, 213, 219, 222
Covent Garden workhouse, 113–14, 295
Crewe, Frances, 41
Crewe, John, 40–1
Crewe Hall, 40, 55
Crimean War, 242, 255

Cromford, 94, 105–6
Crompton, Samuel, 189
Cruikshank, George, 216, 232
Crusades, 65
Culliford, Thomas, 43–4, 47–8, 51–2, 82, 129
currency crisis, 161

Daily News, 255
David Copperfield, 1, 4, 50, 119, 145, 148, 167, 169–74, 178
   as autobiography, 6–12
   and CD's childhood, 159–60
   and CD's reading, 115–18, 131
   Micawber, 38–9, 73–4, 116, 136, 170, 290
   the Orfling, 135–6, 171, 173, 180, 242, 245, 251, 282
   preface, 239, 244
Davis, Eliza, 88, 90–1, 130–1, 223
Day & Martin, 155–6
de Heriz family, 65
Deller, Jeremy, 152
Derrida, Jacques, 151, 299
Derry/Londonderry, 57, 289
Derwent, River, 94–5
Dickens, Alfred Allen (CD's brother, died in Portsmouth), 84, 118
Dickens, Alfred Lamert (CD's brother), 250
Dickens, Augustus (CD's brother), 253
Dickens, Catherine (née Hogarth), 6, 215, 218, 221, 224–5, 252–4
Dickens, Charles
   his beard, 255–6
   'Boz' pseudonym, 6, 215, 218, 232–3, 283–4
   and blacking factory, 6–9, 40, 49–50, 84, 87, 129, 133, 154–61, 163–4, 166, 169–70, 174, 176–7, 180, 187, 211
   charity performances, 246, 248
   Chatham childhood, 114–37
   early reading, 115–18
   early writing and sketches, 210–18
   extended family, 37–52
   horror of dirt, 185
   the 'Inimitable', 12, 126–7, 133, 262
   irony and secrets, 131–2
   jealousy, 233
   male friendships, 124, 127
   marriage, 15, 218
   and money, 38–9
   as moralist, 254–5
   and mother's dame school, 164–5
   and orphan maid, 135–7, 165
   'parish' series, 17–19, 35
   parliamentary reporting, 212, 214
   'Personal Statement', 253
   reading tours, 15–16, 92, 137, 272–5
   and religion, 123–5
   romantic conservatism, 34–5
   self-consciousness, 51
   separation from Catherine, 252–4
   and shame, 11, 38, 54–5, 90–3, 134, 158, 177–8, 266, 280
   smoking, 126
   his statue, 92
   strokes and death, 274–5
   and theatre, 128–9, 133, 163–4, 212–13, 219–21, 223–6, 246–50
   train crash, 275
   and universal audience, 233–4
   and walking, 182

Dickens, Charley (CD's son), 222, 224
Dickens, Elizabeth (née Ball) (CD's grandmother), 40–1, 166
Dickens, Elizabeth (née Barrow) (CD's mother), 10, 37, 42, 74–5, 81–4, 112, 117–18, 135–7, 158–60, 162, 164–5, 174, 242
Dickens, Frances (Fanny) (CD's sister), 82, 84, 87–8, 112, 121, 123, 133, 161–2, 164–5, 212, 216, 220–1, 234, 249, 300
Dickens, Fred (CD's brother), 253
Dickens, John (CD's father), 10, 37–42, 55, 73–5, 77–9, 81–3, 88, 90, 112, 114, 116–17, 119, 121, 136, 158–60, 162, 165–6, 170, 174–5, 204, 242
Dickens, Kate (CD's daughter), 39, 85, 225–6, 249, 252–3
Dickens, Letitia (CD's sister), 118
Dickens, Mamie (CD's daughter), 114, 225, 249
Dickens, Walter (CD's son), 249
Dickens, William (CD's grandfather), 39–41
Dickens, William (CD's uncle), 40–1, 112, 160
Dickens Birthplace Museum, 76–7, 79–83
Dilke, Charles Wentworth, 175–6, 211, 234
Disraeli, Benjamin, 98, 187, 206, 250, 278
Dissenters, 124, 133, 201
Doctors' Commons, 210, 213
Dodds, Henry, 185–6
Doherty, Agnes, 203
Doherty, Ambrose, 203
Doherty, Augustus, 203–4

Doherty, John, 5, 150, 198–205, 208, 211, 226, 229–30, 235
Doherty, Laura, 203–4
Doherty, Mary, 203
Dolby, George, 274
Dombey and Son, 85–8
Don Quixote, 115, 117, 219
D'Orsay, Duke, 278
Dover Beck, 61–2, 65–6
Drury Lane Theatre, 224–5, 295
Dylan, Bob, 250

Eagle, The, 241–2
Eastman, Julius, 259
Edinburgh, 215
Edwin Drood, 240, 247, 251, 263
Employment of Children in Manufactories Committee, 205–9
English language, 130
Enlightenment, 233–4
entrepreneurialism, 13, 97, 155, 215, 231
Evening Chronicle, 215, 221
Everett, Percival, *James*, 60, 68, 91, 280
Examiner, The, 175

Factory Bill, 226
Factory Records, 148
Family Quarrels, or The Jew and the Gentile, 223
Farrow, Mia, 254
Fechter, Charles, 247
Fenton, Roger, 242
Fiddler on the Roof, 278–9
Fielding, Henry (*Tom Jones*), 23, 45, 58, 115–17, 131
Fields, James T., 86
First Sikh War, 255

Fitzgerald, Edward, 228
Fleet, River, 20, 22, 33, 48, 182–3
Fleet Prison, 48, 174, 182
Fleet Street, 5, 50, 183–4, 191, 212–13
forgery, 161
Forster, John, 6–12, 40, 49, 84–5, 87, 116, 123, 125, 129, 132–5, 154–5, 157–9, 161–2, 164, 167, 169, 172, 174–7, 211, 213, 224, 227, 282
Foulkes, Violet, 1–2
Foundling Hospital, Coram's Fields, 24, 269, 286
Franklin expedition, 248
fraternity, 59–60
Freetown, Sierra Leone, 123
French Revolution, 32, 34
Frieze Art Fair, 51
Frozen Deep, The, 226, 249–56, 263

Gad's Hill Place, 114, 134, 247, 272, 275
Gallery of Illustration, 249
Gamble, William, 143
Garrick Club, 220
Gaskell, Elizabeth, 98, 250
Gaza, 45, 261, 294
Geib, John, 129
General Strike (1842), 206
George IV, King, 163–4
Gil Blas, 115, 117
Giles family, 121–7, 132–3, 234, 245
Gilpin, Rev. Martin, 202–3, 315
Glazer, Jonathan, 100
Godwin, William, 33
Golden Cross Inn, 50, 167
Goldoni, Carlo, 219–20
Goldsmid family, 222
Goldsmith, Oliver, 23
Goldsmith, Oliver (*The Vicar of Wakefield*), 23, 115, 283–4

Goldsworth, John, 129
Goldsworth, Mary, 48
Gonalston, 58, 62–4
Good Samaritan, 29
Goodfellas, 174–5
Gordon, Lord George, 89
Gordon Riots, 34, 53, 89
Goswell Street, 243, 273
Grant, James, 211
Grant brothers' mill, 229, 231
grave robbers, 202, 211
Gray's Inn, 163, 165
Great Expectations, 78–9, 88–9, 91–2, 119, 127, 145, 148, 187, 263, 272
Great Fire of London, 25
Great Reform Bill, 200, 212
Grimes, Darren, 121
Grub Street, 188
Guild of Watermen, 49
Gye family, 212, 306

Hall, William, 217
Hansard, 212
Hanway, Jonas, 289
Hard Times, 98, 250
Hardy Tree, 33
Hargate Wall, 94
Harmonicon magazine, 162
Harrison, George B., 265
Hart, Mike, 32
Hawkins, Francis Bisset, 205–6, 209, 217
Hawkins Hospital, 135
Hawksmoor, Nicholas, 258
Haymarket Theatre, 250
Hervieu, Auguste, 101, 229, 258, 310
Higson, Charlie, 32
HMS *Dart*, 82
HMS *Victory*, 83–4
Hogarth, George (CD's

father-in-law), 215–16, 221, 224, 307
Hogarth, Georgina (CD's mother-in law), 252
Hogarth, Georgina (CD's sister-in-law), 114, 119, 247, 249, 252–3, 274–5
Hogarth, Mary (CD's sister-in-law), 224–5
Holocaust, 293–4
homunculus theory, 239
Horton, Priscilla, 225–6, 249, 281
Hospital for Sick Children, 254
Household Words, 98, 240, 253
Hullah, John, 216, 220, 254
Hulton, William, 149–50
Hungerford Stairs, 49, 156–7, 166–7, 172, 174
Hunt, Henry 'Orator', 150, 152, 154, 194, 200, 212
Hunt, Henry Leigh, 175–6, 211, 216, 234, 300
Hyman, Catherine, 225

Idealism, 34
Illustrated London News, 242, 264
Incledon, Charles, 223
Indian Raj, 34, 43
Indian Rebellion, 249, 255–7, 260–4
industrial revolution, 95
initial teaching alphabet (ITA), 193
Ireland, 135, 199, 208
Irwell, River, 148
Is She His Wife?, 221
Isle of Man, 79, 87–8, 112, 165, 215–16
It Happened One Night, 144
Ivey House, The, 243, 266

Jacob's Ladder, 110
Jenkins, Billy, 277

Jesus Christ, 75, 186
Jews, 88–92, 130–1, 133–4, 186–7, 223, 236, 277–9, 292–3, 297, 308

Kean, Charles, 225
Keats, John, 175
Keeling, William Knight, 199–200
King's Theatre, 300
Kingsley, Charles, 158, 293
Kingsolver, Barbara, 241
Kipling, Rudyard, 262
Kolle, Henry, 17–18, 214
Lacy, Edward, 305
Lambert brothers (Lowdham Mill), 57, 60–7, 70–2, 94
Lambeth Marsh, 49
Lambeth Walk, 44, 46–7
Lamert, James, 8, 87, 90, 127–34, 157, 160, 163–4, 166, 174, 187, 245
Lamert, John Thomas, 160–1
Lamert, Matthew, 127–31, 135, 157
Lamert, Sophie, 157
Lamplighter, The, 221
Lancaster gaol, 196, 199, 202–3
Latham, Jane, 112
Lazy Tour of Two Idle Apprentices, The, 252
Lean, David, 26, 276–8, 294
Lee, Janet, 19–21, 32, 46–50, 74–5, 132–3, 167–72, 240–6,
  adoption and care, 35–6, 137, 269–80
  critical theory, 151–3, 299
  Manchester, 146–9, 189
  moving house, 179–1, 266
Lee, Stewart, 270
Lemon, Mark, 253
lice, 101

Lion, The, 5, 106–7, 196–8, 212
Lipkin, Simon, 277
Litton Mill, 98–101, 106, 109–11, 143, 198
'logical families', 35, 232
London Bridge, 49, 170–3
London Symphony Orchestra, 259
London Wine Company, 212
Longman & Broderip, 47–8, 272
Loren, Sophia, 279
Lowdham, 62, 64–5, 206
Luddites, 94
Lynn, Vera, 213

Macready, William, 221, 225–6, 297
Macrone, John, 215–17, 222
Madgwick, George, 78
Magwitch, *see Great Expectations*
Malthus, Thomas, 53–4, 96, 150, 204–5
Manchester, 1–2, 20, 107, 110–11, 133, 135, 139–41, 146–8, 151, 188–91
   Athenaeum Club, 250
   CD in, 228–9, 231–5, 274
   children's employment committee meeting, 205–9
   cholera epidemic, 203
   and *The Frozen Deep*, 226, 249–50, 253–4
   and industrial unrest, 196–205
   Old Church (Manchester Cathedral), 139–41, 147
   'shock city', 234–5
   Short Time Committee, 199–200, 205
   see also Peterloo Massacre
Manchester and Salford Yeomanry, 149
Manchester Grammar School, 207, 238

Manchester Infirmary, 189
Manchester Observer, 150, 152, 197
Marine Society Charity, 289
Marr, Johnny, 148–9
Marshalsea Prison, 165–6, 170, 174
Martineau, Harriet, 204–5
Mary Rose, 84
Marylebone parish, 113
Mathews, Charles, 219
Matthews and Masterman, 183
Maupin, Armistead, 35
Medway, River, 114–15, 119, 127, 130, 134–5, 240
Medway workhouse, 136
Mendelssohn, Felix, 162
Merchant Navy, 55
Methodists, 70, 123
Metropolitan Police, 71
Metropolitan Tabernacle, 257
Milton, John, 195
Mirror of Parliament, The, 212, 214
Mrs Pipchin, *see Dombey and Son*
Montefiore, Moses, 130, 296–7
Monthly Magazine, 17, 213
Moody, Ron, 89, 277, 279
Morning Chronicle, 214–15, 221
Morrissey, 149
Moscheles, Ignasz, 162
Mother Black Cap, 31–2
Mother Red Cap, 21, 31
Mozart, Wolfgang Amadeus, 220
Mudie, Robert, 90
Muggeridge, Malcolm, 279
music halls, 131, 241–2, 278

Napoleonic France, 84–5
Napoleonic Wars, 42, 76, 111, 120–1, 128, 135, 255
National Union of the Working Classes, 208

Navy Pay Office, 42, 51, 73–5, 79, 83, 112, 165, 175
Nazi death camps, 100, 276, 294
Needham, Ellis, 94–6, 98, 101, 104–6, 109–11, 184, 198
Needham, John, 104–6, 111, 184
Nelson, Admiral Horatio, 83, 118, 125
New Mills, 111, 143
Newgate Calendar, 177
Newgate prison, 88–9, 236, 273
Nicholas Nickleby, 5, 222, 227–31, 309
Nonconformists, 125, 133, 150
Norman Conquest, 65
Northern Star, 229
Not So Bad as We Seem, 246
Nottingham, James, 106
Nottingham, 58, 60–1, 67, 69, 72, 99, 104, 208

oakum, 3, 26, 135
Oastler, Richard, 201, 208, 236
Odessa, 278
Old Bailey, 202
Old Bekka, 111
Old Curiosity Shop, The, 4, 136, 173, 177–8, 227, 235, 251, 263
Oldfield, Bruce, 270
Oliver!, 2, 89, 101–2, 136–7, 275–80
Oliver Twist, 2–3, 5–6, 14–15, 18–19, 27–30, 35, 54–5, 90–1, 102, 124, 126, 171–3, 181, 214, 221–4, 226–7, 231–2, 234–7, 244, 261
  adaptations, 275–80
  Artful Dodger, 18, 90, 277
  Bill Sikes, 171–2, 178, 181–2, 235, 263, 273, 275–6, 279
  Mr Bumble, 2–4, 18, 28–9, 31
  and childhood innocence, 158, 176–8

  death of the dog, 235–6
  Fagin, 18–19, 54, 88–92, 130, 171, 176, 187, 223, 227, 234, 236–7, 252, 273, 277–8, 280, 292–3
  Gamfield, 29–30
  Limbkins, 29–30
  Mr Brownlow, 50, 171–2, 236
  Mrs Mann, 25
  model for the workhouse, 113–14, 295
  Nancy, 10, 16, 119, 171–3, 224, 235, 251, 273, 276, 280
  Noah Claypole, 54, 171–3
  Rose Maylie, 119, 171, 224, 232
  serialisation, 5–6, 15, 27, 221–3, 226–7, 235
  Sowerberry, 29
  subtitle, 3, 27
  three-volume publication, 27, 227, 232–3
  Yiddish translation, 278
Oliver Twist (David Lean film), 26, 276–9
One Man Two Guvnors, 219
Ordnance Hospital, 128, 296
Original Sin, 125
Ormrod, Richard, 189
Our Mutual Friend, 49, 55, 91–2, 173, 185
outdoor relief, 26
Oxford, Earl of, 41

Paine, Tom, 183–4
Pains and Penalties Bill (1820), 163
parish beadles, 3–4, 15, 24
Parker, George, 265
Patten, Robert L., 87
Peace, David, 32
Peake, Richard Brinsley, 5
Peel, Robert, 71, 191

People, Places and Things, 167, 172
People's Voice, The, 199
'Perils of Certain English Prisoners, The', 260–1, 267
Peter Pan, 277
Peterloo Massacre, 135, 149–52, 154, 183–4, 195, 197, 303
Pickwick Papers, The, 5, 126, 128–9, 156, 167, 213, 217–22, 243, 273, 276
Pocock, Lucina, 253
Polanski, Roman, 277, 294
police, 15, 71, 77, 120–1, 235
Polygon, *see* Somers Town
Poor Law (1834), 18, 23, 26, 28, 54, 97, 136, 173, 214, 221, 231
Poor Man's Advocate, The, 199
population growth, 18, 26, 53–5, 63, 139, 149–50
Portsmouth, 76–84, 88, 118, 120–1, 127
Portsmouth Independent Party, 78
Portugal Hotel, 212
Pratt, Charles, 1st Earl of Camden, 32
Psalm 23, 95
Punch, 253

Radicals, 32–3, 35, 124, 197, 201, 230
Rag, Phebe, 105–6
railways, 22, 167
Rauzzini, Venanzio, 223
Reed, Carol, 279
Reed, Oliver, 279
Regent's Canal, 22, 185, 224
Republican, The, 154, 183–4, 195–6, 198, 299
Rhodes, Cecil, 32
Richards, Mary, 68, 199, 206
'Roast Beef of Old England, The', 58

Rochdale Canal, 147
Rochester, 114–15, 117, 133–6, 225, 240, 247, 272
Theatre Royal, 128, 133–4, 245–6
Romanticism, 23
Royal Academy of Music, 161–2, 212, 216, 220–1, 300
Royal Literary Fund, 302
Royal Vauxhall Tavern, 45–6
Royal Veteran Battalions, 128
Roylance, Elizabeth, 84–7, 165–6, 170, 174, 253
Russian pogroms, 278

St Aloysius, Somers Town, 33
St Andrew's, Holborn, 183, 187–8
St George's, Wolverhampton, 238, 259
St James's Hall, 272–3, 275
St James's Theatre, 216, 222, 247
St Luke's, Old Street, 241, 244, 257–9, 263
St Luke's workhouse, 241–2
St Martin's Hall, 254
St Martin's Le Grand, 243
St Mary Le Strand, 43, 74
St Mary the Less, 44
St Mary's, Chatham, 127
St Mary's, Lowdham, 64
St Mary's, Widley, 84
St Pancras graveyard, 211
St Pancras parish, 3, 17–19, 22, 24–7, 32–3, 55, 113, 185, 206
  report on apprentices, 70–1
St Pancras parish church, 34, 164
St Pancras workhouse, 19–22, 25–7, 32–3, 55, 143
St Thomas' Hospital, 49
Savage, Richard, 6
Seven Years War, 43, 289

Seymour, Robert, 217–18
Shakespeare, William, 41, 265
   Othello, 224–5
   Richard III, 134
   The Tempest, 225, 249
Shaw, Jemmy, 241
Sheerness, seized by Dutch Navy, 119
Shelley, Mary, 211, 256
Shelley, Percy Bysshe, 175
Sherwin's Political Register, 150, 154, 183, 299
Simpson & Co., 224
Sinclair's Oyster Bar, 139, 147
Sissay, Lemn, 269
Sketches by Boz, 216–17
Skinner, Frank, 132
Slater, Michael, 122, 282
slavery/slave trade, 34, 102–4, 108, 201, 209, 258
smallpox, 26, 33, 101
Smith, Adam, 97–8, 103
Smith, Venture, 60–1
Smith, Zadie, 179–80
Smithfield Market, 182, 185
Smollett, Tobias (*Roderick Random*), 23, 45, 115–17
Society of Merchant Venturers, 291
Solomon, Ikey, 90
Somers Town (Polygon), 32–3, 164, 210–11, 227
Somerset House, 42, 51, 74, 112, 166, 175
Southey, Robert, 118, 183
Southwell, 61–2
Spanish Inquisition, 43
Spring, Howard, 275
Stalybridge, 110–11, 143, 206, 232, 250
Statesman, The, 232

Stein, Gertrude, 51
Stephens, Rev. Joseph Rayner, 232
Sterne, Laurence, 131, 239
Stevenson, Robert Louis (*The Strange Case of Dr Jekyll and Mr Hyde*), 114, 251, 267
Stockport, 149, 202–3, 206, 305
Storey, Gladys, 85, 225, 252
Strand, the, 48–51, 112, 155–7, 167, 174, 191, 213, 256
Strange Gentleman, The, 220
Swettenham Church, 266–7
Swift, Taylor, 92

Taddington, 99
Tait, Bishop Archibald, 264–5
Tale of Two Cities, A, 33, 211, 249, 251, 263
Ten Hour Movement, 5, 11, 108, 200–1, 204–5, 212
Tennyson, Alfred, 175
Tennyson, Charles, 212, 306
Ternan, Ellen, 39, 114, 119, 133–4, 224–6, 240, 246, 249–52, 263, 272, 275, 282, 297–8
Ternan, Fanny, 119, 133–4, 226, 240, 246, 249–50
Ternan, Frances, 39, 114, 133, 224–5, 246, 249, 253–4, 272, 275, 298
Ternan, Mary, 246
Ternan, Thomas Lawless, 224–5, 297
Ternan, William, 225
Three Coney Walk, 46–7
Thurgarton Priory, 65
Tideswell, 99, 109–10
Times, The, 90, 161, 183, 257, 264
Tiny the Wonder, 241
Tomalin, Claire, 41, 73, 81, 133, 250
Tomkison, Thomas, 162

Tories, 35, 201, 208, 230–2
trade union movement, 199
Tree, Herbert Beerbohm, 279
Tripp, Charlotte, 243–4, 266
Trollope, Fanny (*Michael Armstrong*), 5, 95–8, 100–1, 110, 158, 228–33, 235–6, 250–1, 258, 309–10
Trollope, Thomas, 226, 229–30, 309
Turpin, Dick, 215, 235

Uncle John, 250
Uncommercial Traveller, The, 115
Unitarians, 125
University College London, 164
Urania Cottage, 180, 251–2
utilitarianism, 96

Vauxhall Pleasure Gardens, 44–6, 53, 151, 212
Victoria, Queen, 15, 224, 246, 249, 255
Victoria Embankment, 50
Village Coquettes, The, 220, 307–8
Virginia, 57, 289
Voltaire, 91

Waller, John, 63, 283, 285
Warren, Jonathan, 156–7
Warren, Robert, 155–7, 160–1, 167
Warren, Thomas, 156
watermen, 49
Weller, Mary, 119
Wellington, Arthur Wellesley, Duke of, 162, 255
Wentworth Place, 175
Wesley, John, 122

West Indies, 258
West Norwood, 214
Western Dispensary, 205
Westminster Bridge, 49, 167
When Harry Met Sally, 144
Whigs, 201, 204–5, 214, 221, 231
Widley, 84
Wigan, Alfred, 133, 226, 297
Willan, Sophie, 270
Wilson, Edmund, 7, 281, 297
Winterson, Jeanette, 270–1
Wish Street, Portsea, 83–4, 92
Wollstonecraft, Mary, 32
Woodd, William Edward (WEW), 157, 160, 174, 187
Woodford, James, 80
Woodward, Robert, 71, 94, 105
Woodward, William, 107
workhouses, 3–4, 10, 18–35, 48, 54–5, 57, 62–3, 113–14, 135–7, 143, 188, 193, 202, 241–2, 245, 265, 276–7, 295
see also individual workhouses
Wormhill, 98–9, 109
Worms, Henry, 90, 187
Worms, Lewis, 187
Worsley, Thomas, 202–3
Wroe, James, 197–8
Wye, River, 94, 100, 110
Wyman, Bill, 250

Yeats, W. B., 33
Yiddish theatre, 278–9
Yorkshire Mercury, 305
Yorkshire schools, 226–7

Zone of Interest, 100, 277, 293–4